DEMOCRATIC EQUALITY: WHAT WENT WRONG?

Edited by Edward Broadbent

Are the world's oldest democracies failing? For most of the past fifty years democratic governments have made determined and successful efforts to overcome the significant inequalities that are the by-product of a capitalist economy. During this period a new concept of democratic citizenship that added social and economic rights to the liberal legacy of political and civil liberties established roots in most North Atlantic democracies. Since the 1980s this notion of democratic citizenship has been challenged ideologically to such a degree that through either major modification or complete elimination of programs, equality as a fundamental democratic goal is disappearing in many nations, particularly in the Anglo-American democracies.

In this wide-ranging yet coherent collection, top scholars in political science, sociology, philosophy, and economics discuss this radical shift towards inequality in an age of mass capital globalization. They also point out many European democracies have adapted to new circumstances in the global economy without resorting to policies that actively promote inequality. While holding differing views on some important details regarding solutions, the contributors all contend that the political decision-making process is of critical importance in entrenching, or battling, an escalating inequality that is neither necessary nor desirable.

EDWARD BROADBENT is a visiting fellow in the Arthur Kroeger College of Public Affairs, Carleton University. He was a New Democratic Party member of Parliament for twenty-one years, and party leader for fifteen years.

Democratic Equality:

What Went Wrong?

EDITED BY

Edward Broadbent

UNIVERSITY OF TORONTO PRESS
Toronto Buffalo London

Toronto Buffalo London
Printed in Canada

ISBN 0-8020-4787-4 (cloth)
ISBN 0-8020-8332-3 (paper)

Printed on acid-free paper

Canadian Cataloguing in Publication Data

Main entry under title:

Democratic equality : what went wrong?

ISBN 0-8020-4787-4 (bound) ISBN 0-8020-8332-3 (pbk.)

1. Equality. 2. Democracy. 3. Welfare state. I. Broadbent, Ed, 1936– .

JC575.D45 2001 323 C00-932815-7

University of Toronto Press acknowledges the financial assistance to its publishing program of the Canada Council for the Arts and the Ontario Arts Council.

University of Toronto Press acknowledges the financial support for its publishing activities of the Government of Canada through the Book Publishing Industry Development Program (BPIDP).

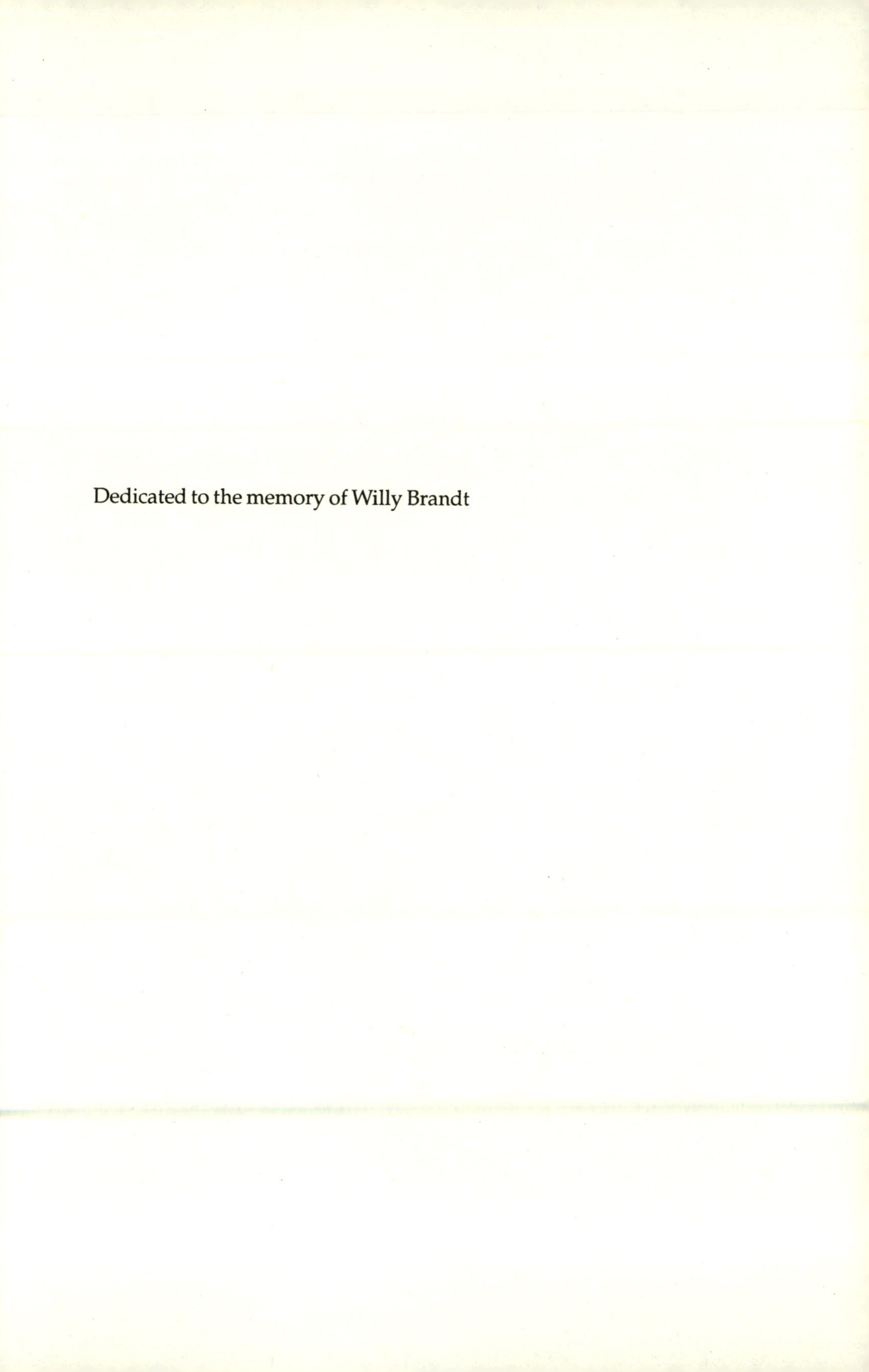

Dedicated to the memory of Willy Brandt

Contents

Acknowledgments

This book results from an international conference on equality and the democratic state that took place in Vancouver in the fall of 1998. It was sponsored by the Institute for the Humanities at Simon Fraser University and attended by scholars, senior government officials, and trade unionists. I want to thank the institute's staff and its then director, Jerry Zaslove, for their enthusiastic support. Thanks are also due to Virgil Duff, executive editor of the University of Toronto Press, and to Frances Shepherd and Laura MacInnis, without whose expeditious and practical work the book would never have come to fruition. Most of all, I want to thank the contributors to *Democratic Equality: What Went Wrong?* for revising their texts two years after the conference in order to incorporate new arguments and the most recent data.

Contributors

Ian Angus is professor of sociology and humanities at Simon Fraser University. His recent books include *(Dis)figurations: Discourse/Critique/ Ethics*, *Primal Scenes of Communication* and *A Border Within: National Identity, Cultural Plurality and Wilderness*.

Edward Broadbent is a visiting fellow in the Arthur Kroeger College of Public Affairs, Carleton University. He was elected to the House of Commons in 1968, and became leader of the New Democratic Party in 1975, a position he held until his retirement from politics in 1989. Since then he has been president of the Centre for Rights & Democracy in Montreal (1990–6) and a visiting fellow at All Souls College, Oxford.

G.A. Cohen, a fellow of the British Academy, was educated at McGill and Oxford universities and is currently Chichele Professor of Social and Political Theory, and a Fellow of All Souls, Oxford. His most recent books are *If You're an Egalitarian, How Come You're So Rich?* and an expanded edition of his 1978 work on *Karl Marx's Theory of History*.

Barbara Ehrenrich is an independent scholar and journalist whose books include *Fear of Falling: The Inner Life of the Middle Class* and *Blood Rites: Origins and History of the Passions of War*.

Robert A. Hackett is professor of communications at Simon Fraser University and co-director of NewsWatch Canada, a media monitoring project. His most recent publications (co-authored) include *Sus-*

taining Democracy? Journalism and the Politics of Objectivity and *The Missing News: Filters and Blind Spots in Canada's Press.*

Jane Jenson is professor of political science, Université de Montréal, director of the Université de Montréal and McGill University Institute of European Studies and director of the Family Network of the Canadian Policy Research Networks. She has worked extensively on the political economies of Canada and Europe and is currently writing about social policy and the redesigning of the welfare state.

Ruth Lister is professor of social policy at Loughborough University in the United Kingdom. She has published widely on poverty and social security and her most recent book is *Citizenship: Feminist Perspectives.*

John Richards was elected to the Saskatchewan legislature in 1971 as a New Democrat. He left the caucus to sit as an 'independent socialist' and was soundly defeated in the subsequent election. He has since mellowed, and become an enthusiastic supporter of the 'third way.' He teaches in the Faculty of Business at Simon Fraser University and is a senior fellow at the C.D. Howe Institute.

Bo Rothstein is the August Rohse professor in political science at Goteborg University, Sweden. He is the author of *The Social Democratic State* and *Just Institutions Matter: The Moral and Political Logic of the Universal Welfare State.*

Dietrich Rueschemeyer is professor of international studies (research) at the Watson Institute of International Studies at Brown University. Among his publications are *Capitalist Development and Democracy* (co-authored with E.H. Stephens and J.D. Stephens) and *Participation and Democracy East and West: Comparisons and Interpretations* (co-edited with M. Rueschemeyer and B. Wittrock).

Daniel Savas is a senior vice-president of the Angus Reid Group in Vancouver.

Jim Stanford is an economist with the Canadian Auto Workers in Toronto. He is the author of *Paper Boom*, published in 1999 by the Canadian Centre for Policy Alternatives and James Lorimer.

Armine Yalnizyan has worked with community-based organizations since the mid-1980s, identifying the economic issues that affect people where they live. She has specialized in analysis about the labour market, income distribution, and government policies from the local to national levels and has delighted in learning and sharing every step of the way.

Introduction

EDWARD BROADBENT

Equality has always been seen as the core democratic value, and for a brief period in the twentieth century it actually became the guiding principle for many governments. Following the Second World War, virtually all of the North Atlantic democracies consciously adopted policies that were radically different from those of the pre-war years.[1] They did what many liberal theorists from James Madison to Friedrich Hayek had always feared: they politicized the distributional struggle of the market place. In the post-war decades, politicians from a variety of ideological backgrounds were no longer willing to accept the inequality and instability inherent to a capitalist economy. Still reeling from the effects of the 1930s, when the market was allowed to dominate the state, they were determined to reverse the emphasis. Capitalism had to be held in check if social stability and the rhetoric of equal citizenship were to have real meaning.

During this period the notion of democratic citizenship took on a completely new dimension. No longer was freedom defined exclusively in the negative terms of traditional liberalism, by which it was understood that a person was free in all those areas in which the state did not set restrictions. To this idea, which had produced important civil and political rights, was added a positive notion of freedom. Freedom for citizens meant individual autonomy, the actual capacity to fulfil oneself and to achieve this goal for all citizens, liberal 'freedom from the state' was seen to be inadequate. Thus democratic governments throughout the North Atlantic region initiated myriad social and economic programs explicitly aimed at furthering equality and security. In most of these democracies, pensions, health care, and education came to be viewed as a citizen's right, precisely because they were established for all citizens regardless of income.

Although the most important ideology of social equality based on citizen's rights was social democratic (stretching back to the end of the nineteenth century, with Edward Bernstein's concept of the new citizen), other important belief systems underlay the new broad-ranging political consensus on the positive role of the state. Conservatives could draw upon their idea of a 'social market economy,' which had always distinguished itself from laissez-faire capitalism; liberals in quest of a positive notion of freedom could invoke T.H. Green, Leonard Hobhouse, and, above all others, John Stuart Mill.

It was no accident that when the Universal Declaration of Human Rights was adopted by the United Nations in 1948, it contained not only the civil and political freedoms of the Western tradition but also the new egalitarian social and economic rights. The Canadian John Humphrey, who prepared the first draft of the Declaration, wrote that it 'attempted to combine humanitarian liberalism with social democracy.'[2] Like Humphrey, most political leaders in most democracies had come to believe that without social and economic rights traditional political and civil liberties had little meaning for the majority.[3] And without continuing intervention by national governments in the vagaries of unstable capitalism there could be neither social stability nor social rights.

When the contributors to this volume consider equality as a value of fundamental importance to democracy, they have at least one reasonably precise idea in mind: economic or material equality in substance or in outcomes. Thus when they advocate organizing society to ensure that a higher degree of equality prevails, they take into consideration the distribution of income and other forms of personal wealth, such as stocks, bonds, and housing. They see more economic equality as being desirable for two reasons. First, those not separated by a wide gap in wealth are more likely to be able to communicate and empathize with each other as citizens living in the same political structure. Without denying the importance of other significant differences which frequently result in other kinds of inequality – for example language, religious, ethnic, cultural, and gender differences – a significant gap in wealth not only weakens the general possibility of positive communication in society but also makes each of these other differences more likely to be seen as sources of conflict rather than forms of positive diversity. It is also the case that most liberal democracies have made significant progress in dealing with inequalities of these kinds, at the very time when economic inequality related to class has been on the increase. A second reason for favouring greater economic equality in outcomes as opposed to the classical liberal and neo-liberal (or neo-conservative) equality of opportunity, is that economic equality is seen to be fundamentally connected to the notion of free and participatory citizenship. This is particularly evident in a capitalist economy, grounded as it is on private property, differentials in market-based incomes, and the majority of individual choices being exercised in the context of purchasing goods and services.

In such a society, to make choices in exercising one's talents, capacities, or interests is to participate in the market place, precisely because the means of their realization has to be purchased. Whether we are talking about going to a movie, taking a skiing holiday, acquiring a television set, having music lessons, or deciding to take a day off from work, the vast majority of the choices we make to give substance to the abstract notion of freedom require money. The more choices we can make, the more freedom we have. Since choices require money, the more money we have, the more free we are. In a market economy the rich not only have more money, they have more freedom. Thus equal citizenship in a market-based democracy, grounded in the notion of the equal freedom to make choices, necessarily implies that the state must take strong measures to achieve higher degrees of material equality than would result from the market when left alone. Material inequalities cannot be left alone if the democratic goal of each citizen having an equal moral claim to the right of self-development is to be a reality.

'Equality in substance' is a direct challenge to the neo-liberal 'equality of opportunity' favoured by most non-social democratic parties and promoted by the mainstream media in most liberal democracies. What might be called the weak version of this liberal notion of equality of opportunity emphasizes the need for formal legal equality of all citizens as they confront real life in a capitalist democracy. If legal equality is provided by the state then any resultant inequalities in outcomes should be understood as just, that is, they result from differences in original capacities or effort in the market place. A stronger version of the liberal theory of equality of opportunity takes into account the need to compensate for inequalities of circumstance that individuals may be confronted with at birth or that result from market conditions. 'Strong' liberals would therefore justify intervention by the state to enable individuals to have a 'fair start.' State intervention can take the form of special regulations and programs to compensate for systemic discrimination in the market place – discrimination based on gender, ethnicity, sexual orientation, or even class – and particularly in education or retraining. What unites both weak and strong liberalism is the view that all individuals (after compensatory action is taken by the proponents of strong liberalism) should then compete in the market place and that whatever inequalities result from this competition are just.

What unites virtually all of the authors in this book, in contrast, is a rejection of the outcomes of economic liberalism even of the strong kind. They make the almost self-evident point that the view of life as a race in the market place, with its unequal incomes and right to acquire property, inevitably results in unequal outcomes that bestow on children and other individuals in the families at the top of the income and wealth scale a range of clearly identifiable choices that are unavailable on the same terms to the vast majority of allegedly equal citizens. It is not too much to say that for the poor in particular, the liberal notion of equal citizenship is at best an oxymoron and at worst cruel propaganda.

Some of the contributors to this volume would reject outright any version of liberal equality of opportunity. Others see it as self-limiting and requiring serious supplementary action by the democratic state if the goal of equal citizenship is to be at least approximately realized. For this reason all of the authors strongly believe in the necessity of the equalizing state, which, by means of universal social programs and redistributive taxation, makes greater substantive or material equality a leading policy objective for a modern democracy.

Beginning in the 1980s, following the elections of Margaret Thatcher in Britain and Ronald Reagan in the United States, a programmatic and ideological assault was launched against the welfare state in general and the social equality concept of citizenship in particular. Not content, as many continental European governments were, to deal with fiscal pressure as a practical problem that had arisen by the end of the 1970s, they attempted to undo all governmental institutional and policy attempts initiated to facilitate the growth of social citizenship. Although their nations had by far the weakest social rights foundations in the North Atlantic region, Thatcher and Reagan provided the most virulent attacks on the welfare state. Their campaign against social equality, always done with an emphasis on the pre-war concept of anti-government personal liberty, spread to Commonwealth democracies and in the 1990s to conservative governments in France and Germany. Neo-liberal policies which had flourished in the Anglo-American world began to spread their wings.

The social consequences of almost two decades of neo-liberalism are quite clear. A growth in inequality unprecedented in the post-war period in Britain, other Commonwealth democracies, and the United States ensued. The social damage done by inequality to the body politic led to a massive electoral rejection of the Conservative government in Britain in 1997. Shortly after, voters in France and Germany reacted in a similar way to conservative governments which had just begun to adopt a similar neo-liberal agenda.

The authors contributing to this book share two notable characteristics: they believe that the values of equality and democracy are linked in a fundamental way, and, from quite different intellectual perspectives, they contend that the policies that produced such unequal citizenship near the end of the twentieth century were unnecessary and should be reversed. As will be seen in the chapters that follow, a significant number of North Atlantic democracies did not revert to prewar liberalism. They continued with the post-war commitment to greater equality. While other democracies reversed themselves, they managed to adapt to a changing world without putting the new social citizenship in jeopardy.

Austria, Denmark, the Netherlands, Norway, and Sweden demonstrated great flexibility in policy in confronting domestic and global economic challenges. Maintaining high levels of economic productivity, they also retained strong egalitarian social policies. The Socialist government of France, while putting a new emphasis on the private sector (the preceding five countries have always emphasized the private sector) seems committed to retaining its strong equalizing social programs. Britain is much more problematic. New Labour has taken serious political initiatives to improve citizens' equality by increasing the regional political authority of the Scots and the Welsh. It has also brought into British law the European system of human rights. At the same time, the government has barely scratched the surface in dealing with the market's unequal distribution of income or with the seriously underfunded health and education programs. Ironically while 'New Labour' is the only remaining European social democratic party with structural ties to the trade unions, the Blair administration has also been less open to the concerns of organized workers than any other European social democratic government. At the close of the twentieth century in Germany, the Social Democrats were elected on a campaign promise to preserve the social programs that the Christian Democrats had planned to weaken. In the short run, the new government moved to alter the same programs in order to resolve a serious financial situation. It remains to be seen whether the strong ideological commitment to equality of the large majority of the party's membership will prevail in shaping the government's agenda over the long haul of its term in office. While the United States has had notable success in the past decade in creating jobs, the American government has adopted policies that produce escalating inequality in income and wealth.

The contributors to this collection make clear that whether equality is extended or reduced in the future will depend primarily, as it has in the past, on the politics of each nation, and not on the alleged insuperable economic forces of the global economy. Institutional traditions buttressed by public opinion favouring strong universal social programs are an empirical reality in the majority of North Atlantic democracies. Greater equality will thus depend on the willingness and ability of political leaders to use the institutions of both civil society and the state to subordinate the destabilizing and inequality-creating forces of the market. To some extent it will also depend on their willingness to collectively challenge the hegemonic position of the United States in shaping the direction of global financial institutions.

This volume is divided in four sections. I begin with an overview of the historical relationship between democracy and equality, stretching from the time of Socrates (who opposed democracy) to the universal social rights-based welfare states of the second half of the twentieth century. Many of the considerations I touch upon are discussed in detail in subsequent chapters by other authors.

Part Two consists of five essays which provide assessments of the current democratic reality from the perspectives of philosophy, economics, and sociology. For the most part, the authors present their views concerning the adequacy of existing welfare states in delivering higher degrees of equality. In so doing they range from outright rejection to revisionist reform to its strong defence. Bo Rothstein makes a persuasive case for the universal rights welfare state, for reasons of both equality and economic efficiency. Based in part on recent studies of electoral behaviour that demonstrate the complexity of motives people have in voting, he also points to empirical evidence showing that contemporary democratic citizens will support such a welfare state provided certain feasible normative and practical conditions are met. While Gerald Cohen would agree that social democracy more adequately fulfils the democratic requirement for equality than does liberal democracy, he contends that the available evidence does not warrant ruling out the feasibility of socialism. Furthermore, he argues persuasively that only such 'socialist aspiration' can extend the value of community to all of our economic life. John Richards, in contrast, argues that Tony Blair's Third Way is the most relevant option for a contemporary party of the left if it wants to be electorally competitive. Assigning to social democrats the 'parental responsibilities' for the equality that can derive from a welfare state – because no one else will take on such an obligation – he contends that accepting balanced budgets, no further increase in income taxes, and the primacy of the market are current democratic electoral requirements that parties of the left must meet in order to obtain political power. If Richards sees existing degrees of equality, for instance in universal health, education, and pension programs, more likely to be preserved by parties of the left moving in the more traditionally liberal direction of favouring strong markets, Ian Angus offers contradictory considerations. Angus asserts that traditional left concerns of community and social rights require even further limitations on the dominating role of the market. It is only by shifting away from the industrial priorities of market capitalism to an economy based on 'healthy and sustainable development' that a desirable form of human life can be achieved. His appeal is for a coalition of First Nations, feminists, and social democrats to work with environmentalists to concentrate their joint efforts at the local level to break away from the powerful dehumanizing force of globalizing capitalism.

Dietrich Rueschemeyer also sees the need for politics to triumph over economics. While claiming that there is an important positive role for markets in providing goods and services, he strongly defends the importance of non-market values to democracy. Rueschemeyer is apprehensive that the current strength of neo-liberals will result in market criteria being misused as the measurement for assessing democracy's collective goals. He sees strong welfare states as having done much more than liberal-capitalist regimes in providing support to facilitate autonomous participation in the democratic process by those with less status and power: workers, women, visible minorities. For him it remains an open question, however, as to whether or not universal welfare states will be any more successful than liberal democracies like the United States in containing the drive for more and more consumption that has become a pervasive characteristic of life in all market-based societies.

It has frequently been asserted or assumed that social life, and in particular concern about equality, has taken on virtually identical characteristics in all of the advanced democracies. This is not the case. Although in 1960 most advanced democracies were at approximately the same level in terms of the percentage of gross domestic product (GDP) going to social programs (whose broad goal was to bring about higher degrees of equality), since then considerable divergence has occurred. During the 1980s and '90s this difference intensified when quite different national policy options were pursued. While all countries have been experiencing increasing economic 'globalization,' by which I mean the reduction of national barriers to the international flow of goods, services and capital, there has been no common domestic response to its effects in terms of social and economic policies. Thus the impact on equality has varied considerably. Although confronted with the common global pressure to reduce corporate and upper income taxes, Northern and Western European continental governments, whatever their ideological stripe, managed to preserve (sometimes precariously) the post-war commitment to social rights. Such rights have become strongly imbedded characteristics of citizenship. These rights are now more fragile in the Anglo-American democracies, where neo-liberal ideology on taxation and social programs found more fertile ground.

Part Three includes assessments of three of the Anglo-American democracies: the United States, Britain, and Canada. These countries share many similar neo-liberal policies, although the governments of all three would reject such labelling.

Jane Jenson portrays a drift in Canadian social policy away from the post-war citizenship regime, which comprised a mixture of universal social rights aimed at equality of condition (health care, unemployment insurance, family allowances) as well as a variety of measures designed to alleviate the poverty of certain groups but which were not intended to generate equality. This mixture in social policy was complemented by initiatives intended to produce more equality in political participation for disadvantaged groups as well as a significant number of changes – constitutional, affirmative action, and pay equity – directly beneficial to half of the population in terms of citizenship: women. Jenson shows how social, political, and gender adult-focused equality of citizenship politics have recently shifted to a neo-liberal model of individualism with its emphasis on equality of opportunity. The new initiatives are not only intended to promote equality of opportunity (with its inequality in outcomes) but are concentrated on children. While acknowledging that there may be real benefits for many children, she notes there could well be negative direct and indirect equality consequences for those adult citizens who previously were the beneficiaries of social, political, and gender policies: trade unionists, women, and the poor.

Armine Yalnizyan's discussion of inequality focuses on Canada. However, she provides two important documented arguments based on the Canadian experience which have broader implications. The first is that a general economic upswing does not lead automatically either to reductions or to increases in inequality. Government social and taxation policies make the difference. The data she provides show that between 1989 and 1993 the gap between the rich and the poor narrowed; between 1993 and 1997 it widened. In both periods government intervention significantly changed what would have been the results of the market alone. In the earlier period government policies had an equalizing effect on the direction of the market. In the latter period deepening inequality was made even worse as a result of governmental policy. After looking at recent data from different Canadian provinces she also concludes that there is no economic rule that can explain the relationship between market performance and the distribution of income. And when the issue of a nation's overall prosperity is considered, she argues that the same data lead to the conclusion that recent public debate in the developed democracies has exaggerated the positive role of markets and undervalued that of governments.

Barbara Ehrenreich provides a moving description of the effects of Clinton-era tax and welfare 'reform' legislation at both the national and local levels in the United States. The results have been negative for average and poor citizens alike: inequality has grown to record postwar levels. While Ehrenreich draws attention to the harm done to women and children in particular, she also underlines the negative citizenship effects of underfunding in schools, pensions, and health services. As these services deteriorated increasing numbers of the upper middle class withdrew to finance and use private alternatives. They ceased to be advocates for the 'wider community and the common good.' Life became more privatized and even public services like pensions and the administration of welfare were turned over to corporations, although there was no empirical evidence indicating the result would be an improvement either in quality or in costs.

In her analysis of Britain, Ruth Lister begins with an outline of the society Tony Blair's New Labour inherited when they came to power on May Day in 1997. She points out that during the 1980s the British had experienced the fastest growth in inequality among advanced democracies. In the decade following Margaret Thatcher's election in 1979 the percentage living in poverty increased by about 150 per cent. During the same period the real incomes of the richest 10 per cent grew by 70 per cent. Although she does not blame Thatcher entirely, she contends her policies made a bad situation worse.

While John Richards emphasizes what he sees as the positive aspects of Tony Blair's Third Way, Lister has a more critical response. She praises New Labour for their promise to reduce some disparities but raises serious questions about the government's general approach to inequality and its emphasis on obligations in preference to rights. She notes that when Tony Blair talks about inequality he uses the language of social inclusion, not social justice and cites with approval critics who pointed out that 'inclusion' in society via a job can be inadequate if the job itself leaves the young man or woman working at or below the poverty level. As part of her conclusion Lister questions the possibility of achieving even Blair's limited equality commitments without changing Thatcher's policies on taxation and economic globalization.

Part Four contains chapters dealing with three subjects directly relevant to a more adequate explanation of the variations in inequality in the modern democratic state: the role of privately owned media in shaping public opinion on equality issues, what that opinion was in a number of democracies at the end of the twentieth century, and the importance to a democratic nation of the distribution of financial wealth as opposed to other sources of income. In his wide-ranging contribution Robert Hackett notes that media owned by individuals independent of the state played an important role historically in breaking down aristocratic privilege in pre-democratic Europe and authoritarian government in North America. More recently, journalists linked with commercial media have helped to undermine dictatorships in Asia, Africa, and the former Soviet Union. In liberal democracies today such media have often been sympathetic in their portrayal of equality concerns of certain minorities, including gays and lesbians, as well as documenting corruption by politicians. However, these 'watch dog' roles on behalf of democracy in general and social equality concerns in particular must be balanced against what Hackett calls the 'lap dog' and 'mad dog' functions of privately owned and profit-motivated modern media. Without ascribing conscious motivation, he shows how such media give much less attention to matters that could result in public opinion more favourable to equality than they do to sensational and commercially supported subjects. He demonstrates that in Canada reports and opinions of right-wing think-tanks are quoted more often and more favourably than those from their left-wing competitors. Such priorities reinforce rather than challenge existing inequalities.

Daniel Savas discusses public opinion data resulting from a survey of thirty-two countries. Savas does not deal with the causes that shape such opinion but he does find results that have clear implications for the kinds of pressures that would influence politicians in democratic and non-democratic societies alike. In May and June of 1998, in a comprehensive sample of global opinion, the Angus Reid Group asked two related questions: one on the right to accumulate unlimited amounts of wealth even while others live in poverty and the other on whether governments should be obligated to intervene to reduce the resulting disparities. Among OECD countries the United States was at one end of the spectrum, with strong majorities cutting across class lines favouring the right of unlimited accumulation and opposing state intervention to redress inequalities. In Western Europe, on the other hand, there exists a strong egalitarian disposition in most of the population, favouring government intervention. Women everywhere were found much more likely to favour state action to narrow the gap.

By the close of the twentieth century many governments in capitalist democracies had adopted policies favouring the financial sector over those parts of the economy producing the goods and services consumed by ordinary people and which are reflected in their real standard of living. Using Canada as an example, Jim Stanford argues that the wealthy minority who owned the vast majority of stocks and bonds had been successful in getting government policies that worked to their advantage. An emphasis on keeping inflation down and reducing the size of the public sector, even when unemployment is high, rewards those in the 'paper' economy. And contrary to the impression created by talk about 'people's capitalism' and the alleged widespread holding of shares either by individuals directly or indirectly through pension funds, the reality is quite different. According to data for that time, only one adult in five owned shares and 93 per cent of capital gains tax deductions were claimed by the top 11.7 per cent of the taxpayers. The concentration of wealth in a few hands combined with government policies skewed in their favour, Stanford shows, are major reasons why the wealthy became richer precisely at the time when increasing poverty and static real incomes were the experience of the large majority.

As noted earlier, all the contributors to this book believe in the moral connection between democracy and equality. They also reveal in their contributions a shared understanding that the causes and remedies of existing inequalities are to be found in specific national political *choices* made in an increasingly common global economy. Many advanced democracies have retained an uninterrupted commitment to the post-war goal of expanding our notion of equal citizenship by progressive tax policies and by adding social rights to our legacy of political and civil liberties. Others have not. Established institutions, ideology, and political leadership have had material consequences. Most authors in this volume share the view of the politically ecumenical group of leaders who took the initiative following the Second World War to launch the social rights-based welfare state. They believe more substantive equality ought to be a morally driven goal of democratic governments, even if parties can win elections without making such a commitment. Some of us also believe, though empirical evidence is inconclusive, that those democracies which continue to become more unequal are also likely to become more unstable. In any case, Auden got it right when he wrote:

> We have no destiny assigned us,
> No data but our bodies: we plan
> To better ourselves; bleak hospitals alone remind us
> Of the equality of man.[4]

NOTES

1 They were joined in this goal by Australia and New Zealand. Very soon after the war both West Germany and Japan pursued similar nation-building agendas.

2 John Humphrey, *Human Rights and the United Nations: A Great Adventure* (New York: Transnational Publishers, 1984), 39.

3 *Ibid*.

4 W.H. Auden, *Collected Shorter Poems 1927–1957* (London: Faber & Faber, 1966), 122.

PART ONE

AN OVERVIEW

1

Ten Propositions about Equality and Democracy

EDWARD BROADBENT

Democracy has been with us since the time of Pericles. However, the form of democracy most citizens of the world are familiar with at the close of the century, representative government within a nation state, is a mere two hundred years old. The modern welfare state, found principally in the North Atlantic region, is the youngest version yet of democracy. What distinguishes all forms of democracy, whether ancient or modern, from other kinds of society is the importance of equality. I offer ten propositions about democracy, equality, and the welfare state.

Proposition One: Equality has been the value most persistently associated specifically with democracy. From Classical Greece until the twentieth century, concern with the effects on equality has led to both support and rejection of democracy.

Throughout the larger part of human history most intellectuals not only saw equality as a defining characteristic of democratic government but also opposed it for precisely this reason. Although Aristotle and Plato disagreed about a great many things, each saw democracy as a form of class rule in which, as Plato said in his *Republic*, the majority has gained the day. And he agreed with the argument made later by Aristotle in his *Politics* that constitutions reflect class interests. With the few and the rich in charge, the result is oligarchy. With power in the hands of the many or the poor (the demos), the product is democracy. In each case, power is used not impartially but to favour the dominant group or class, that is, democracies work to equalize conditions of life for the majority.

Proposition Two: The link between democracy and equality persisted in theoretical discussions right up to the eighteenth and nineteenth centuries, when for the first time nation-state representative democracy became a serious possibility in North America and Europe. Countrywide people's movements had produced revolutionary social and political demands, including universal (male, white) voting rights. The assumption by both those promoting and resisting this change was the same: democracy with equal political rights would lead to demands for greater equality in the conditions of life. The most important democratic theorist of the age had this to say: 'The working classes have taken their interest into their own hands, and are perpetually showing that they think the interest of their employers are not identical with their own, but opposite to them.'[1]

That theorist was, of course, John Stuart Mill. In *Utilitarianism,* he argued that everyone not only has an equal claim to happiness but also that this 'involves an equal claim to all the means of happiness.'[2] Equality, he stressed, is the norm of justice, first justifying political democracy and then economic and social arrangements within a society. Those wanting inequality have the responsibility of justifying it.[3] This Millian idea that democracy entailed not only formal legal rights and high levels of participation but also material substance was to be picked up in the twentieth century by supporters of the welfare state and provides, for example, the moral foundation for the social and economic rights found in the Universal Declaration of Human Rights.

Proposition Three: North American and European liberals who supported or acquiesced to the coming of democracy feared the majoritarian desire for more equality would result in political threats to minorities and to the inequality in wealth inherent in a capitalist economy. Both Alexis de Tocqueville and Mill liked much of what the former had observed when he visited America early in the nineteenth century. Each, however, was concerned that majorities in the world's first modern 'democracy' (except for blacks and women) might use their power to suppress minorities' freedoms of expression and association. Most other liberals of the day, including a number of the Founding Fathers of the United States, had more material concerns. They deliberately constructed a constitution that restricted the power not only of the executive branch but also of the legislators. In the well-known *Federalist* paper no. 5, James Madison concocted a distinction between 'republicanism,' which he favoured, and a majority-based 'pure democracy,' which could lead to demands for equalizing wealth.[4] Such a 'faction,' even when made up of the majority, he believed, should be held in check by the constitution. In

Canada there were similar economic concerns about democracy. Our first Prime Minister justified an appointed Senate by asserting that minorities needed protection. The rich, he pointed out, would always be a minority.

Whether in Europe or North America, however, most of those with wealth and power finally came to accept democracy based on equal political rights. What many of them have continued to fear about democracy, however, is that the inherent inequality of capitalism might be challenged. Historically, they have wanted the distributional struggle to be left in the market place, where working people are of course subordinate. They were apprehensive that ordinary people, once in control of the state, would use it to tip the balance in favour of greater equality – equality in substance, not in opportunity.

Proposition Four: With the sole exception of the United States, major social democratic parties emerged early in this century in the North Atlantic democracies, whose goal was the creation of social citizenship. This was seen as a democratic struggle, the institutional objective of which was to embed the political and civil rights of liberalism in a context of substantial social and economic equality. One hundred years ago Edward Bernstein, the leading German social democratic theorist, expressed this new citizenship goal in these words: 'No man thinks of destroying civic society as a civilized ordered system of society. On the contrary, social democracy does not wish to break up this society and make all its members proletarians together; it labours rather incessantly at raising the worker from the social position of a proletarian to that of a citizen, and thus makes citizenship universal.'[5]

Proposition Five: More equality, it was increasingly understood, is not only an ethical requirement of democracy but is also needed to ensure stability in a capitalist society. Following the Second World War, significant elements of traditional liberal and conservative political parties joined with social democrats and other socialists in urging the structural modification of capitalism. After assessing the Depression of the 1930s and the rise of fascism and communism, a number of Christian Democrats, Conservatives, Liberals, and Democrats (U.S.A.) came to believe that a capitalist economy could and should be moderated in its effects in order to create greater equality. They believed this could only be achieved through a continuous degree of state involvement in the economy to ensure that the ever expanding benefits of capitalism be more widely dispersed.

Otherwise inequality would deepen and instability would result. In 1942 Churchill's coalition cabinet (with Labour) made the decision to launch a post-war national and international system of human rights that included social and economic entitlements. And in his last presidential address to Congress, two years later, President Roosevelt attempted, without success, to convince American legislators that political and civil liberties were insufficient for the pursuit of happiness in a capitalist democracy. Economic rights were also required.[6]

Proposition Six: During the period 1945–1980, increasing substantive equality became the stipulated broad political goal of most developed democracies. This was achieved with substantial degrees of success. Some states established a wide range of universal social programs (pensions, health care, university education) based on the social democratic principle of citizenship rights, while others relied upon liberal means-tested 'safety net' provisions. All democratic states pursued reasonably progressive taxation policies and aimed at maximizing economic growth. And for most, full employment became the labour market objective. The modern welfare state had come into being in the North Atlantic region.

Although critics of the welfare state from both the left and the right emerged during this time, the reality is that this emphasis on building greater equality – by reducing the effect of market-derived income inequalities with progressive taxes and by providing a significant range of social goods – had the dual results of increasing the real freedom of millions of human beings to the highest level in history and of reducing internal conflict to its lowest level in this century. During this period, parties at the left and right extremes of the political spectrum lost most of their support. With the exception of the United States, a growing consensus about a new kind of 'social citizenship' emerged in all North Atlantic democracies. In the European Union and Canada, important social equality provisions were added to the older civil rights, either as legislated universal entitlements or as constitutional rights. Again, with the exception of the United States, all of these democracies went on to ratify the new United Nations Covenant on Economic, Social and Cultural Rights which came into being in 1966. Although in 1960 the United States was spending at about the same level as other advanced democracies on social expenditures, by 1985, this had changed significantly. As a percentage of gross domestic product, much less is now spent by governments in the United States on social expenditures. 'Bail-out' or 'safety-net' welfare states like the United States, cost less in taxes because they deliver less for their citizens.

Proposition Seven: The coming together of a series of developments during the 1970s made possible an ideological assault on equality that came in the 1980s. Lower growth rates, higher oil prices, an aging population, and the transformation of industry from large, unionized, blue-collar enterprises into smaller, unorganized manufacturing and service employment produced unanticipated problems for the welfare state.

Virtually all developed democracies experienced new fiscal pressure, resulting in many cases in large budgetary deficits. All governments were compelled to deal with this situation and a radical form of nineteenth-century liberalism re-emerged. Notably associated with Margaret Thatcher and Ronald Reagan, this old set of ideas was simply an ideology in waiting. Deficits provided the catalyst. Neo-liberals, particularly in the Anglo-American democracies, used the new or looming deficits to legitimate a reduction in equalizing activity by the state. For the first time in half a century, heads of democratic governments began to use industrial, taxation, and social policy initiatives not as a means of promoting equality but as necessary political instruments to re-establish the complete dominance of the market in civil society. This was accompanied, sanctioned, or reinforced by a political vocabulary that denigrated government and promoted the virtue of self-reliance. With few exceptions, corporations had never been committed to the equality-building agenda of post-war democracies. On the contrary, their prevailing ethic emphasized competitively differentiated incomes, private consumption over public projects, and lower taxes in preference to social programs. The privately owned mass media and the newly established conservative think tanks, promoted the same set of values. Thus when Thatcher and Reagan came along to add the influence of the head of government to the equation, the breadth of the ideological assault on social programs and citizens' equality became overwhelming. The re-marketization of life was underway.

When politicians with power attack taxes to pay for social programs as intrusions by the state, portray unions not as democratic institutions but as 'special interests,' equate unregulated capital flows with free trade in goods and services, undervalue the pleasures of public parks in comparison with the benefits of new consumer gadgets, and even argue that there is no such thing as society, only individuals, is it any wonder that many ordinary people in the Anglo-American world started to call into question the welfare state foundations of the post-war order?

Proposition Eight: In many democracies, the march to equality has not only stopped, it has been reversed. Neo-liberals in power consciously rejected burden sharing as a solution to the fiscal problems that emerged in most welfare states. Instead, they embarked on a political agenda that intensified inequality both within the developed democracies and on a global basis. This change in social policy direction came precisely at the time when changes within the market place itself were creating new polarities in income. Fewer and poorly paid jobs at the bottom of the scale are combining with new demands for highly paid educated workers at the upper end.

The policy trend for most advanced democracies during the past two decades, as revealed in OECD data, has been the opposite of the four decades following the Second World War. In addition to the freezing or reduction of social programs, there has been an increasing reliance on regressive consumption taxes, a reduction in the marginal tax rate at the top end of personal incomes, and a widespread policy of reducing corporation taxes. Legislated minimum wages in real value have been allowed to remain at the level prevailing in the early 1970s.

The result of these policies ought to have surprised no one: there has been a reversal of the post-war march to equality. For most countries, middle-income earners have had stagnant real market incomes and as a group their overall national share has dwindled. At the extremes, both the rich and the poor have increased in numbers. However, while the share going to the rich increased, that to the poor has declined. And for a majority of industrial democracies, there has been an overall increase in household inequality in incomes even after consideration of the impact of taxation.

A similar ideological approach was taken internationally. In the 1980s, the major conservative parties in government, including British Conservatives, American Republicans, Japanese Liberals, Canadian Tories, and Australian Liberals, in tandem with the international business community, vigorously promoted a new global order characterized by limited democracy and capitalism without borders. These modern conservatives rejected outright the post-war democratic commitment to greater equality and the related need for government involvement in the economy. International Monetary Fund policies, the North American Free Trade Agreement, the new World Trade Organization, and the proposed Multicultural Agreement on Investment all reflected the new philosophy of marketization without rights – or, more precisely, without human rights. Intellectual property rights are protected in the WTO; workers' civil right to organize a union, is not. The International Democratic Union, a new global body of conservative political parties initiated by Thatcher and Reagan, and officially launched by the former at a major conference in London in 1983, has as its goal the development of a world characterized by states with market economies and minimal government. The rule of law, the protection of property, and international enforcement of trade agreements, all promoted by the more than seventy parties in the International Democratic union, constitute a seriously different agenda from that of the older and now much weaker grouping of conservative parties, the International Christian Democratic Union. While the ICDU supports the notion of a 'social market economy' and specifically endorses the International Covenant on Economic, Social and Cultural Rights, the new neo-liberal International Democratic Union consciously rejects both.

Proposition Nine: Globalization has been a contributing cause of the increase in inequality in the North Atlantic democracies. The meaning, the newness, and the impact of globalization are all contested concepts. I use 'globalization' in the restrictive economic sense to mean the growth in international flows of goods, services, and capital. That such recent growth, quite disproportional to that of any previous period, including the end of the nineteenth century, has occurred, should be now beyond dispute.[7] The relaxation or abolition of virtually all state barriers on such flows has reduced the capacity of the developed welfare state to set its own monetary and fiscal policies. The consequence has been new power and greater freedom for both corporations and the educated elite to move, whether or not they do so. The net effect has been a significant reduction in their share of the tax burden, with a resulting increase for everyone else, that is, more inequality for the majority.

Proposition Ten: Having witnessed the negative social consequences of increasing inequality, most North Atlantic democracies have sought to make inequality more acceptable. Instead of the stipulated post-war democratic goal of creating greater equality, among many OECD countries there is instead increasing talk of achieving 'cohesion' or 'inclusion.' More recently, so-called Third Way politics has become the new mantra, and with the seeming conversion of Chancellor Schroeder in Germany it is no longer restricted to the Anglo-American democracies. Instead of challenging the increasing dominance of the market in our lives, there is growing acquiescence. Instead of rights, governments talk of obligations (mostly for the poor and the unemployed, not the rich and the corporations). Instead of equality, they propose cohesion. The goal is no longer to persuade electorates of the need for more economic justice but to make compliance with the basic thrust of a market economy more acceptable. Put positively, those marginalized or excluded are being targeted by education programs designed to enable them to get a job in the market system. Instead of the post-war discourse of democratic equality, which would provoke confrontation with the existing trends, there have been exhortations about the sharing of undefined values and an emphasis on policies (often quite desirable) that have no immediate effects on existing maldistributions of power and income. A new job for an unemployed British youth is not to be sneered at. But what if his or her wage is below the poverty level while the rich continue to get richer? In the United States the most recent data show that the real incomes of 'middle-class' workers have finally started to move beyond the level of the 1970s. However, the data also indicate the same workers cannot afford to purchase a home, obtain adequate health insurance, or send their children to good universities, all of which were possible in the early 1970s.[8] In short, middle-class Americans can no longer afford what were taken to be defining characteristics of what it meant to be 'middle class' in the post-war period. Is durable cohesion likely or desirable in such circumstances?

As I write, the 'working definition' of social cohesion used at senior levels of the Canadian government provides a further illustration of the problem. At a time when the average family income has actually dropped by $4,000 (between 1989 and 1996 for families with children over eighteen) and that of the richest 10 per cent has escalated to 314 times the bottom 10 per cent[9] there is Alice-in-Wonderland talk of social cohesion. We are told that social cohesion is an 'ongoing process of developing a community of shared values' and there is a reference to 'a sense of trust, hope and reciprocity among all Canadians.' However, there is no expression of the need to build communities involving reciprocity in power-sharing or generating a sense of trust because of a commitment to a more equitable distribution of wealth. Similarly, while the Blair government in Britain has taken commendable initiatives on political and civil rights, it has essentially left alone the unequal distributional struggle of the market. The same government released a report on 'social exclusion' which showed that between 1979 and 1995, the share of income going to the poorest 10 per cent dropped by 8 per cent. That of the top 10 per cent increased by about 70 per cent.

While it is clearly possible to construct an acceptable statement of social goals for a modern democratic state that includes the language of community and cohesion, to do so without linking such concepts to the need to seriously reduce existing inequalities in income and power is to abandon the democratic citizenship goal of social equality. There are now many in Anglo-American countries who use 'community' and 'cohesion' the way neo-conservatives once co-opted 'family values,' fine phrases that can disguise or gloss over brutalizing inequality.

Concluding Thoughts – Politics and Values Matter

I believe the principal barriers to further equality in income and power are political and institutional, not economic. For reasons already indicated, it is true that there are some new economic constraints at both the national and international levels. When it comes to social policy, however, it is clear that the internal political values, priorities, and preestablished structures of social programs of a given nation matter a great deal. The particular circumstances of each of the advanced democracies are the primary determinants of what kind of programs will emerge from the impact of globalization, which is affecting them all.

Important differences exist between Norway and the Netherlands. But each of these countries retains policy commitments aimed at furthering equality in the distribution of income and the maintenance of workers' rights, which are significantly superior to those found in most other OECD states. Similarly, Germany, Sweden, and France differ in important ways from each other. However, the rich in each of these countries send their children to the same well-funded public school system as all other families, with significant consequences favouring social equality. In contrast, in intensely class-divided Britain, rich and many middle-class families continue to use private schools and health services qualitatively superior to those available to the majority. The fact is that if the British paid the same level of taxes as the Germans and the French, they could double their level of spending on their deplorably underfunded health and education systems.[10] It is the absence of British willingness to pay more taxes and nothing else that perpetuates such serious inequality in the delivery of two of the most important social services.

Although most developed democracies have not been adversely affected by the expansion of international trade in goods and services, the recent removal of virtually all national barriers to the movement of capital has created fiscal and monetary problems that limit steps to further equality. Government autonomy to determine desired levels of social spending and taxation has been reduced. National currencies and governments' capacities to establish their own interest rate policy have been put at risk by the absence of any controls on the flow of short-term capital. This reality exacerbated currency crises that did great harm to the lives of millions in Mexico and in a number of Asian countries. How long will the established democracies in North America and Europe remain exempt? It was political decision making that liberated capital from any serious regulation, and only political decision making can put the genie partially back in the bottle.

Whether at the national or international level, that elusive entity known as 'political will' seems to be the most important problem. When the determined march to greater equality was launched towards the end of the Second World War, the heterogeneous group of leaders and political parties who provided the initiative had no reason to believe their action would be met with such a prolonged period of success. While they benefitted from strong post-war public support, the evidence is clear that major decisions were taken *before* the war's end, by leaders who had come to understand that laissez-faire capitalism, whatever its productive merits, is inevitably deeply unequal in its distributional effect, destructive of communities, and seriously prone to intermittent depressions. They believed change was needed, and made it happen.

A two-decade-long experience of neo-liberalism at a global level is providing alarming evidence that their understanding was sound. Recent elections in the United States, Britain, and Germany demonstrate that skilful politicians leading parties which once had the goal of furthering equality are capable of winning majorities over conservative opponents. It remains to be seen whether they have the interest or capacity to produce the policies needed to reverse the disturbing increase in inequality within and between nations.

The question 'Will we need another great depression before the required national and international institutional changes are made?' can have no sensible answer. Politics, now as ever, is unpredictable. Looking at the past we can always find something that, while at the time seemed merely possible, did in fact happen. We are then inclined to think the possible was inevitable. Such thinking, whether about the past or the future, is illusory. Politicians do not create the social and economic circumstances to which they must respond. But in responding they make value-based choices that can give new direction to those circumstances. They will not know how today's uncertain populations will react to new egalitarian initiatives for the state, civil society, and the private economy until such steps are taken. Nor can they be certain of other consequences such policies might have. However, they are aware of the terrible injustice neo-liberalism is imposing on the world. Politicians must be told that exclusive reliance on policies designed simply to integrate people into changing markets is a dangerous abandonment of our democratic commitment to equality. Political morality in a democracy has little to do with the morality of family or personal life. As the ancient Greeks understood, it has everything to do with attempts to build more equal societies.

NOTES

1 J.S. Mill, *Principles of Political Economy* (Toronto: University of Toronto Press, 1965), 3:762.

2 J.S. Mill, *Utilitarianism* (London: J.W. Dent and Sons, 1954), 58.

3 Ibid.

4 Robert Dahl has recently pointed out that Madison created this distinction for his own political purposes. At the time 'republicanism' and 'democracy' were used as synonyms. See R. Dahl, *On Democracy* (New Haven: Yale University Press, 1998).

5 Edward Berstein, *Evolutionary Socialism* (New York: Schotkin Books, 1961), 147–8.

6 Franklin Delano Roosevelt, State of the Union Address, United States Congress, 11 January 1944.

7 See David Held et al., *Global Transformations* (Stanford: Stanford University Press, 1999).

8 See Jeff Madrick, 'How New Is the New Economy?' *New York Review of Books*, 23 Sept. 1999.

9 See Armine Yalnizyan, *The Growing Gap* (Toronto: The Centre for Social Justice, 1998).

10 See the article by Andrew Dilnot, Director of the Institute for Fiscal Studies in London, in *The Observer*, 30 Mar. 1997.

PART TWO

THE PERSPECTIVES OF PHILOSOPHY, ECONOMICS, AND DEMOCRACY

2

Understanding the Universal Welfare State: An Institutional Approach

BO ROTHSTEIN

The Puzzle of Increased Variation

In the comparative welfare state research, two major findings are of interest when thinking about the possible future of the welfare state. The first and most well-known of these findings is the differences which exist in the quality and scope of welfare state programs among the industrialized Western democracies (Esping-Andersen 1990). Quantitatively, in the mid-1990s, the Scandinavian countries spent almost twice as much as a percentage of gross domestic product (GDP) on social insurance and social assistance than did the United States (30 per cent compared to 14 per cent). Most other European countries fell somewhere in between. The less well-known finding is that this huge difference in welfare state ambitions is a fairly recent phenomenon. In the early 1960s these countries spent almost the same percentage of GDP on welfare policies (OECD 1994). Given the internationalization of values, increase in trade, and globalization of capital, for example, this is a rather unexpected development. After all, these are countries with basically the same type of social, economic, and political structures, meaning they are all Western democratic capitalist market economies. Most social scientists working in the early 1960s would probably have predicted convergence in social policy between these countries, not such a dramatic divergence.

One way to explain the differences in welfare state programs would be through standard political variables: the ideological orientation of dominant political parties in Scandinavia are different (read: more Social Democratic) from those in the United States or Canada. This is of course true, but it should also be said that all Scandinavian countries have had extended periods with non-socialist/conservative parties in government. Furthermore, these periods have been marked more by expansion than contraction of welfare state spending (Rothstein 1998). A second type of explanation would point to general norms and values, for example, that Scandinavians, for whatever historical and cultural reasons, are more inclined to embrace norms such as equality and social justice. The problem, however, is that comparative studies based on survey data find very little, if any, support for this type of explanation. To the contrary, such studies report a striking similarity in basic values and norms about justice and equality, for example, between countries with very different ambitions in welfare state measures (Svallfors 1996). A third type of explanation is directed at differences in class power and class formation. This has become known as the 'power-resources' approach (Korpi 1983) and has provided a fruitful way of explaining the puzzle of increased variation. However, there are two main problems which the power-resources approach cannot solve. While there is definitely a strong relationship between the strength of the labour movement and social spending, the causal mechanism is double-linked. The strength of the labour movement in Sweden, Finland, and Denmark, for example, can be explained to a large extent by the character of social policy initiatives and forms of institutionalization that took place in the 1930s (Rothstein 1992). The implication is that the organizational power of the working class is as much an effect, as it is a cause of social policy. In the Scandinavian countries, support for the welfare state goes far beyond the working class or the Social Democratic parties. In fact, it can be argued that some of the most expansionary periods have taken place with non-socialist governments in power (Lindbeck 1997). So, we are left with a genuine puzzle – standard theories about economic development, political power or social norms seem not to be able to explain the differences in welfare state programs.

The Universal Welfare State and Procedural Justice

I propose that this puzzle can be understood from a neo-institutionalist perspective (cf. Rothstein 1996a; Steinmo 1993). The argument is that the explanation of the puzzle of increased variation has to do with how the institutions of the welfare state programs have been historically established. In order to highlight the differences, I will concentrate the analysis on Sweden, which in various studies has been shown to be the most expansive welfare state.

TABLE 2.1
The redistributive effect of the universal welfare state

Group	Average income	Tax (40%)	Transfers	Income after taxes and transfers
A (20%)	1000	400	240	840
B (20%)	800	320	240	720
C (20%)	600	240	240	600
D (20%)	400	160	240	480
E (20%)	200	80	240	360
Ratio between groups A & E	5/1	(=1200)	(1200/5=24)	2.33/1

Speaking from an institutionalist perspective, what characterizes the Swedish and the other Scandinavian (and some other North European) welfare states is that most programs are universal, not selective. This means that social programs such as old-age pensions, health care, childcare, education, child allowances, and health insurance are not targeted only for 'the poor,' but instead cover the entire population without consideration of their ability to pay.

Many scholars have maintained that, since benefits and services are distributed in roughly equal shares to everyone, and since the tax system is proportional on the whole, no real redistribution between income groups takes place in a universal welfare state (Barry 1990; Gutman 1990). Some economists have even claimed that a universal welfare system amounts largely to a costly bureaucratic roundabout with very little redistributive effects (Tullock 1983). Nothing could be further from the truth. The data presented in Table 2.1 serve to illustrate why.

The redistributive logic of the model is as follows. In the first column, income earners are divided, for the sake of simplicity, into five groups of equal size and according to average income. We assume the average income of the group earning most is five times that of the group earning least. This difference, which we may call the inequality quotient, is 5/1. We further assume, *nota bene*, not a progressive but rather a strictly proportional system of income taxes. We set the tax rate at 40 per cent, which corresponds roughly to that part of the Swedish public sector currently 56.2 per cent of gross national product (GNP), which is spent on social, educational, and other welfare policy. Finally, we assume that all public benefits and services are universal, which means that the individuals in each group receive *on average*, the same sum in the form of cash benefits and/or subsidized public services. The result, as seen in the last column, is a dramatic reduction in inequality between group A and group E, from 5/1 down to 2.33/1. The level of inequality has thus been reduced by more than half in this model of how the universal welfare policy works. Note that this redistributive logic works the same if you take the groups' (or persons) income over a lifetime or compare it at one single point in time. Only if you can argue that over time, the persons in groups A and B will switch with the persons in groups D and E, will the redistributive effect decrease.

This model is strongly supported by empirical data depicting how different welfare states redistribute income (McFate, Smeeding, and Rainwater 1995). It turns out, perhaps contrary to one's intuition, that the states which tax and give 'equally' to everyone, that is, the universal systems, effectively redistribute economic resources, while the systems intended to tax rich in order to give to the poor end up with much less redistribution. The reason for this paradox in redistribution, as shown in Table 2.1, is that while taxes are usually relative (a fixed percentage of income for example), benefits or services are usually nominal. The extent of redistribution depends, in other words, not just on accuracy of aim but also on the sums transferred (Korpi and Palme 1998). To put it in other words: if you tax the rich and give to the poor, the rich will not accept high taxes.

Procedural Justice and the Universal Welfare State

Most discussions of social policy are concerned only with the condition of substantial justice. However, several studies show that people are also interested in procedural justice (Levi 1998; Tyler 1996, 1998). The public discussion of social policy in a selective system often becomes a question of what the well-adjusted majority should do about 'the others,' – the socially marginalized minority. The substantial justice of the system can thereby come under question by the majority, who might start asking questions about its procedural justice: first, where the line between the needy and non-needy should be drawn, and second, whether the needy ('the others') themselves are not to blame for their predicament (and therefore unable to legitimately claim assistance). We may refer to the first as the general and the second as the individual boundary-drawing problems. In the selective model, the discussion often comes to focus on how to separate the 'deserving' from the 'undeserving' poor (Katz 1989). This translates into a seemingly unending debate about where and how to draw the boundary lines. Leading politicians are therefore likely to find themselves in a situation in which it becomes increasingly difficult to argue that the selective programs are normatively fair. Public consent to the system is undermined, rather, because the social policy debate comes to turn not on what is generally fair, but on what is specifically necessary for 'the others.'

Furthermore, in a selective system, the moral logic of the discourse tends in itself to undermine the legitimacy of the system. Most selective types of policies that are structured to integrate a specific group with the rest of society seem to entail a paradox. To motivate selective measures, such as affirmative action, the targeted group must first to be singled out as inherently different from ordinary citizens. But if the group is so different, how can its members, by any social policy initiative, become like 'ordinary citizens'? If the selective policy has only marginal effects, the usual strategy for those advocating it is to argue that the group is even more different (and thus has even more special needs) than what had initially been presumed, and therefore needs more selective/targeted policies.

Under a universal system, in which the idea is that the state furnishes all citizens with what Amarty Sen has labelled basic capabilities, the moral logic is altogether different (Sen 1983). The public discourse about social policy in a universal system cannot be conducted in the terms indicated by the question: 'what shall we do about these deviant groups/individuals?' Or, as former U.S. Vice-President Dan Quayle put it in a debate: 'those people' (Katz 1989, 236). Since the universal welfare policy embraces all citizens, the debate assumes quite another character. Social policy is now thought to concern the entire community, and the question becomes what, from a general standpoint, is a fair manner in which to organize social policy. There is no need for a public discussion concerning boundary lines for 'the others,' simply because no lines need to be drawn. Welfare policy does not, therefore, turn into a question of what should be done about 'the poor' and 'the maladjusted,' but considers instead what constitutes general fairness in respect to the relation between citizens and the state. The question becomes not 'how shall we solve *their* problem?' but rather 'how shall we solve our common problems with social insurance'?

If people care about procedural as well as substantive justice, they are also likely to focus on whether welfare policy can be carried out in a fair manner. How does the choice of a universal or selective welfare policy affect the public's view of state capacity? One should bear in mind that a typical universal welfare program, like flat-rate pensions or child allowances, is a great deal simpler, cheaper, and easier to implement than its selective counterpart. This is largely because there is no need, in a program of a universal type, for an administrative apparatus charged with carrying out the two types of eligibility tests which are a necessary concomitant of a selective program. These tests would have to be administered to ascertain (1) whether a given applicant is entitled to support, and (2) if so, the amount of support required. Social policy can instead be designed as a form of specified citizen rights, and the social duties of the state can be rigorously defined in order to respect the integrity of citizens. The point is, depending on the institutions we select for furnishing citizens with basic capabilities, we create different types of moral logic in the social policy discourse. In the case of a selective policy, the state separates those citizens unable to provide such basic capabilities for themselves and furnishes them with said capabilities. To do this, however it must first determine whether or not these citizens belong to the needy group, and if so, how much they need. The problem that arises is that it is very hard to do these things without violating the principle that the state should treat all citizens with, as it has been stated by Ronald Dworkin, 'equal concern and respect' (Dworkin 1977, 180ff). The very act of separating out the needy almost always stamps them as socially inferior, as 'others' with other types of social characteristics and needs, and results most often in stigmatization (Salonen 1993, 176–80). In his important book *Spheres of Justice*, Michael Walzer argues that social policy of this sort is incompatible with the maintenance of recipients' self-respect (Walzer 1983, 227f).

Selective programs present serious problems of procedural justice because they must allow local administrators a wide field for discretionary action. The difficulty of finding usable criteria for selecting recipients can often become unmanageable. This creates a 'black hole of democracy,' in which citizens find themselves faced with an administration or system of rules that no one really understands, and in which no one can be held responsible. In sum, the selective model leads, as Robert Goodin has stated to 'unavoidable,' 'insurmountable,' and 'insoluble' problems in respect to the arbitrary treatment of citizens seeking assistance (Goodin 1988, 219f).

The difficulty of handling the discretionary power of administrators in selective programs has two important consequences. These consequences are often thought to be opposites, but in fact they are two sides of the same coin. They are the bureaucratic abuse of power, and fraud on the part of clients. Applicants in a selective system, if rational, will claim that their situation is worse than it actually is, and describe their prospects for solving their problems on their own as small to nonexistent. The administrators in such a system, for their part, often have incentives from their superiors to be suspicious of clients' claims. In game theory, this is known as 'the control game,' a rather sad game because it has no stable equilibria and thus no solution. Fraud by a few clients feeds into increased control, which in its turn feeds into increased fraud by more clients, and so on (Hermansson 1990).

The question of procedural justice therefore looms large in selective systems. Even if cases of cheating, fraud, and the abuse of power are in fact relatively rare, the sensationalistic logic of mass media means that such cases will receive great attention and thereby influence the majority's 'cognitive maps' on what social policy is about. It is very difficult to combine means-testing with procedural justice, for means-testing entails a violation of citizens' integrity – either in the means-test itself, or in the verification checks that often follow.

Attitudes towards Different Types of Social Program

One consequence stemming from modern social science is that citizens are asked now and again about their attitudes towards various matters, including welfare policy. How does the empirical evidence look, then, in relation to the institutionalist theory? Can empirical support be found for the proposition that, if the institutions of social policy are structured according to the principles of this theory, they will by themselves create support for the reproduction of the policy? Axel Hadenius in 1986 and Stefan Svallfors have conducted survey research that speaks to this problem. They have asked identical questions of representative samples of the Swedish population about their support for different welfare state programs. The results may be seen in Table 2.2.

At least two results of these studies are worthy of note. The first is the marked and stable difference in support for different types of programs over time. Support for the universal programs is unambiguously strong and stable, while the opposite is true for the two selective programs (housing allowances and social assistance). Following our prediction from above, the programs with strong support are (with one exception), more universal than selective, while the two programs with weak support are clearly selective. The most crucial difference is that both hous-

TABLE 2.2
Attitudes towards public expenditures. (Answers to the following question: 'Taxes are used for various purposes. Do you think the revenues spent on the purposes mentioned below should be increased, held the same, or reduced?' The figures in the table repre-sent the percentage of those wishing to increase expenditures minus the percentage of those wishing to reduce them.)

	1981	1986	1992	1997
Health Care	+42	+44	+48	+75
Support for the elderly	+29	+33	+58	+68
Support to families with children	+19	+35	+17	+30
Housing allowances	−23	−23	−25	−20
Social assistance	−5	−5	−13	+−0
Primary and secondary education	+20	+30	+49	+69
Employment policy	+63	+46	+55	+27
State and municipal administration	−54	−53	−68	−65

Sources: Hadenius 1986; Svallfors 1996, 1998.

ing allowances and social assistance are means-tested programs and thus difficult to implement with respect to procedural justice.

One program that stands out is employment policy which is, for most parts, selective. Nevertheless, such policy has fairly strong support, although it has declined somewhat in the latest survey. One reason may be that this is a program which, at least in Sweden, does not serve 'the poor' only, but for historical reasons has a much broader range in what is known as 'active labour market policy.' Not only unemployed workers, but also workers who in the future risk unemployment, including many white-collar workers, attend job-counselling and vocational training. Secondly, this is a program in which historically the ruling Social Democratic Party has paid special attention to the problems of legitimacy in the implementation process. For example, decisions about who is eligible for unemployment insurance are taken by union representatives (Rothstein 1996b).

There is reason to compare Sweden with the United States on this point. As Margaret Weir has noted, it is striking that no form of active labour market policy has been successfully established in the United States, despite the fact that a strong work ethic pervades American society (Weir 1992). The attempt made beginning in the 1960s – CETA (Comprehensive Employment and Training Act) – was that social program which the Reagan administration found easiest to dismantle upon assuming office in 1981. The CETA was equated, in public opinion, with waste, bureaucracy, and a focus on helping only certain socially distinct minority groups; it was, in short, a program exhibiting all the problematic features of selective policies. An American scholar puts it this way: 'The legitimacy of CETA was seriously eroded by the stream of 'bad press' it was receiving – adverse publicity on waste, nepotism, patronage and corruption. Perhaps nothing contributed more to the loss of confidence and legitimacy in CETA and, ultimately, to its demise' (Mucciaroni 1990, 1976).

While part of the explanation presented here is ideological, relying on what political leaders hold forth as substantially just, how the government arranges the administrative institutions of the welfare state is also crucial. The evidence from the Swedish system of welfare policies provides empirical support for the institutionalist approach that procedural justice is important. The universal programs command widespread support in the population while the two programs (social assistance and housing allowances) which appear most clearly to violate the principles of this theory enjoy the least support. These programs are difficult (not to say impossible) to implement in a procedurally fair manner. They make it easy for those who want to attack the welfare state to argue that those receiving benefits do not contribute according to ability to defraying the costs of the program. It should be added that in the Swedish case, the construction of the institutions that made it possible to solve the collective action problem by no means came into existence by chance or as unintended consequences of other political decisions. Instead, they were deliberately crafted by centrally placed political actors, very much with the problem of procedural legitimacy in mind (Olsson 1993; Rothstein 1998).

The Future Economic Viability of the Universal Welfare State

I would like to conclude by addressing the problem of the economic viability of the universal welfare state. I have come to realize that the welfare state is, by most economists, understood as a sort of altruistic luxury established to take care of 'the poor' (Freeman 1997; Lindbeck 1997). The major flaw in this analysis is that the demand side is totally neglected. What is missing is that in a universal system, as should be clear from the argument made above, the major part of the demand does not come from the 'poor minority' or from any altruistic ideals within the majority to help the disadvantaged part of the population. Instead, because the system is universal, the demand comes from the vast majority of the population. To present this argument, I must ask the reader to follow me in a simple thought experiment. Assume that all welfare state programs in the Nordic countries were abolished, and that the taxes people pay for these services were to be reduced as well. What would the majority living in these countries do? My guess, which is substantiated by survey research (Svallfors 1998) as well as by the American example, is that the vast majority of the population would buy health insurance, pension plans, education and day care for their children, unemployment insurance, and so on on the market. Contrary to what the public choice approach tells us, what governments in democratic welfare states produce, for the most part, cannot be explained by budget maximizing bureaucrats or politicians seeking re-election, because the demand is there.

Secondly, would a private market system be more efficient than the universal and mandatory systems that exist in the Nordic countries? This we cannot say for sure, but there are strong theoretical arguments as well as empirical indications that private market systems are less cost-efficient than universal systems with regard to social insurance and social services. Social insurance systems are particularly sensitive to what is known as problems of assymetric information between producers and consumers. For example, insurance companies will have to make very costly efforts to screen applicants to get rid of 'bad risks.' They must also engage in costly surveillance to ensure that the (naturally rent-seeking) providers of health care and other such services do not engage in various kinds of fraud. This surveillance turns out to be very difficult because the provider (i.e., the doctor or the hospital) and the consumer (the patient) have ample opportunities as well as a mutual interest to shield information about treatments and costs from the insurance companies. Thirdly, those who apply for social insurance will do whatever they can to try to hide the fact that they may be bad risks (by economists labelled 'lemons'), making it all the more necessary for insurance providers to obtain and run costly information systems. In sum, the transaction costs in private insurance systems tend to become much higher than in universal and public systems. Nicholas Barr has stated that these information problems 'provide both a theoretical *justification of* and an *explanation for* a welfare state which is much more than a safety net. Such a welfare state is justified not simply by redistributive aims one may (or may not) have, but because it does things which private markets for technical reasons would either do inefficiently, or would not do at all' (Barr 1992).

Another question in this thought experiment is whether we would increase social utility if we let people decide to take the 'James Dean' option in life. This means letting people choose to stand the risk of becoming old, unemployed, or ill without relying on any public assistance (and of course allowing them to spend the money as they wish while they are young, healthy, and in demand on the labour market). Theoretically, the answer is yes. The utility for both the James Dean types as well as the more cautious types would be increased. In practice though, there seems to be no democratic country in which the public or the politicians have been able to muster the moral strength to actually say no to the James Dean types when the day of reckoning arrives. Thus, these persons will be taken care of, and this is the argument for making the basic forms of social insurance mandatory.

The empirical side of this argument is more problematic, but it has not been possible to show a negative relation between high public spending and economic growth (Dowrick 1996; Korpi 1996). In health care, there seems to be ample evidence that the U.S. system of private insurance is much less cost-efficient than the Nordic model with universal insurance (Gerdtham and Löthgren 1998).

My point is, the Nordic type of welfare state is not an altruistic luxury established to take care of 'the poor' and should thus not be evaluated simply by comparing efficiency costs with gains in the form of increased equality. Since the demand for social insurance and social service exists, the costs will be there, whether or not the demand is filled by government provision or by market forces. Most of the evidence seems to show that, due to the problem of assymetric information in this area, mandatory and universal systems are more cost-efficient than private insurance systems.

Still, one could add that the level of social insurance and social services in the Nordic welfare states are so high, that a large part of the population (i.e., 'the poor') would not be able to, or chose to, afford it if provided by market forces at production costs. This is of course correct, but it may also be the case that the efficiency gains with mandatory and universal systems compared to a private market system covers these 'costs.' This we do not know, but the possibility should not be ruled out without further empirical research.

In conclusion, it seems as if the economists analysing the Nordic welfare states have forgotten the oldest of all economic lessons, namely, that if there is a credit account, there should be a debit account. They seem to take for granted that anything provided for by the government is not truly in demand. Why this is so, and why their analysis of the universal welfare states have such a marked ideological leaning to the right, I leave for others to speculate. Let me finish by stressing that it should be remembered that behind the macroeconomic figures describing the differences between welfare states are the lives of real people. These figures compare the economic situation of single-parent families in the mid-1980s, 54 per cent in the United States and 46 per cent in Canada of whom live in severe poverty (defined as having less than half of the median income), compared to 6 per cent in the Netherlands and 7 per cent in Sweden (McFate, Smeeding, and Rainwater 1995). Another interesting figure here is the difference in prison interns. Of 100,000 persons, 580 are in prison in the United States compared to an average of 40 in the Scandinavian countries (Wacquant 1998). There are of course many different reasons behind crime and imprisonment, but severe poverty would clearly count as one.

NOTE

This essay builds on many discussions with Peter Mayers, whose ideas and suggestions have been most valuable.

REFERENCES

Barr, Nicholas. 1992. 'Economic Theory and the Welfare State: A Survey and Interpretation.' *Journal of Economic Literature* 30: 741–803.

Barry, Brian. 1990. 'The Welfare State vs. the Relief of Poverty.' *Ethics* 100 (3): 503–29.

Dowrick, Steve. 1996. 'Swedish Economic Performance and Swedish Economic Debate: A View from Outside.' *Economic Journal* 106 (November): 1772–9.

Dworkin, Ronald. 1977. *Taking Rights Seriously*. London: Duckworth.

Esping-Andersen, Gosta. 1990. *The Three Worlds of Welfare Capitalism*. Cambridge: Polity Press.

Freeman, Richard B. 1997. 'Are Norway's Solidaristic and Welfare State Policies Viable in the Modern Global Economy?' In J.E. Dokvik and A.H. Steen, eds., *Making Solidarity Work?* Oslo: Scandinavian University Press.

Gerdtham, Ulf G., and Mikael Löthgren. 1998. *'Health Care System Effects on*

Cost Efficiency in the OECD Countries'. Stockholm: Stockholm School of Economics.

Goodin, Robert E. 1988. *Reasons for Welfare: The Political Theory of the Welfare State*. Princeton: Princeton University Press.

Gutman, Amy. 1990. Introduction. In Amy Butman, ed., *Democracy and the Welfare State*. Princeton: Princeton University Press.

Hadenius, Axel. 1986. *A Crisis of the Welfare State?* Uppsala: Almqvist and Wiksell.

Hermansson, Jorgen. 1990. *Spelteorins nytta. Om rationalitet I politik och vetenskap*. Uppsala: Statsvetenskapliga Föreningen.

Katz, Michael B. 1989. *The Undeserving Poor: From the War on Poverty to the War on Welfare*. New York: Pantheon Books.

Korpi, Walter. 1983. *The Democratic Class Struggle*. London: Routledge & Kegan Paul.

– 1996. 'Eurosclerosis and the Sclerosis of Objectivity: On the Role of Values among Economic Policy Experts.' *Economic Journal* 106 (2): 439–56.

Korpi, Walter, and Joakim Palme. 1998. 'The Paradox of Redistribution and Strategies of Equality: Welfare State Institutions, Inequality, and Poverty in the Western Countries.' *American Sociological Review* 63 (5): 661–87.

Levi, Margaret. 1998. *Consent, Dissent and Patriotism*. New York: Cambridge University Press.

Lindbeck, Assar. 1997. *The Swedish Experiment*. Stockholm: SNS Förlag.

McFate, Katherine, Timothy Smeeding, and Lee Rainwater. 1995. 'Markets and States: Poverty Trends and Transfer System Effectiveness in the 1980s.' In K. McFate, R. Lawson, and W.J. Wilson, eds., *Poverty: Inequality and the Future of Social Policy: Western States in the New World Order*. New York: Russell Sage Foundation.

Mucciaroni, Gary. 1990. *The Political Failure of Unemployment Policy 1945–1982*. Pittsburgh: University of Pittsburgh Press.

OECD. 1994. *New Orientations for Social Policy*. Paris: Organization for Economic Development.

Olsson, Sven E. 1993. *Social Policy and Welfare State in Sweden*. Lund: Arkiv.

Rothstein, Bo. 1992. 'Labour-Market Institutions and Working-Class Strength.' In S. Steinmo, K. Thelen, and F. Longstreth, eds., *Structuring Politics. Historical Institutionalism in a Comparative perspective* Cambridge: Cambridge University Press.

– 1996a. 'Political Institutions – an Overview.' In R.E. Goodin and H.-D. Klingemann, eds., *A New Handbook for Political Science*. Oxford: Oxford University Press.

– 1996b. *The Social Democratic State: The Swedish Model and the Bureaucratic Problem of Social Reforms*. Pittsburgh: University of Pittsburgh Press.

– 1998. *Just Institutions Matter: The Moral and Political Logic of the Universal Welfare State*. Cambridge: Cambridge University Press.

Salonen, Tapio. 1993. *Margins of Welfare: A Study of Modern Functions of Social Assistance*. Lund: Hällstead Press.

Sen, Amarty. 1983. *Choice, Welfare and Measurement*. Cambridge, Mass.: MIT Press.

Steinmo, Sven. 1993. *Taxation and Democracy: Swedish, British and American Approaches to Financing the Modern State*. New Haven: Yale University Press.

Svallfors, Stefan. 1996. *Välfärdsstatens moraliska ekonomi*. Umea: Borea Förlag.

– 1998. *Mellan risk och tilltro: Opinionsstödet för en kollektiv välfärdspolitik*. Umea: Department of Sociology, Umea University.

Tullock, Gordon. 1983. *Economics of Income Redistribution*. Boston: Kluwer and Nijhoff.

Tyler, Tom. 1996. 'Understanding Why the Justice of Group Procedures Matters: A Test of the Psychological Dynamics of the Group-Value Model.' *Journal of Personality and Social Psychology* 70 (5): 913–30.

– 1998. Trust and Democratic Governance. In V. Braithwaite and M. Levi, eds., *Trust & Governance*. New York: Russell Sage Foundation.

Wacquant, Loic. 1998. 'Lémprisonnement de "classes dangereuse" aux Etats-Unis.' *Le Monde Diplomatique*, July 1998, 21–2.

Walzer, Michael. 1983. *Spheres of Justice: A Defense of Pluralism and Justice*. New York: Basic Books.

Weir, Margaret. 1992. *Politics and Jobs: The Boundaries of Employment Policy in the United States*. Princeton: Princeton University Press.

3

The Party's Over: What Now?

JOHN RICHARDS

> [Labour Party] ideology was out of date; and yet the structures of the Party had no means of bringing that home. In the end, of course, the country brought it home, by rejecting – repeatedly – the prospect of a Labour government.
>
> Tony Blair (1995), address to Fabian Society celebrating the fiftieth anniversay of the 1945 Labour victory

Canadian social democrats began the 1990s with unprecedented electoral success. Following elections in Ontario (in 1990) and in British Columbia and Saskatchewan (in 1991), New Democrats governed the majority of Canadians, at least at the provincial level. At the end of the decade, the Ontario New Democratic Party (NDP) had not only been defeated; its Queen's Park caucus was below the threshold required to maintain official party status. In British Columbia, the NDP tenuously clings to power at time of writing (November 2000) but, based on contemporary opinion polling, the party would suffer a humiliating defeat were an election held in the near future. In the last three federal elections (in 1993, 1997, and 2000) the NDP received, on average, less than 10 per cent of the popular vote. This is roughly half the average received in the nine other federal elections held subsequent to the party's 1961 founding (elections between 1963 and 1988).

A few small candles relieve this electoral gloom. At both the federal and provincial level, the party has realized gains in Atlantic Canada, and it retains a large measure of public confidence in two of the three prairie provinces. The party retained office in the 1999 Saskatchewan election.[1] In another 1999 election, the Manitoba NDP returned to office after eleven years in opposition.

I. The Defining Moment

The thesis of this article is simple. Building a mass political party on the foundation of organized labour has become a fundamentally flawed strategy; those who seek to advance the heritage of the left must find another. Before I formally lay out the thesis and its implications, let me sketch the tumultuous events in Ontario in 1993, events which I take to be the defining moment for understanding the fate of Canadian social democrats.

The Ontario New Democrats came to power in 1990, in the opening months of a severe recession, and governed at a time when the majority of Canadians were en route to deciding that public sector deficits must be eliminated and that further tax increases were unjustified. Premier Bob Rae's cabinet initially resisted fiscal restraint and, in constructing their first two budgets (for fiscal years 1991–2 and 1992–3), applied traditional Keynesian ideas about providing fiscal stimulus.

By late 1992, economic advisers at Queen's Park underwent a traumatic loss of faith in the province's attempt to stimulate economic activity via deficit spending. The open nature of the provincial economy plus general public misgiving about the longer term implications of rising public debt had led to disappointing results. Extrapolating trends from their first two budgets, the advisers projected a provincial deficit growing to rival that in Ottawa. Rae and his cabinet were part of that collective loss of faith; they became convinced that expenditure restraint was required in order to maintain majority willingness to pay for core provincial programs. The NDP caucus more or less acquiesced to this new direction but most party members were far from convinced. They perceived their government succumbing to what militants disparaged as a 'neoconservative corporate agenda of budget slashing.'

Canadian provinces devote roughly 60 per cent of program spending (i.e., spending other than debt service costs) on salaries for civil servants, teachers, nurses, social workers, and others who provide valuable but labour-intensive services. Given the relative weight of salaries, serious spending restraint inevitably meant public sector pay cuts and/or lay-offs. Throughout the first half of 1993, the cabinet doggedly attempted to reach a compromise with union allies, whereby the government would guarantee job security in exchange for salary cuts. Union leaders balked at the proposed 'social contract' and in the summer of 1993, amidst tumultuous labour opposition, the cabinet unilaterally imposed payroll cuts via legislation.

One of the prominent labour leaders adamantly opposed to the social contract legislation was Buzz Hargrove, head of the Canadian Auto Workers. Writing five years later, he had lost none of his outrage that a NDP government constrain workers in the exercise of collective bargaining: 'To the Canadian Auto Workers, Bill 48 [the Ontario social contract legislation] was so odious that we felt we had no recourse but to withdraw our support of the NDP ... Our decision to refuse financial support to the NDP did not mean we had abandoned the social democratic movement. But our commitment to the party could only have credibility with our members if it was mutual, a commitment that respected the principles working people have fought so long to achieve: the right to organize, the right to collective bargaining, and the right to strike. What the Rae government did was violate the trust of members of the labour movement' (Hargrove 1998, 159–60).

The political ramifications of the social contract were far larger than the fiscal. The NDP's restraint measures came nowhere near to eliminating the provincial deficit; they merely stabilized it (at an annual level of roughly $10 billion). On the other hand, the events of 1993 decisively destroyed public confidence in the NDP's ability to manage public affairs. In the subsequent election (held in 1995), Ontario voters opted for a conservative populist regime that promised – much as had Margaret Thatcher in Britain – to cut spending and put the unions in their place. Relative to 1990, the NDP popular vote fell by half. The NDP passed from government to third-party status in Queen's Park.

Admittedly, Hargrove represents the militant left among organized labour. Most union leaders were somewhat less aggressive in damning the NDP's attempted social contract, but no major union or NDP leader explored the case that public sector unions had become an excessively powerful interest group whose demands were unjustifiable. Instead, the NDP behaved like the French royalty after 1791. What the French say of the Bourbons can be said of the remnants of the Ontario NDP: they remember everything and have learned nothing from their exercise of power. During the past legislature (1995–9), the much reduced caucus avoided the painful dilemmas raised by the events of 1993. They attempted to refurbish relations with interest groups allied to the party, including public sector unions, by relentlessly opposing the conservative fiscal policies of the new government. Ontario voters were unimpressed. In the most recent election (held in June 1999), the NDP popular vote declined again, to one third its 1990 level. As already mentioned, the provincial NDP caucus fell below the minimum size required to obtain official party status at Queen's Park.

When they founded it in 1961, David Lewis and his colleagues consciously modelled the New Democratic Party on the British Labour Party, with the hope that here as in Britain it would replace the Liberals on the electoral stage. It would be churlish not to acknowledge the tenacity and sincerity with which David Lewis – and many others – strove to build a mass political party on the foundation of organized labour. But intellectual honesty demands that we admit the obvious: the party's over.

What now? The answer is far from clear. In due course, I provide some – very tentative – answers.

Part II of this article provides a synopsis of the history of collective bargaining since the Second World War. The conclusion is that the rise of public sector unions within the labour movement poses a 'fundamental contradiction' to a labour-based electoral party. Part III emphasizes that, across most industrial countries, citizens have collectively said 'enough' to politicians and interest groups contemplating further tax increases to fund further expansion of the welfare state. If it is to be credible with the majority, the left must respect this desire for a limit to the size of the state. The intent in Part IV is to suggest that political parties laying claim to the heritage of the left retain an important role: they remain well placed to 'parent' the welfare state. Part V surveys the ideological changes in the British Labour Party wrought by New Labour, and their potential relevance to Canada.

II. The Fundamental Contradiction of the Traditional Left

The fate of the Ontario NDP illustrates what might be labelled the 'fundamental contradiction' that has beset the 'traditional left' over the last quarter of this century, in other industrial countries as well as Canada. The public sector strikes in Quebec in the winter of 1982–3 (which came close to destroying the credibility of the Parti Québécois) and the public sector strikes against the British Labour government in the winter of 1978–9 (which served as catalyst to transform many into supporters of Margaret Thatcher) are two other high profile illustrations of this contradiction.

I use 'traditional left' here to encompass a range of political organizations intimately dependent on organized labour, including the New Democratic Party (leaving Saskatchewan aside), the Parti Québécois (at least during its first terms in office, 1976–85), Old Labour (as opposed to New Labour) in Britain, and many parties of western Europe. There are differences among them, as measured by the degree of commitment to civil liberties and by the degree of hostility to market activity. But they all share key features. They afford a privileged status to unions as source of electoral financing, of members and candidates, and of political ideas; and they endorse a political culture according to which union collective bargaining demands are – almost always – right, and the arguments of those who oppose are – almost always – wrong.

In many industrial countries, this contradiction has destroyed the credibility of parties of the traditional left as legitimate contenders to govern a modern welfare state. Intuitively, the majority understand that unions engaged in collective bargaining may or may not be deserving of popular support. Sometimes they enhance equality and efficiency; sometimes they do the opposite. Intuitively, the majority also understand that the modern welfare state is of immense value. The challenge for those wanting to sustain the heritage of the left is to disentangle the interest of their potential electoral supporters, those who want a generous, well-managed welfare state, from the interests of unions, whose leaders expect support from 'their' political party in realizing collective bargaining goals.

Another way to state this is that unions can, at least in the short run, strengthen their bargaining power by promoting a culture based on union solidarity, but by doing so they lower social trust across the society. The stronger the union culture becomes, the weaker become the shared elements of a communitywide culture encompassing the majority. When the shared culture is weak, citizens will not democratically endorse parties advocating generous social programs and the taxes required to pay for them.[2]

A good way to appreciate this 'fundamental contradiction' is to sketch the history of collective bargaining since the Second World War.

In all industrial countries, workers legitimately organize unions to advance their collective interests. Marx may have been wrong in his prediction that conflict between capitalists and workers would bring an end to market economies, but he was right inasmuch as the ideological and economic conflict between workers and corporate owners is often intense. Accordingly, governments in all countries have put in place rules to regulate it. Whether the political rationale was to encourage collective bargaining or to contain it, such rules exist. The key regulatory concepts in Canada are twofold: first, governments establish procedures whereby a particular union can obtain and retain the legal monopoly to represent a group of workers in collective bargaining; second, industrial conflict resolution has been diverted from the courts to special tribunals (i.e., to labour relations boards). Ottawa and the provinces adopted these concepts during the 1940s, borrowing from the 1935 Wagner Act, a key piece of New Deal legislation during Franklin Roosevelt's first term. Here, incidentally, is an example to illustrate that, at the time, the United States had more developed social policy than Canada.

The rules were originally designed by Senator Wagner and his aides to manage bargaining between private sector workers and corporate owners. That they still do, but the nature of collective bargaining has changed from the 1930s. The private sectors in which workers rely most heavily on unions have been the traditional crafts, primary and secondary manufacturing. As a share of the private sector workforce, these sectors have declined relative to the service sector, which now includes many low skill Macjobs and many high skill knowledge-based activities. This evolution in the distribution of private sector jobs has meant an overall decline in the unionized share of the private sector workforce in most industrial countries. On the other hand, the welfare state has expanded, and the heavily unionized public sector has become an important component of the unionized workforce. In many countries, the unions with the most members and the most influence are now in the public sector.

Immediately following the Second World War, both academic economists and ordinary workers feared that declining military spending would trigger a major international depression, such as occurred following the First World War. From 1945 to, say, 1960, public sector workers accepted overall wages lower than their private sector counterparts, seeing in this a reasonable trade-off for greater job security. But such a depression did not occur and, by the 1960s, fear of a major depression faded from public debate. Public sector workers no longer accepted the terms of the trade-off. Their unions became more militant, undertaking campaigns to catch up with their private sector counterparts.

In summary, public sector workers in Canada have done very well over the last four decades. They not only caught up; they established a premium over comparable private sector compensation and also imposed some highly restrictive work rules on public sector employers. Any particular measure of this compensation premium is subject to controversy, but it was probably in the 10–20 per cent range in the early 1990s, and concentrated among low paid workers.[3] This premium is, in effect, an expensive social program. Direct expenditures on salaries for public employees loom large as a share of public expenditures, particularly at the provincial level. To put the point crudely, Ottawa writes cheques to individuals and to other governments, while the provinces and municipalities (the latter are under the jurisdiction of the provinces) hire teachers, nurses, and social workers to deliver services. Direct federal expenditures on incomes for public employees amount to roughly 15 per cent of federal program spending; as mentioned above, spending on salaries accounts for 60 per cent of provincial program expenditures.

The ultimate constraint on private sector collective bargaining is competitive behaviour in the marketplace. Workers can leave a firm if wages are too low; customers can refuse to buy a firm's products if wage costs (and hence prices) are too high. The situation in the public sector is different. In many cases, public sector workers are more mobile than taxpayers: they can find alternate jobs if wages are too low, but taxpaying citizens who rely on public services are in the short term captive. Unless they emigrate from the relevant jurisdiction, they have no analogue to customers' switching to a competitor. In the medium term, citizens vote out governments whose policies diverge from majority preferences. Public dissatisfaction with government conduct of public sector bargaining figured prominently in the defeat of Labour in Britain in 1979, of the PQ in 1985, and of the Ontario NDP a decade later. Electoral democracy is not, however, as immediately binding a constraint on public sector collective bargaining as is market competition on private sector bargaining.

In the case of health and education services, the modern welfare state entails a virtual public monopoly on supply. Few private sector jobs exist for nurses or teachers. Where the state is effectively the sole employer, collective bargaining takes on the character of a prisoners' dilemma game. It is tempting for both union as agent of employees and government as agent of citizens to exploit cooperative strategies by the other. If both sides pursue noncooperative strategies, however, they both wind up with a worse outcome than if they cooperated. In such cases, politicians have a politically complex task in generating an outcome fair for public sector workers and for citizens. Neither a party beholden to unions nor one beholden to private business interests is well placed to undertake this task with credibility.

By the early 1990s, the consequences of protracted deficits among Canada's eleven senior governments became undeniable. Debt servicing costs had become a cancerous growth squeezing program spending. Uncertainty in financial markets over policies to be pursued by debt-laden governments induced unnaturally high long-term real interest rates, which exacerbated debt service costs and discouraged private investment. The relative size of public debt constrained government's freedom to use tax cuts or spending increases as countercyclical policy because potential lenders doubted the ability of government to manage further increases in debt. Public opinion shifted. These matters became real issues determining election outcomes.

Citizens choose their governments for many reasons and, in some instances, governments retained power despite running deficits. The narrow electoral victory of the British Columbia NDP in 1996 is a case in point.[4] But, in general, Canadians have electorally refused further tax increases; they want the books balanced without tax increases and, preferably, with tax reductions. In this context, the public sector compensation premium became vulnerable and governments bargained more aggressively with their employees. In some instances, governments bargained too aggressively, and unions generated sufficient public support to make governments back down. But amidst considerable political controversy and some bitter strikes, Canadians have tended to support governments and not their employees.

Marx inherited the Hegelian sense of historical forces impersonally transforming society. He disagreed with Hegel, insisting that changing material class interests and not changing ideas underlie major historical transformations. As every Marxist treatise on history explains, the fundamental contradiction of feudal society was the bourgeoisie that grew within the womb of feudal towns and ultimately transformed it into capitalism. The fundamental contradiction of capitalism would be the growth of a self-conscious industrial working class that brings about socialism. This particular contradiction turned out to be a good deal less fundamental than earlier generations of Marxists thought. As industrial societies shared the wealth, the great majority have accepted the legitimacy of a market economy. Nonetheless, growth of the welfare state and the changing composition of organized labour produced a fundamental contradiction. Unfortunately, it has afflicted the socialists, not the capitalists.

III. Setting Limits to the Welfare State

At its peak in 1992, program spending (total spending less debt service costs) by Canadian governments was 46.0 per cent of gross domestic product (GDP); by 1999, it had fallen 9.6 points to 36.4 per cent of GDP.[5] The only Organization of Economic Cooperation and Development (OECD) countries to experience larger declines were two Nordic countries, Finland and Sweden. Like Canada, they faced severe economic recessions early in the decade and an unwillingness of electorates to increase already high taxes.

Assar Lindbeck, a prominent Swedish economist, headed a government commission charged in the depths of Sweden's early 1990s recession with analysing his country's welfare state. His commission identified many flaws, but Lindbeck (1995, 9) has always prefaced his critiques by describing the welfare state as a 'triumph of western civilization.'

Defining this triumph more precisely is elusive. My own attempt is to identify the welfare state as simply all government programs that redistribute in an egalitarian manner. Redistribution is more complex than it initially appears: it is inseparably linked to other collective goals of the community. In bullet form, here are a few observations:

- The most obvious welfare state programs are those that redistribute income from nonpoor to poor (such as social assistance and the progressive income tax).
- Marxists are right inasmuch as private market outcomes in important sectors (such as education and health) are less efficient than what a public bureaucracy can achieve. If well managed, certain welfare state programs simultaneously improve on the efficiency of private market alternatives and enhance equality. They do so by redistributing not income but 'merit goods' (such as health services and K-12 education).
- Welfare state programs inevitably pose trade-offs between preserving individual liberty for a dissenting minority and realizing majority values within the community. For example, the majority may wish that no one be without basic health services and legislate mandatory participation in a public insurance program providing such services. This imposes constraints on a dissenting minority who prefer to contract individually for health services. The state may structure the income tax such that, at all income levels, families

with children pay less than those without. This may reflect a majority value that favours public support for families raising children, but it nonetheless amounts to fiscal discrimination against those who choose not to raise children and gives offence to those who believe the state should be neutral over such lifestyle choices.

Viewed historically, the traditional union-based left was one of the welfare state's parents. The other parent were organizations that translated traditional religious concerns with charity into secular political action. Sometimes singly, often together, the two mobilized public support for the core programs of the welfare state: universal primary/secondary education, universal insurance for basic health needs and unemployment, reasonably generous income transfers for the truly needy and the old. Whatever the present-day contradictions besetting the traditional left and whatever the difficulties experienced by organized religion in a secular age, the present beneficiaries of the welfare state owe a debt to its parents.

From Sweden to Canada, the traditional left has predicted dire consequences from cuts to public spending. But, in many instances, the previous spending levels were realized only because countries incurred unsustainable public sector deficits. One very robust conclusion to draw from the past decade is that the majority in industrial countries concluded that the consequences from extrapolating deficits were worse than the consequences from cutting expenditures. A second is that citizens collectively said 'enough' to politicians and interest groups contemplating further tax increases to fund further expansion of the welfare state. (By a reasonable estimate, expenditures for social programs now comprise about two-thirds of program spending for the typical government.)[6] At some point, it was inevitable that the majority say 'enough.' The seemingly inexorable growth of the relative size of the welfare state since the Second World War could not go on forever.

One means to appreciate whether these conclusions make sense is to look at what has actually happened among OECD member countries in terms of taxing effort and expenditures.[7] (See Figures 3.1 and 3.2.)

If countries are ranked in any year in terms of taxing effort, the top quartile divides them such that one-quarter have higher revenue/GDP ratios, and the remaining three-quarters all have lower ratios. The cutoff revenue/GDP ratio defining this quartile has risen over time; it approached 50 per cent of GDP by the early 1980s, and has scarcely budged since. Analogously, the bottom quartile divides countries such

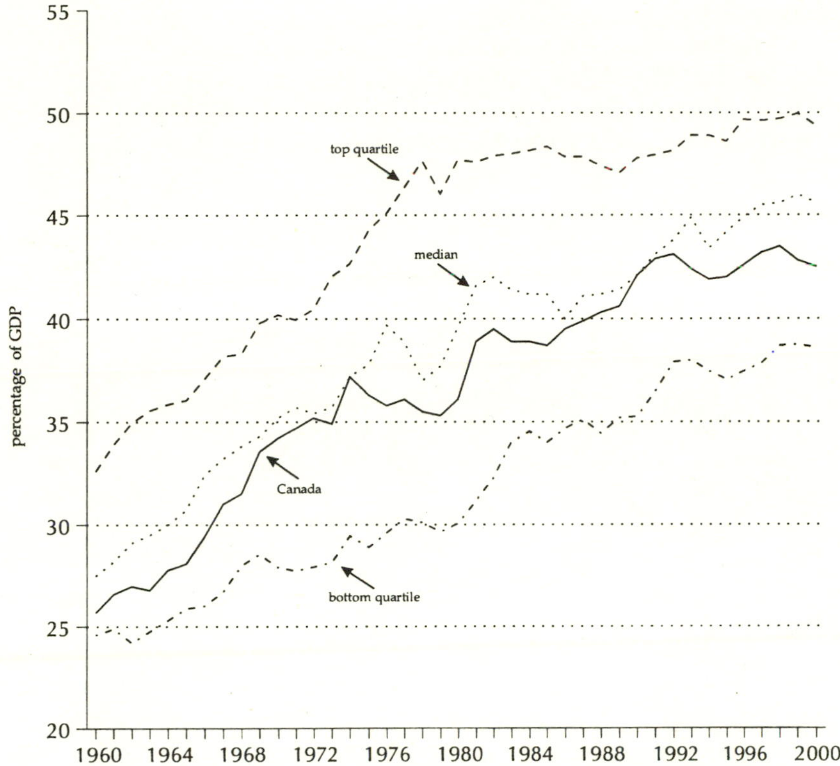

Figure 3.1 Government revenues, 19 OECD countries, 1960–2000.
Source: Author's calculations from data in OECD *Economic Outlook*, various issues through no. 66 (December 1999).

that one-quarter have lower revenue/GDP ratios and three-quarters higher ratios. The bottom quartile has slowly risen over the last four decades from about 25 per cent of GDP in 1960 to slightly less than 40 per cent today. Finally, the median is a measure of the central tendency. By definition, the median divides in two: one-half have lower and one-half higher revenue/GDP ratios. Measured by the median, taxing effort among OECD countries rose from below 30 per cent in 1960 to 45 per cent by the mid-1990s. The final statistic traced in each figure is for Canada. In terms of taxing effort, Canada has consistently been in the third quartile, but usually within two to three percentage points of the median.

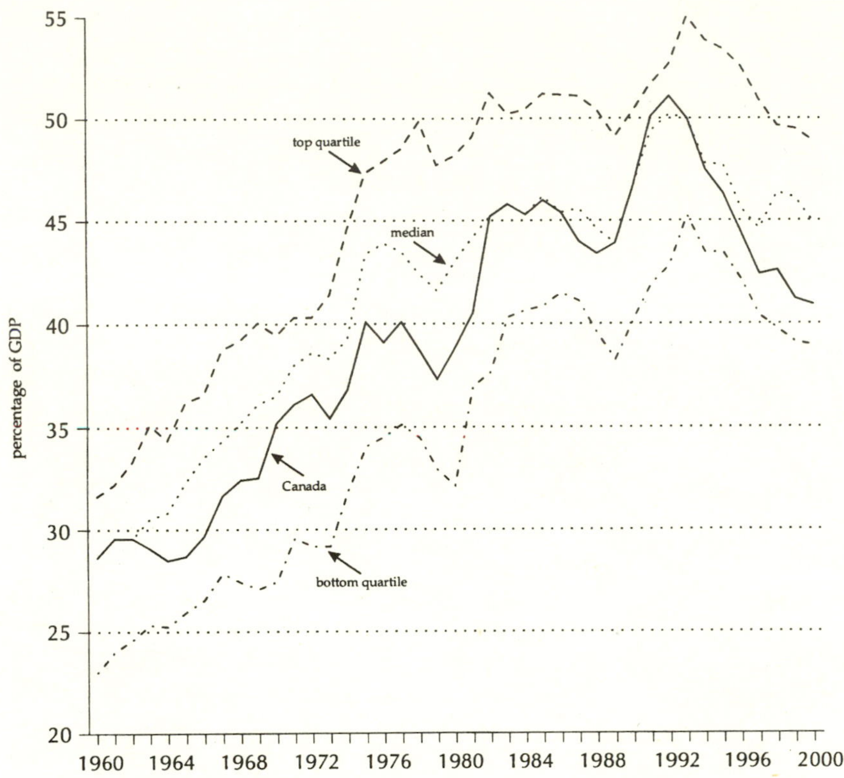

Figure 3.2 Government outlays, 19 OECD countries, 1960–2000.
Source: Author's calculations from data in OECD *Economic Outlook*, various issues through no. 66 (December 1999).

Prior to the Canada–U.S. Free Trade Agreement of 1988, many on the left argued that Canadian participation in regional free trade agreements would force Canadian convergence to lower U.S. taxes. To date, that has not happened: the Canadian revenue to GDP ratio has increased since 1988 and the tax gap between Canada and the United States has also increased slightly.[8] Neither this agreement nor the subsequent North American Free Trade Agreement have forced convergence, although increased north-south trade probably constrained divergence.

Measured by the median, government expenditures among major

industrial countries rose from under 30 per cent in 1960 to a peak above 50 per cent of GDP in the early 1990s. Since then, the top quartile, median, and bottom quartile have declined by roughly five percentage points and, as measured by these three statistics, the distribution of public spending among OECD countries in the year 2000 is projected to coincide closely with what it was in the mid-1980s.

Until the 1980s, Canada's public sector was on average about two percentage points below the median. For fifteen years (1982 to 1996 inclusive) Canada's spending was remarkably close to the median: over the plateau of the mid-1980s, over the increase in the early 1990s recession, and over the subsequent decline.

From the Roosevelt New Deal until the 1960s, social programs were about as generous in the United States as in Canada. The Canadian welfare state became notably more generous when particular governments – Tommy Douglas's CCF/NDP in Regina, the Pearson Liberals in Ottawa, the Lesage Liberals in Quebec City – introduced universal Medicare and other major social programs. Canadians collectively opted in the 1960s for a European-style welfare state; unfortunately, they never agreed to pay for it. From the mid-1970s to the mid-1990s, the aggregate federal-provincial sector was continuously in deficit and, over much of that period, our deficit was much larger than in the median OECD country. Canada's public sector net debt/GDP ratio grew and, when it peaked in 1996, it ranked third among OECD countries.[9]

When, finally, Canada's senior governments determined to set their respective accounts in order, they made remarkably rapid progress. They taxed more aggressively and constrained expenditures. In 1991 and 1992, Canada ranked among the bottom quarter of OECD countries in terms of aggregate government balances (i.e., among those with the largest deficit/GDP ratios). Most OECD countries improved their fiscal balances during the decade, but Canada did better than most. Since 1996, it has been close to or among the top quarter (i.e., among those having achieved either the smallest deficits or, for a few like Canada, budget surpluses). Canada has realized consecutive budgetary surpluses since 1997.[10]

Deficits have been eliminated, and quite reasonably, Canadians are demanding selective spending increases and tax reductions. Potentially, these are contradictory expectations, but provided economic growth continues and debt service costs continue to decline, Canadian senior governments can simultaneously realize some combination of increased program spending, tax cuts, and debt reduction. To pull this off will require better parenting of the welfare state than occurred in the previous two decades.

IV. So What if the Left Faces a Fundamental Contradiction?

To play the devil's advocate, so what if parties of the traditional left face a fundamental contradiction? Why not add the NDP to the list of extinct or endangered political species? The NDP may indeed join them. Or, building on its recent success in Atlantic Canada, it may settle into a narrow political niche, specializing in the art of lobbying Ottawa for interregional transfers to 'have not' regions.

The best reply to the devil's advocate is the danger that *no* political organizations opt for parenting the welfare state as their prime electoral strategy.

The welfare state is, in part, tax-benefit programs that transfer income from the nonpoor to the truly poor. Achieving sufficient redistribution to avoid abject poverty is a relatively easy task in a wealthy industrial society.[11] A good welfare state is, however, much more: it requires good social workers, teachers, and nurses, and good administrators to manage them. Finally, a successful welfare state requires political organizations engaged in an ongoing community debate over certain ethical questions that arise in civilized societies. The vocabulary of these questions changes according to whether the society is openly religious, in which case church leaders often lead the debate, or secular, in which case politicians substitute.

People want answers to questions such as the following. How generous should welfare programs providing income to the very poor be? More generally, how generous should social programs be, and how redistributive should be the taxes required to pay for them? Should the state oblige all parents to send their children to school, and to what age? Should the state oblige everyone to subscribe to mandatory pensions and publicly administered health insurance? Where the state is in effect a monopoly employer, how much should it pay in wages? To what extent should the tax system favour families with children relative to families without children? What should be done – if anything – to encourage two-parent families, to discourage divorce and single parenthood? Should the state increase the minimum wage or will that merely deny employment to those with few skills? Should the state subsidize earnings among low-income parents with children? In a federation, what should be the allocation of jurisdiction for supplying services and raising the taxes to pay for them, and to what extent should the central government redistribute revenue to equalize uneven fiscal capacity among provinces?

Rigorous analysis can reduce uncertainty and resolve some controversies, but uncertainty and controversy inevitably surround these questions and good answers will usually be tentative answers. Successful welfare states are those in which the political answers to the above questions are reasonably consistent with majority preferences and with what academics know. Realizing this double convergence requires political organizations that make 'parenting' the welfare state their *raison d'être*, organizations whose leaders take an active interest in these questions and are prepared to defend a coherent set of answers.

To belabour the argument made in Part III, in an age when the average citizen has concluded that the welfare state is big enough, it is not good enough to answer each question with a brief from relevant interest groups insisting the state either spend more, or regulate private market behaviour more aggressively. Given its fundamental contradiction, the answers of the traditional left lack credibility. On the other hand, questions about the welfare state are not central to the agenda of politicians closely allied to business interests in the community. Hence, contemporary society faces the prospect that *no* political organizations will come forward with credible answers, and that debate over public priorities will degenerate into a series of narrow interest groups – including public sector unions – making their respective claims.

Relative to other industrial countries, the United States is uniquely cursed by this problem. A central reason, I suggest, is that Americans in the 1930s abandoned the culture of 'states' rights' in matters of social policy, and thereby sacrificed much of the necessary local texture required for an intelligent political dialogue on social policy. Admittedly, some states – Wisconsin is an example – have kept alive local traditions of good government. But Wisconsin is the exception. Since the New Deal, the locus of most social policy debate has been among coalitions of Congressmen, presidential advisers, or activist judges. In countries of continental dimension, political debate in national institutions inevitably suffers from information overload, and falls prey to the oversimplifications of interest groups whose long tentacles reach to the capital. This is equally true of Washington, Ottawa, Delhi, or Moscow.

Canada and the United States are two federations of continental dimension; both have productive industrial economies and both share

European cultural origins. Since the 1930s they have performed a natural experiment. Canada did not copy the U.S. New Deal; Canadian provinces preserved more autonomous taxing and spending authority relative to Ottawa than U.S. states relative to Washington. The most important reason for this difference is francophone Quebec resistance to centripetal forces. Not as consistently as Quebec, the western provinces developed a tradition of local political autonomy and refused to accept Ottawa-directed social policy. A third reason is the residual colonial authority exercised by the Judicial Committee of the Privy Council which, until after the Second World War, served as Canada's final court of constitutional appeal.

Whatever the right weight to accord to the various reasons, Canada has preserved a stronger culture of provincial responsibility and innovation with respect to social policy than has the United States. For countries of continental size, this is undoubtedly a good thing. Overall, it has proved more conducive to a generous and effective welfare state than reliance on the once-in-a-century coalition that was Roosevelt's New Deal.

So long as the NDP retained within its counsels a respectable contingent of leaders like Tommy Douglas, Woodrow Lloyd, and Allan Blakeney, men and women fully aware of the pragmatic problems of running a government, the NDP performed a truly important role in Canadian public life. The pragmatic reformers within the NDP complemented the federal Liberals, one of whose fundamental flaws is too great an attraction to politically centralized power and whose record of managing what they undertake is correspondingly poor.

Now, however, the NDP no longer plays that role. Most of the pragmatists have departed; prairie NDP politicians keep their heads down and manage their local affairs, leaving the federal party to the unions and their allies. In effect, the federal NDP is a crude echo of ideas prevalent among the federal Liberal caucus. Liberals want to use Ottawa's spending power to launch new nationwide social programs and impose national standards on provincial programs; the federal NDP agree but are critical that the Liberals have not done this more aggressively. The Liberals mistrust provincial governments; the NDP mistrust them more. The Liberals mistrust the Quebec government more than any other, due to its consistent opposition to nationwide programs; so too do the NDP.

On occasion, federal NDP leaders still play a useful role in telling truth to power, but the overwhelming majority of Canadians instinctively understand that the federal NDP and most provincial sections of the party have abandoned any interest in responsible parenting of the welfare state.

V. New Labour's Third Way

In order to gain support, politicians constantly attempt to simplify and place ideological order on complex, imperfectly understood social dynamics. There is nothing wrong with this, provided it does not degenerate into dogma that frustrates public debate and provided it does not preclude formation of the necessary minimum communitywide shared culture. On the left, the communists have been the most guilty of fomenting a dogmatic and divisive discourse, but the noncommunist traditional left have done likewise.[12]

One such example is Labour after their initial defeat by Margaret Thatcher in 1979. Following that defeat, Labour elected a leader (Michael Foot) whose convictions conformed to those of interest groups closely allied to the party, and the party adamantly reaffirmed its traditional verities. The result was secession by a large centrist faction and a worse electoral defeat in 1983. Throughout the 1980s, it was uncertain whether Labour could survive as a major political party.

Obviously the Labour Party has survived, and since 1997 has returned to office, but only after undertaking major revisions to its ideological discourse. 'New Labour' have defined their strategy as a 'Third Way' between those of pre-1979 Labour governments and post-1979 Conservatives. Many 'Old Labour' supporters are decidedly leery – as are, I would guess, nearly all those who continue to support the New Democrats in Canada.

Critics of New Labour see a politically opportunistic syncretic mix of ingredients, and conclude that this new mayonnaise will inevitably come apart. They may be right. In any democracy, much of politics is an ad hoc succession of compromises among competing interests. Maybe, in retrospect, it will turn out that there was nothing more to New Labour than the exhaustion of the Thatcherite agenda after two decades, and the skill with which Tony Blair and his colleagues articulated the interests and culture of middle-class Britain. On the other hand, at the risk of dogmatically imposing intellectual order where not much exists, let me suggest there is an operational code underlying New Labour and furthermore that it has relevance for a deeply dispirited left in Canada.[13]

In summary, I think the operational code can be reduced to three grand themes.

1. The Need to Overcome the Left's Fundamental Contradiction

Speaking at the 1998 annual Labour Party conference, Blair insisted that the electorate wanted a government 'not in the pocket of the trade unions, not taxing them through the roof, not chasing after every passing fad of the political fringe' (quoted in Preston 1998). It is hard to be more blunt than that in addressing the traditional left's fundamental contradiction.

Keith Joseph was an intellectual in Parliament who, in the 1970s, helped turn the Conservatives from 'wets' into 'drys.' Joseph argued that macroeconomic stability was necessary to realize the supply-side productivity-enhancing reforms that he thought crucial to overcome what was popularly called the British disease. He attacked Keynesian fiscal and monetary policy as accommodation of interest group pressures, and advocated 'monetary continence' as the requisite cure. Predictably, Joseph was a *bête noire* to Old Labour, but this is no longer the case. The lead essay in a recent *New Statesman* (Leadbeater 1999) was a sympathetic review of his career and analysis of the parallels between Joseph's themes and those stressed by New Labour.

There is no direct line from Joseph's speeches in the 1970s to those of Blair in the 1990s, and Labour politicians would never publicly admit they are intellectually indebted to such a controversial politician. Admit it or not, over the intervening generation, his ideas have permeated the barrier between political parties:

- *New Labour insist they will not return to the tax-and-spend habits of former Labour governments.* The OECD projects a modest improvement in the U.K. budget balance between 1997, the year Labour was elected, and 2000. As a share of GDP, public expenditures are estimated to fall modestly (from 40.9 per cent to 39.5 per cent); public revenues will rise modestly (from 38.9 per cent to 40.3 percent) (OECD 1999, Tables A28, A29).
- *New Labour accept 'monetary continence.'* Given their past record, New Labour sought means to make credible their promise of fiscal prudence. One of the first acts of the new Labour government was to give autonomy to the Bank of England, with a mandate to pursue a low inflation target.

- *New Labour endorse the 'flexible' labour market inherited from the Conservatives.* Many of Thatcher's supply-side reforms entailed controversial initiatives to render the labour market more flexible. Flexibility is something of a euphemism for weakening union power and strengthening managerial discretion to hire and fire. In 1998, the British unemployment rate was 6.3 per cent, scarcely more than half the 11.1 per cent average for Italy, France, and Germany (OECD 1999, Table A22). In an address before the French National Assembly in 1998, Blair vowed to preserve Britain's flexible labour markets – to the delight of the conservative *députés* and consternation of the socialists.
- *New Labour reject much of the ideology of anti-poverty advocacy groups.* Keith Joseph accepted the culture-of-dependency thesis according to which long-term beneficiaries of social assistance and unemployment insurance develop a self-destructive entitlement ideology that legitimizes nonwork as a normal status that can be sustained intergenerationally if need be. Writing in the *New Statesman*, Leadbetter (1999, 13) summarizes the transition of ideas on this subject: 'The evidence [adduced by Keith Joseph on dependency culture] was at best patchy, but the "cycle of deprivation" mutated in the 1980s into Charles Murray's underclass and from there into new Labour's advocacy of an active approach to welfare in which rights go with responsibilities.' Needless to say, most advocacy groups among the poor vehemently deny the culture-of-dependency thesis, blame joblessness on the state of the labour market, and favour generous transfer programs. In effect, New Labour have separated their analysis of poverty from the ideology of anti-poverty groups representing the poor. To understate matters, this is controversial for a party of the left.
- *New Labour accept the international market economy as the benchmark for productivity and the constraints of international free trade arrangements as desirable.* In the 1970s, conservatives like Keith Joseph talked of the British disease, of the need for the country's unions and management to abandon old ways and adopt international standards for productivity. The left were divided over British participation in (what was then) the Common Market. There is nothing novel in New Labour's discussion of all this, except that it comes from a party of the left. The only difference with Thatcher or Joseph here – and it is a matter of degree – is a greater stress on the responsibility of the state to help workers and industry to adapt. The limit to New

Labour's acceptance of international market arrangements may turn out to be the euro which, to date, Britain has refused to adopt. British opinion is deeply divided on this matter, and Labour may refuse to abandon the pound as an independent currency.

2. The Key Social Problem Is Social Exclusion, Not Unemployment

Tony Giddens is to Tony Blair what Keith Joseph was to Margaret Thatcher. Giddens is a sociologist, director of the London School of Economics, and public academic closely associated with New Labour. The term social exclusion is central to his writings.[14] Like all such expressions adopted into political discourse, its meaning has become amorphous. Roughly, it refers to the idea that identifiable groups in society remain for long periods, even intergenerationally, excluded from the mainstream British community and – this is crucial – the reasons for groups' remaining excluded are multiple. These groups include single-parent families on public housing estates in Midland cities, residents of low-income, low-education, low-employment neighbourhoods in south London, etc. The short-term unemployed are not 'excluded,' the long term are.

Under New Labour, the public discourse on causes of unemployment has become more eclectic and linked to diverse strands of academic research. Whereas Old Labour emphasized Keynesian aggregate demand explanations for unemployment, New Labour subsume demand-related explanations for unemployment as part of a broader discussion of social exclusion. Below is a summary paragraph taken from the 1999 U.K. budget. In qualified terms typical of official documents, it lists four causes of unemployment: (1) no jobs 'for people without qualifications' (i.e., a mismatch between supply of and demand for labour skills), (2) 'distortions in the tax and benefit system,' (3) absence of suitable 'family-friendly work practices' to accommodate women, and (4) the phenomenon of the excluded who are 'outside the work force altogether'

> The traditional approach to full employment relied heavily on the levers of macroeconomic demand management to secure full-time male employment. Active Welfare to Work policies were not so important when a high proportion of those looking for work could find it relatively quickly. Skills mattered less when there were plentiful job opportunities for people without qualifications. Distortions in the tax and benefit system had a much

> lesser impact when work took people substantially above the level of benefits. Family-friendly work practices were less relevant when fewer women were in work and fewer people needed to balance work and family responsibilities. And it was more valid to focus on the claimant unemployed when those outside the work force altogether were not denied the chance of employment opportunity. (United Kingdom 1999, para. 4.4)

The proposed solutions are implied by the causes listed. Rather than use 'the levers of macroeconomic demand management,' it is more important, suggest New Labour, to improve job skills, eliminate poverty traps generated by high marginal effective tax rates,[15] assure flexible labour markets, and prod the socially excluded into work.[16]

3. *New Labour Are Communitarians: Shared Community Values, Not Working Class Solidarity, As the Basis for Political Activity*

Blair has been described as a Victorian scold, and parallels have been drawn to William Gladstone's moralizing liberalism (Beer 1998). Blair's speeches frequently contain religious themes and emphasize the concepts of mutual responsibilities in civil society: 'The only way to build social order and stability,' states Blair, 'is through strong values, socially shared, inculcated through individuals, family, government and the institutions of civil society' (quoted in Shaw 1999, 121). Socialism is a question of ethics, not class analysis: 'Since the collapse of communism, the ethical basis of socialism is the only one that has stood the test of time. This socialism is based on a moral assertion that individuals are interdependent, that they owe duties to one another as well as themselves' (Blair 1995, 12).

Tony Giddens has suggested as 'the prime motto of the new politics *no rights without responsibilities*' (emphasis in original, quoted in Shaw 1999, 118). Shaw (1999, 119) contrasts New Labour's communitarian vision of responsibility to Old Labour's vision of social rights:

> Perhaps the major point of attack by New Labour on the collectivism of 'Old Labour/left' turns on the doctrine of social entitlements, the belief that people have a right – derived from their status as citizens – to expect the state to meet their basic needs.
>
> This doctrine overlooked, argues New Labour, corresponding responsibilities or duties. Absolute social rights to benefits from the state has been

> a morally corrosive idea, for it undermines (able-bodied) recipients' self-reliance and, ultimately, their self-respect. It is a modern day equivalent of the Roman's free distribution of bread. A social security system which fails to tie handouts (to use the parlance New Labour has inherited from the right) to matching responsibilities chains people to passive dependency instead of helping them to their full potential ... Once large numbers of people grow accustomed to relying on state benefits, a culture of dependency emerges. In turn, this culture of dependency severs people from the structure and rhythms of work which alone can promote self-discipline, diligence and independence.

Over the last generation the traditional left became feminists: single-parent mothers are to be praised for escaping abusive partners and deserve generous transfers in order to raise their children with dignity and free from poverty. No, argue the social conservatives: government transfers targeted to single parents encourage women to adopt single-parenthood as a lifestyle and only traditional two-parent families can hope to socialize children, boys in particular, successfully. New Labour leaders have, with mixed success, attempted to define a 'Third Way' through this ideologically mined landscape. As to be expected, many of the explosions have been in Labour territory and not in that of the enemy.

New Labour have quite rightly resisted the full agenda of the social conservatives, who want benefits solely for the traditional two-parent family. In general, however, New Labour agree with the social conservatives about the significance of government fiscal incentives. Since coming to power, Labour have lowered untied benefits to poor single parents, and new programs more aggressively tie benefits to work. For example, Labour have relabelled and massively expanded a program that directs income to low-income families as a supplement to wages.[17]

VI. Conclusion

Most of the world have concluded that the utopian ideals of early socialists were at best naïve, at worst conducive to tyranny. But lowering expectations and viewing the world more stoically, as have New Labour, does not come easily.

There may again come a time of serious international depression (will the asset price bubble on Wall Street burst and generate an international recession?) and a need for an aggressive Keynesian agenda of demand stimulation and public works. The Third Way may wither into an amorphous dialogue among moralizing elites and become detached from the way ordinary people view the world. New Labour may allow the rich to avoid their fair share of taxation. Under such circumstances, New Labour's emphasis on shared community values, welfare-to-work programming, and limits on the public sector may appear irrelevant.

All this is possible. But the here-and-now problems for those who subscribe to the heritage of the left are to reinvigorate the welfare state in a time of fiscal restraint and increased domestic exposure to international markets. These problems are more powerfully present in Canada than in most industrial countries. New Labour's Third Way is, I suggest, an encouraging international example of the left's attempting to resume its parental responsibilities.

NOTES

1 Even this candle flickered. The NDP enjoyed a comfortable majority in the 1995–9 legislature; in the 1999 election its caucus was reduced to precisely half the seats in the legislature. To secure a working majority, the NDP formed a coalition with the small provincial Liberal Party.
2 I have avoided use of the term social capital. But readers familiar with the social capital thesis will appreciate this discussion draws on that intellectual tradition. See, for example, Fukuyama (1995).
3 For a survey of the evidence on public relative to private compensation, see Brown (1994).
4 The case of the British Columbia NDP is an exception to the generalization that Canadians have electorally opted for fiscal restraint. The NDP was elected in this province in 1991 and undertook proportionately larger program spending increases than any other senior government over the decade. It has tabled nine consecutive budget deficits (from 1992–3 to 2000–1 inclusive). Prior to the 1996 provincial election, the NDP undertook an exercise in dubious accounting in order to table a budget that projected a fiscal surplus for fiscal years 1995–6 and 1996–7. Subsequent revisions revealed both fiscal years to be in deficit. Revelation of this accounting legerdemain contributed to the loss of credibility of the NDP in its second term of office. For more detail see Richards (1997, 57–60, and 2000).
5 These statistics are calculated from data in OECD (semi-annual, various issues through no. 66).
6 What is and is not to be included as a welfare state social program is open

to alternate interpretations. (I define a country's welfare state as simply the sum of its social programs.) The two-thirds estimate is based on the following calculation. For fiscal year 1999–2000, Ottawa proposed program spending of $97 billion (including here $6 billion in tax expenditures via the Canada Child Tax Benefit but excluding transfers to other governments). Social program spending items sum to $56 billion. Included as social programs are the following items: elderly benefits, EI benefits, agricultural subsidies, international aid, budgets for several departments (Health, Human Resources Development, Indian and Northern Development), and CMHC. By this categorization, federal social program spending is 58 per cent of all program spending. At the provincial level, the ratio is higher. Social program spending in Saskatchewan, for example, is estimated at $3.6 billion for 1999–2000, 75 per cent of total program spending of $4.8 billion. Included as social program spending are the following: agriculture, education, health, and social services. Federal program spending is estimated to be 44 per cent of the total; the provincial 56 per cent. Based on these weights, the overall share of welfare state spending in public budgets is two-thirds (Canada 1999; Saskatchewan 1999).

7 Comparative statistics on government expenditures, revenues and balances are drawn from various issues of the OECD *Economic Outlook*. The figures plot trends among the nineteen OECD countries for which continuous data stretch back to 1960: Australia, Austria, Belgium, Canada, Denmark, Finland, France, Germany, Greece, Ireland, Italy, Japan, Netherlands, Norway, Portugal, Spain, Sweden, the United Kingdom, and the United States. The statistics are in terms of standardized national income accounting concepts. These differ somewhat from public accounts systems used by individual countries.

8 The difference between the Canadian and U.S. revenue/GDP ratios grew from about ten percentage points of GDP in 1988 to twelve percentage points in 1998 (OECD 1999).

9 In 1996 Canada ranked third in terms of net public debt, fourth in terms of gross public debt. The difference in ranking is attributable to the absence of OECD data on Greece for net debt. The 1996 statistics for these four countries in terms of gross (net) debt to GDP are as follows: Belgium 127 per cent (120 per cent), Italy 122 per cent (109 per cent), Greece 111 per cent, and Canada 99 per cent (69 per cent) (OECD semi-annual, no. 66 Tables A34, A35).

10 This statement refers to the aggregate Canadian public sector. Two important jurisdictions were still incurring deficits in 1999: Ontario, because the

Conservatives cut taxes before balancing accounts; and British Columbia, because the NDP did not constrain expenditure growth.

11 Recalling the 20 per cent cut in welfare benefits made by the Ontario Conservatives after their election in 1995, some readers may balk at this statement. However, real welfare benefits rose over the previous two decades by roughly 20 per cent and the cuts effectively returned them to real levels prevailing in the mid-1970s. Elsewhere, I have argued that welfare benefits in most Canadian provinces became too generous and too readily accessible by the early 1990s, that good anti-poverty policy required lower benefits and more incentives to encourage welfare beneficiaries to enter training or undertake paid work (Richards 1997, 1999). Such an alternative would still be expensive: it would not save taxpayers money.

12 After the Russians, the French left have probably been the most consistently drawn to the politics of dogma. Although, even in Paris, left wing ideological doubt is now in vogue. The Parisian press has been fascinated by the contrast between the British Labour government under Tony Blair and their own socialist administration headed by Lionel Jospin. For a sample, see several articles in *Le Nouvel Observateur* (1999).

13 I have borrowed the term operational code from an interesting survey of what New Labour are attempting. Eric Shaw has written extensively on U.K. politics. In a recent article, Shaw (1999, 118) refers to the 'Third Way as New Labour's "operational code" – a frame of reference that defines the key problems as its adherents see them, provides a diagnosis of these problems, identifies the values and goals to be realized and supplies the criteria for selecting appropriate policies.' Shaw's sympathies are with 'Old' as opposed to 'New' Labour, but he is unstintingly fair in his attempt to define this operational code.

14 A recent work by Giddens (2000) is *The Third Way and Its Critics*.

15 Marginal effective tax rate (METR) refers to the total gap between gross and net income per additional dollar – or pound – earned. The relevant marginal income tax is one component. For the working poor, clawbacks of government transfer programs are often larger than income tax. Once people adjust, the disincentive effect on work of transfer clawbacks is probably similar to the effect of explicit income taxes. Hence, reference to government-generated poverty traps. The 1999 U.K. budget estimates the number of families facing a METR above 60 per cent, and discusses initiatives directed at lowering the METR among the working poor (United Kingdom 1999, paras 4.64–4.66).

16 As an example of a willingness to prod the unemployed, Frank Field

(1997), at the time Labour minister responsible for welfare reform, participated in a conference whose main speaker was Lawrence Mead, an American policy analyst, who extolled the workfare programs undertaken by the Republican governor of Wisconsin.

17 Labour have relabelled and greatly expanded what is now called the Working Families Tax Credit (WFTC), an earnings supplement program that directs income to low-income families as a supplement to wages earned. The WFTC will cost an estimated C$12 billion annually when fully phased in by 2000 (United Kingdom 1998, para. 2.08). For a discussion of earnings supplements as social policy see Richards (1999). For an overview of the family debate within Labour see Lloyd (1998).

REFERENCES

Beer, S. 1998. 'The Roots of New Labour: Liberalism Rediscovered.' *The Economist*, 7 Feb. 1998, 23–5.

Blair, T. 1995. 'Let Us Face the Future.' Address to Fabian Society conference on the 50th anniversary of election of the 1945 Labour government. Fabian pamphlet 571. London: Fabian Society.

Brown, D. 1994. 'No Sense of Direction.' In R. Harris et al., *Paying Our Way: The Welfare State in Hard Times*. The Social Policy Challenge no. 3. Toronto: C.D. Howe Institute.

Canada. 1999. *Economic and Fiscal update*. Ottawa: Department of Finance.

Field, F. 1997. 'Re-inventing Welfare: A Response to Lawrence Mead.' In L. Mead et al., *From Welfare to Work: Lessons from America*. London: Institute of Economic Affairs.

Fukuyama, F. 1996. *Trust: The Social Virtues and the Creation of Prosperity*. Reprinted. London: Penguin.

Giddens, A. 2000. *The Third Way and Its Critics*. Cambridge: Polity Press.

Hargrove, B., with W. Skene. 1998. *Labour of Love: The Fight to Create a More Humane Canada*. Toronto: Macfarlane Walter & Ross.

Le Nouvel Observateur. 1999. 'Blair-Jospin: le choc des gauches.' 'Le blairisme est-il de gauche?' 'Moscovici: non à Tony Blair.' no. 1807 (24–30 June 1999), 28–31.

Leadbetter, C. 1999. 'New Labour's Secret Godfather.' *New Statesman*, 10 May 1999, 13–14.

Lindbeck, A. 1995. 'Hazardous Welfare State Dynamics.' *American Economic Review* 85. Papers and proceedings, 9–15.

Lloyd, J. 1998. 'How the Left Hijacked the Family.' *New Statesman*, 27 Nov. 1998, 9–10.

OECD (Organization for Economic Cooperation and Development). Semi-annual. *Economic Outlook*. Various issues to no. 66 (Dec. 1999). Paris: OECD.

Preston, R. 1998. 'Blair Outlines Reform Package to Party.' *Financial Times*, 30 Sept. 1998), 10.

Richards, J. 1997. *Retooling the Welfare State: What's Right, What's Wrong, What's to Be Done*. Policy study 31. Toronto: C.D. Howe Institute.

– 1999. 'The Case for Earnings Supplements: The Devil's in the Detail.' In D. Allen and J. Richards, eds., *It Takes Two: The Family in Law and Finance*. Policy study 33. Toronto: C.D. Howe Institute.

– 2000. 'Now That the Coat Fits the Cloth ... Spending Wisely in a Trimmed-down Age.' *Commentary*, no. 143. Toronto: C.D. Howe Institute.

Saskatchewan. 1999. *Moving Forward Together.* Budget Address. Regina: Department of Finance.

Shaw, E. 1999. 'New Labour's Third Way.' *Inroads* 8, 117–30.

United Kingdom. 1998. *The Modernisation of Britain's Tax and Benefit System: The Working Families Tax Credit and Work Incentives*. Supplementary document to 1998 budget. London: HM Treasury.

– 1999. *Financial Statement and Budget Report* (March). London: HM Treasury.

4

Why Not Socialism?[1]

G.A. COHEN

The question that forms the title of this paper is not intended rhetorically. I begin by presenting what I believe to be a compelling preliminary case for socialism, and I then ask why that case might be thought to be merely preliminary, why, that is, it might, in the end, be defeated.

To summarize more specifically: In Part I, I describe a context, which I call 'the camping trip,' a context in which most people would, I think, strongly favour a socialist mode of organization over feasible alternatives. I proceed, in Part II, to specify two principles, one of equality and one of community, that are realized on the camping trip, and whose realization explains, so I believe, why the camping trip mode of organization is attractive. In Part III, which is brief, I ask whether those principles also make (society-wide) socialism desirable. But I devote more attention (in Part IV) to whether socialism is feasible, by discussing difficulties that face the project of promoting socialism's principles not in the mere small, as on a camping trip, but throughout society as a whole. I then (Part V) offer an excursus on market socialism, in which I commend it as a good second-best in response to the difficulties of implementing the ideals of socialism proper, but I criticize market socialist enthusiasts who believe market socialism to be more than a good second-best. Part VI is a short coda.

I. The Camping Trip

You and I and a number of other people go on a camping trip. There is no hierarchy among us; our common aim is that each of us should have a good time, doing, so far as possible, the things that he or she likes best (some of those things we do together; others we do individually). We have facilities with which to carry out our enterprise: we have, for example, pots and pans, oil, coffee, fishing rods, canoes, a soccer ball, decks of cards, and so forth. And, as is usual on camping trips, we avail ourselves of those facilities collectively: even if they are privately owned things, they are under collective control for the duration of the trip, and we have shared understandings about who is going to use them when, under what circumstances, and why. Somebody fishes, somebody else prepares the food, and another person cooks it. People who hate cooking but enjoy washing up may do all the washing up, and so on. There are plenty of differences, but our mutual understandings, and the spirit of the enterprise, ensure that there are no inequalities to which anyone could mount a principled objection.

It is commonly true on camping trips, and on certain small-scale projects of other kinds, that we cooperate within a concern that, so far as is possible, everybody has a roughly similar opportunity to flourish. In these contexts most people, even most *anti*-egalitarians, accept, indeed, take for granted, a norm of equality. So deeply do most people take it for granted that there is no occasion to question it: to question it would contradict the spirit of the trip.

You could imagine a camping trip where everyone asserts her rights over the pieces of equipment and the talents that she brings, and where bargaining proceeds with respect to who is going to pay what to whom to be allowed, for example, to use a knife to peel the potatoes, and how much he is then going to charge others for those now peeled potatoes which he bought in an unpeeled condition from another camper, and so on. You could base a camping trip on the principles of market exchange and strictly private ownership of the required facilities.[2]

Most people would hate that. Most people would be more drawn to the first kind of camping trip than to the second, primarily on grounds of fellowship.[3] And this means that most people are drawn to the socialist ideal, at least in certain restricted settings.

To reinforce this point, here are some conjectures about how most people would react in various imaginable camping scenarios.

a. Harry loves fishing, and Harry is very good at fishing. Consequently, he brings back more fish than others do. Harry says: 'It's unfair, how we're running things. I should have better fish when we dine. I should have only perch, not the mix of perch and catfish that we've all been having.' But his fellow campers say: 'Oh, for heaven's sake, Harry, don't be such a shmuck. You sweat and strain no more than the rest of us do. So, you're very good at fishing. We don't begrudge you that special endowment, which is, quite properly, a source of satisfaction to you, but why should we *reward* that pre-eminence?'

b. Following a three-hour, time-off-for-personal-exploration period, an excited Sylvia returns to the campsite and announces: 'I've found a huge apple tree, full of perfect apples.' 'Great,' others exclaim, 'now we can all have apple sauce, and apple pie, and apple strudel!' 'Provided, of course,' so Sylvia rejoins, 'that you reduce my labour burden, and/or furnish me with more room in the tent, and/or with more bacon at breakfast.' Her claim to (a kind of) ownership of the tree revolts the others, but exactly such a claim, expressed or implicit, is, of course, at the heart of the constitution of private property: private property renews itself, every day, because such a claim is enforced, and/or accepted.[4]

c. Morgan recognizes the campsite. 'Hey, this is where my father camped thirty years ago. This is where he dug a special little pond on the other side of that hill, and stocked it with specially good fish. Dad knew I might come camping here one day, and he did all that so that I could eat better when I'm here. Great. Now I can have better food than you guys have.'

The rest frown, or smile, at Morgan's greed.

Of course, not everybody likes camping trips. I do not myself enjoy them much, because I am not outdoorsy, or, at any rate, I am not outdoorsy overnight-wise. There is a limit to the outdoorsiness to which an urban Jew can be expected to submit: I would rather have my communism in the warmth of All Souls College than in the wet of the Laurentians, and I love modern plumbing. But the question I am asking is not: wouldn't you like to go on a camping trip? but: isn't this the socialist way, with collective property and planned mutual giving, rather obviously the right way to run a camping trip, whether or not you actually like camping?

II. The Principles Realized on the Camping Trip

I want to state two principles that are realized on the camping trip, an egalitarian principle, and a principle of community. The community principle constrains the operation of the egalitarian principle, by forbidding certain inequalities of outcome that the egalitarian principle permits. (The egalitarian principle in question is, as I shall explain, one of radical equality of opportunity, and that principle is consistent with inequalities of outcome.)

There are, in fact, a number of competing egalitarian principles with which the camping trip, as I have described it, complies,[5] because the circumstances of the trip, unlike more complex circumstances, make it unnecessary to choose among them. But the only egalitarian principle realized on the trip that I shall bring into focus is the one that I regard as the correct egalitarian principle, the egalitarian principle that justice endorses, and that is a radical principle of equality of opportunity, which I shall call 'socialist equality of opportunity.'[6]

Equality of opportunity, whether moderate or radical, removes obstacles to opportunity from which some people suffer and others do not, obstacles that are sometimes due to the enhanced opportunities that privileged people enjoy. We can distinguish three obstacles to opportunity and three corresponding forms of equality of opportunity: the first form removes one obstacle, the second form removes that one and a second, and the third form removes all three.

First, there is what might be called bourgeois equality of opportunity, the equality of opportunity that characterizes (at least in aspiration) the liberal age. Bourgeois equality of opportunity removes socially constructed status restrictions on life chances, of both formal and informal kinds. An example of a formal status restriction is that under which a serf labours in a feudal society: it is part of the law of that society that he must remain where he is, socially speaking. An example of an informal status restriction is that from which a person whose skin is the wrong colour may suffer in a society free of racist law but nevertheless possessed of a racist consciousness.

This first form of equality of opportunity widens people's opportunities by removing constraints on opportunity caused by rights assignments and by bigoted and other prejudicial[7] social perceptions. Notice that it does not widen everyone's opportunities, since it perforce reduces the opportunities of those who enjoy special privileges. I underline this point because it shows that promoting equality of opportunity is not only an equalizing but also a redistributing, policy. Promoting equality of opportunity, in all its forms, is not merely giving to some what others continue to enjoy.

Left-liberal equality of opportunity goes beyond bourgeois equality of opportunity. For it also sets itself against the constraining effect of social circumstances by which bourgeois equality of opportunity is undisturbed, the constraining effect, that is, of those circumstances of birth and upbringing that constrain not by assigning an inferior *status* to their victims, but by casting them into poverty and related types of deprivation. The deprivation targeted by left-liberal equality of opportunity derives immediately from a person's circumstances and does not depend for its constraining power on social perceptions or on assignments of superior and inferior rights.[8] Policies promoting left-liberal equality of opportunity include head-start education for children from deprived backgrounds. When left-liberal equality of opportunity is fully achieved, people's fates are determined by their native talent and their choices, and, therefore, not at all by their social backgrounds.[9]

Left-liberal equality of opportunity corrects for social disadvantage, but not for native (that is, genetic) disadvantage. What I would call socialist equality of opportunity treats the inequality that arises out of native differences as no less unjust than that imposed by unchosen social backgrounds. Socialist equality of opportunity seeks to correct for *all* unchosen disadvantages, disadvantages, that is, for which the agent cannot herself reasonably be held responsible, whether they be disadvantages that reflect social misfortune or disadvantages that reflect natural misfortune. When socialist equality of opportunity prevails, differences of outcome reflect nothing but differences of taste and choice, not differences in natural and social capacities and powers.[10]

So, for example, under socialist equality of opportunity income differences are acceptable when they reflect nothing but different income/leisure preferences. People differ in their tastes, not only across consumer items, but also between working only a few hours and consuming rather little on the one hand, and working long hours and consuming rather more on the other. Preferences across income and leisure are not in principle different from preferences across apples and oranges, and there can be no objection to differences in people's benefits and burdens that reflect nothing but different preferences, and do not, therefore, constitute inequalities of benefits and burdens.

Let me spell out the analogy at which I have just gestured. A table is laden with a dozen apples and a dozen oranges. Each of us is entitled to take six pieces of fruit, with apples and oranges appearing in any combination to make up that six. Suppose, now, I complain that Sheila has five apples whereas I have only three. Then it should extinguish my (totally idiotic) sense of grievance if you point out that Sheila has only one orange whereas I have three, and that I could have had a bundle just like Sheila's had I forgone a couple of oranges. So, similarly, under a system in which each gets the same income per hour but can choose how many hours she works, it is not an intelligible complaint that people who work longer hours have more take-home pay than others.

The income/leisure trade-off is relevantly like the apples/oranges trade-off: that I have more income than you do no more shows, just as such, that we are unequally placed than my having four apples from the table when you have two represents, just as such, an objectionable inequality.[11]

Now, you might think that I have misused the term 'socialist' in the phrase 'socialist equality of opportunity,' for the simple reason that it is a familiar socialist policy to insist on equality both of income and of hours of work: have not kibbutzim, those paradigms of socialism, worked that way?

In reply, I would distinguish between socialist principles and socialist modes of organization, the first, of course, being the putative justifications of the second. What I call 'socialist equality of opportunity' is, as expounded here, a principle, which, so I say, is satisfied on the camping trip, but I have not said what modes of organization would, and would not, satisfy it in general. And, although the suggested strictly equal work/wage regime would indeed contradict it, I acknowledge that socialists have advocated such regimes, and I have no wish, or need, to deny that those regimes can be called socialist work/wage regimes. What I do need to insist is that such systems contradict the fundamental principles animating socialists, when those principles are fully thought through. No defensible fundamental principle of equality, or, indeed, of community, taken by itself, warrants such a system, which may nevertheless be justifiably advocated by socialists as an appropriate 'second-best' in light of the constraints of a particular place and time.

What I have called socialist equality of opportunity is consistent with three forms of inequality, the second and third forms being sub-types of one type.[12] The first form of inequality is unproblematic, the second form is a bit problematic, and the third is very problematic.

(i) The first type, or form, of inequality is unproblematic because it does not constitute an inequality, all things considered. Variety of preference across lifestyle options means that some people will have more goods of a certain sort than others do, but that is no inequality to which anyone can object when those who have fewer such goods have simply chosen differently, and therefore have more goods of another sort. That was the lesson of the apples/oranges example, and of its application to income/leisure choices.

(ii) The second type of inequality *is* an inequality, all things considered. For socialist equality of opportunity tolerates inequalities of outcome, inequalities, that is, of benefit in outcome, where those inequalities reflect the genuine choices of parties who are initially equally placed and who may therefore reasonably be held responsible for the consequences of those choices. And this type of inequality takes two forms: inequality due to differences in amounts of *chosen effort*, and inequality due to differences in amounts of *chosen option luck*.

(ii-a) To illustrate the first of these forms, imagine that one apple/orange chooser (but not the other) carelessly waits so long that, by the time he picks up the number of them to which he is entitled, they have lost their full savour: the resulting inequality of benefit represents no grievance. And the same holds true for someone in a work/pay regime whose ultimate fortune is inferior because she did not bother to examine her job opportunities properly.

These inequalities of outcome are justified by differential exercises of effort and/or care by people, who are, initially, absolutely equally placed, and who are equal even in their capacities to expend effort and care. If you believe (against the grain, I wager, of your reactions to people in ordinary life)[13] that there is no such thing, ultimately, as being 'truly responsible,' if you believe that greater negligence, for example, can reflect nothing but a smaller capacity for attentiveness, in the given circumstances, than others have, which should not be penalized, then you will not countenance this second form of inequality. But even if, like me, you are not firmly disposed to disallow it,[14] then the question remains, how large is this inequality likely to be? That is a very difficult question, and my own view, or hope, is that it would not be very large, on its own. It can, however, contribute to very high degrees of inequality when it is in synergy with the third and truly problematic form of inequality that is consistent with socialist equality of opportunity.

(ii-b) That truly problematic inequality, the substantial inequality that is consistent with socialist equality of opportunity, is the inequality that reflects differences in what Ronald Dworkin calls option luck. The paradigm case of option luck is a deliberate gamble. We start out equally placed, each with $100, and we are relevantly identical in all respects, in character, in talents, and in circumstances. One of the features that we share is a penchant for gambling, so we flip a coin on the understanding that I give you $50 if it comes up heads, and you give me $50 if it comes up tails. I end up with $150 and you end up with $50, and with no extra anythings to offset that monetary shortfall.

This inequality is consistent with socialist equality of opportunity, and it does not occur only as a result of gambling narrowly so called.

Some market inequalities have that sort of option luck genesis, or are sufficiently marked by option luck, within a complex causal story, that justice, understood as socialist equality of opportunity, cannot condemn them, or, better, cannot condemn them entirely. Such inequalities are broadly compatible with, and, indeed, justified by, socialist equality of opportunity.

Although inequalities of type (ii) are not condemned by justice, they are nevertheless repugnant to socialists, when they obtain on a sufficiently large scale, because they then contradict community: community is put under strain when large inequalities come to obtain. The sway of socialist equality of opportunity must therefore be tempered by a principle of community, if society is to display the socialist character that makes the camping trip attractive.

'Community' can mean many things,[15] but the requirement of community that is central here is that people care about, and, where necessary and possible, care for, one another, and, too, care that they care about one another. There are two modes of communal caring that I want to discuss here. The first is the mode that curbs socialist equality of opportunity. The second mode of communal caring is not strictly required for equality, but it is nevertheless of supreme importance in the socialist conception.

We cannot enjoy full community, you and I, if you make, and keep, say, ten times as much money as I do, because my life will then labour under challenges that you will never face, challenges that you could help me to cope with, but do not, because you keep your money. Compare the case where you and I have radically different physical vulnerabilities. You have serious ones, and I could assist you, but I turn my back on you: community cannot, therefore, obtain between us. Analogously, widely divergent incomes produce widely divergent social vulnerabilities, and they, too, destroy community, when those who could attenuate them let them persist.

To be sure, the sick and the healthy can enjoy community with each other. But, so I am suggesting, they can do so only when the healthy are fully prepared, as they may be, to do what they can for the sick, within reasonable limits of self-sacrifice. And if the rich do what they can for the poor, even within reasonable limits of self-sacrifice, then they will give away rather a lot of their money, and community will indeed obtain, but inequality will be reduced. Community is consistent with widely different earnings, but not, in relevantly realistic ranges,[16] with, so to speak, widely different keepings, and, therefore, widely different powers to care for oneself, to protect and care for offspring, to avoid danger, and so forth.

So, to return to the camping trip, if we eat meagrely, but you have your special high-grade fish pond, which you got neither by inheritance nor by chicanery nor as a result of the brute luck of your superior exploratory talent, but as a result of an absolutely innocent option luck that no one can impugn from the point of view of justice: you got it through a lottery that we all entered; then, even so, even though there is no injustice here, you are cut off from our common life, and the ideal of community condemns that.[17]

The other expression of communal caring instantiated on the camping trip is a communal form of reciprocity, which contrasts with the market form of reciprocity, as I shall presently explain. Where starting points are equal, and there are independent (of equality of opportunity) limits put on inequality of outcome, communal reciprocity is not required for equality, but it is nevertheless required for human relationships to take a desirable form.

Communal reciprocity is the non-market principle according to which I serve you[18] not because of what I can get in return but because you need my service, and you, for the same reason, serve me. Communal reciprocity is not the same thing as market reciprocity, since the market motivates productive contribution not on the basis of commitment to one's fellow human beings and a desire to serve them while being served by them, but on the basis of cash reward. The immediate motive to productive activity[19] in a market society is typically[20] some mixture of greed and fear, in proportions that vary with the details of a person's market position and personal character. In greed, other people are seen as possible sources of enrichment, and in fear they are seen as threats. These are horrible ways of seeing other people, however much we have become habituated and inured to them, as a result of centuries of capitalist civilization.[21]

I said that, within communal reciprocity, I produce in a spirit of commitment to my fellow human beings: I desire to serve them while being served by them. To be sure, there is, in such motivation, an expectation of reciprocation, but it differs critically from the expectation of reciprocation in market motivation. If I am a marketeer, then I am willing to serve, but only in order to be served: I would not serve if doing so were not a means to get service. Accordingly, I give as little service as I can in exchange for as much service as I can get: I want to buy cheap and sell dear. I serve others either in order to get something that I desire – that is the greed motivation – or in order to ensure that something I seek to avoid is avoided – that is the fear motivation. A marketeer, considered just as such, does not value cooperation with others for its own sake: she does not value the conjunction, serve-and-be-served, as such.

A non-marketeer relishes cooperation itself: what I want, as a non-marketeer, is that we serve each other. To be sure, I serve you in the expectation that (if you are able to) you will also serve me. I do not want to be a sucker who serves you regardless of whether you are going to serve me[22] (unless you are unable to), but I nevertheless find value in each part of the conjunction – I serve you and you serve me[23] – and in that conjunction itself I do not regard the first part – I serve you – as simply a means to my real end, which is that you serve me. The relationship between us under communal reciprocity is not the market-instrumental one in which I give because I get, but the wholly non-instrumental relationship in which I give because you need, or want, and in which I enjoy a comparable generosity from you.

Because motivation in market exchange consists of greed and fear, nobody cares fundamentally, within the economic game, about how well or badly anyone other than herself fares.[24] You cooperate with other people not because you believe that cooperating with other people is a good thing in itself, not because you want yourself and the other person to flourish,[25] but because you seek to gain and you know that you can do so only if you cooperate with others. In every type of society people perforce provision one another: a society is a network of mutual provision. But in market society, that mutuality *is* only a by-product of a wholly unmutual and non-reciprocating attitude.

III. Is the Ideal Desirable?

It is the aspiration of socialists to realize the principles that structure life on the camping trip on a national, or even an international, scale. Socialists therefore face two distinct questions, which are often not treated as distinctly as they should be. The first is: would that realization be desirable? The second is: is that realization feasible?

Some might say that the camping trip is itself unattractive, that, as a matter of principle, there should be scope for much greater inequality and instrumental treatment of other people, even in small-scale interaction, than the ethos of the camping trip permits: people have a right to make personal choices, even if the result is inequality and/or instrumental treatment of people. These opponents of the camping trip ethos would not, therefore, recommend societywide equality and community as extensions to the large of what is desirable in the small, and they are unlikely to recommend for the large what they disparage even in the small.

But this criticism seems to me to be misplaced, or, at any rate, to be misstated, as presented here. For there is a right to personal choice on the camping trip, and there are plenty of private choices on it, in leisure, and in labour (where there is more than one reasonable way of distributing it), under the constraint that those choices must blend with the private choices of others. Within market society, too, the choices of others confine each individual's pursuit of her own choices, but that fact is masked in market society. By contrast with the camping trip, the unavoidable mutual dependence of human beings is not brought into common consciousness, as a datum for formal and informal planning.

Others would say that, while the camping trip itself is undoubtedly attractive, the cooperation and unselfishness that it displays are appropriate only among friends, or within a small community. But, remembering that we are now discussing desirability, and not feasibility, I find this thought hard to fathom. Why should those of us who do find the camping trip attractive reject the sentiment in a left-wing song that I learned in my childhood, which begins as follows: 'If we should consider each other, a neighbour, a friend, or a brother, it could be a wonderful, wonderful world, it could be a wonderful world?'

What troubles me more, however, are questions not of desirability but of feasibility.

IV. Is the Ideal Feasible? Are the Obstacles to It Human Selfishness or Poor Social Technology?

Whether or not the socialist, or, one could say, communist, modus operandi of the camping trip is attractive, and whether or not it would (also be) an attractive modus operandi for society as a whole, most people who have thought about the matter would judge communism to be infeasible for society as a whole.

There are two contrasting reasons why societywide communism might be thought infeasible, and it is very important, both intellectually and politically, to distinguish them. The first reason has to do with human motivation, the second with social technology. People are, so it is often said, by nature insufficiently generous and cooperative to meet communism's requirements, however generous and cooperative they may be within the frame of limited time and special intimacy in which the camping trip unrolls. And even *if* people are sufficiently generous, we do not know how to harness that generosity, how, through appropriate rules and stimuli, to make generosity turn the wheels of the economy. Contrast human selfishness, which we know how to harness very well.

Of course, even if neither of these problems, and no comparable ones, obtained, communism might still be unattainable, because political and cultural forces – including the enormous force of the belief that communism is impossible to sustain[26] – that would resist movement towards it are, or would be, too strong. But the feasibility that I am discussing here is not accessibility from where we are, and burdened as we are with all the contingencies that compose our current social condition, but the stability of communism, the question whether it could last, under the assumption that we do have the power to institute it.

In my view, the principal problem that faces the socialist ideal is that we do not know how to design the machinery that would make it run. Our problem is not, primarily, human selfishness, but our lack of a suitable organizational technology: our problem is a problem of design.[27] It may be an insoluble design problem, and it is a design problem that is undoubtedly exacerbated by our selfish propensities, but a design problem, so I think, is what we have got.

Selfishness and generosity exist, after all, in (almost?) everyone. Our problem is that, while we know how to make an economic system work on the basis of selfishness, we do not know how to make it work on the basis of generosity. Yet even in the real world, in our own society, a great deal depends on generosity, or, to put it more generally and more negatively, on non-market incentives. Doctors, nurses, teachers, and others do not, or do not comprehensively, gauge what they do in their jobs according to the amount of money they are likely to receive as a result, in the way that capitalists and workers in non-caring occupations do. (The aforementioned carers will not, of course, work for nothing, but that is like the fact that you need to eat on the camping trip: it does not follow, and it is false, that carers tailor their work to expected monetary return.) And the reason for the difference is not that carers are made of morally superior clay, but, in good part, the more cognitive reason that their conception of what is to be produced is given by human need: market signals are not necessary to decide what diseases to cure or what subjects to teach, nor are they good at deciding that. But once we pass out of the sphere of need, or, more generally, of 'merit goods,'[28] to the wide sphere of optional commodities, and we pass increasingly to that as economies progress and as life therefore becomes easier and more elegant, it is more difficult to know what to produce, and how to produce it, without the device of market signals. Very few socialist economists would now dissent from that proposition. (One reason why the camping trip can readily do without market exchange is that the information that the campers need to plan their activities is modest in extent, and comparatively easy to aggregate).

Now, it is logically possible to use markets to determine what to produce and how to produce it, without using them to determine the distribution of rewards.[29] And in light of the infirmities of comprehensive planning on the one hand and of the injustice of market results and the moral shabbiness of market motivation on the other, it is natural to ask whether it might be more than merely logically possible, whether it might, that is, also be practically feasible, to preserve the allocative function of the market, to retain the benefits it provides of information generation and processing, while extinguishing its normal motivational presuppositions and distributive consequences.

Precisely that project of differentiation is the aspiration of a groundbreaking book by Joseph Carens, who works in the Political Science Department at the University of Toronto. The book is called *Equality, Moral Incentives, and the Market*,[30] and its significant subtitle is *An Essay in Utopian Politico-Economic Theory*. Carens describes a society in which what looks like a standard capitalist market organizes economic activity, but the tax system cancels the disequalizing results of that market by redistributing income to complete equality. There are (pre-tax) profit-maximizing capitalists, and workers who own no capital, but people acknowledge an obligation to serve others, and the extent to which they discharge it is measured by how close their pre-tax income is to what it would be in the most remunerative activity available to them, while taxation effects a fully egalitarian post-tax distribution of income. Here, then, producers aim, in an immediate sense, at cash results, but they do not keep the money that accrues, and they seek it out of a desire to contribute to society: a market mechanism is used to solve the social technology problem, in the service of equality and community.

As Carens has recognized, there are plenty of problems with his scheme,[31] but it seems to me to be a scheme that is amply worth refining. I do not know whether the needed refinements are possible, nor do I know, speaking more generally, whether the communist ideal is feasible, in the Carensian, or in some other form. We socialists do not at present know how to replicate camping trip procedures on a nationwide scale, amid the complexity and variety that comes with nationwide size. We do not *now* know how to give collective ownership and equality the real meaning that it has in the camping story but which it did not have in the Soviet Union and in similarly ordered states. The camping trip's confined temporal, spatial, and population scale mean that within those confines the right to personal choice can be exercised, without strain, in a way that preserves equality and community.[32] But we do not know how to honour personal choice, consistently with equality and community, on a large social scale. Yet I do not think that we now know that we will never know how to do these things: I am agnostic on that score.

The technology for using base motives to productive economic effect is reasonably well understood. Indeed, the history of the twentieth century encourages the thought that the easiest way to generate productivity in a modern society is by nourishing the motives of which I spoke earlier, namely, those of greed and fear, in a hierarchy of unequal income. But we should never forget that greed and fear are unattractive motives. Who would propose running a society on such motives, and thereby promoting the psychology to which they belong, if they were not known to be effective, if they did not have the instrumental value which is the only value that they have? In the famous statement in which Adam Smith justified market relations, he pointed out that we place our faith not in the butcher's generosity but in his self-interest when we rely on him to provision us. Smith thereby propounded a wholly extrinsic justification of market motivation, in face of what he acknowledged to be its unattractive intrinsic character. Old-style socialists often ignore Smith's point, in a moralistic condemnation of market motivation that fails to address its extrinsic justification. Certain contemporary over-enthusiastic market socialists tend, contrariwise, to forget that the market is intrinsically repugnant, because they are blinded by their belated discovery of its extrinsic value. The genius of the market is that (1) it recruits low-grade motives to (2) desirable ends, but (3) it also produces undesirable effects, including, notably, significant unjust inequality.[33] In a balanced view, all three sides of that proposition must be kept in focus,[34] but many market socialists now self-deceptively overlook (1) and (3).

Let me now offer some further remarks about market socialism.

V. Market Socialism

Nineteenth-century socialists were for the most part opposed to market organization of economic life. The pioneers favoured something which they thought would be far superior, to wit, comprehensive central planning, and their later followers were encouraged by what they interpreted as victories of planning, such as Stalin's industrialization drive and the early institution of educational and medical provision in the People's Republic of China. But central planning, at least as practised in the past, is, we now know, a poor recipe for economic success, at any rate once a society has provided itself with the essentials of a modern productive system. Accordingly, socialist economists have in recent years done important work on how a socialist market might work. The extensive historical association of socialism with central planning and the hope that central planning could realize the socialist ideal of a truly sharing society meant that economists of a socialist persuasion did not study non-central planning ways of organizing what would remain in one key respect a socialist economy, in that the assets used to produce things are shared. But now there are various designs for workers' ownership, for different forms of semi-public ownership, for example, at a municipal level, and other attempts to formulate a realization of the principle of collective ownership in the absence of state direction of all economic activity.

There is, then, today, among socialist intellectuals an intelligent movement in the direction of a non-planning or minimally planning market socialist society, but there is also, I believe, an unthinking and fashion-driven rush in that direction. Market socialism is socialist because it overcomes the division between capital and labour: there is, in market socialism, no class of capitalists facing workers who own no capital, since workers themselves own the firms. But market socialism is unlike traditionally conceived socialism in that its worker-owned firms confront one another, and consumers, in market-competitive fashion. It is also, and relatedly, unlike traditionally conceived socialism in that it reduces, even though it does not eliminate, the traditional socialist emphasis on economic equality. Equality is prejudiced because market competition leads to inequality between winners and losers. And community, too, is prejudiced because exchange under market socialism is no less market exchange than it is under capitalism:[35] true reciprocity, express rather than merely implicit reciprocity,[36] does not prevail at the heart of market transactions.

I believe that it is good for the political prospects of socialism that market socialism is being brought to the fore as an object of advocacy and policy: these socialist economists, even some of the fashion-driven ones, are performing a useful political service. But I also think that market socialism is at best second best, even if it is the best (or more than the best) at which it is reasonable to aim for the more or less immediate future. I believe that many socialist intellectuals who think otherwise are indulging in 'adaptive preference' a process in which the agent's preference ordering is distorted by his conception of the feasible set. Many socialists have concluded that market socialism is wonderful simply because they believe that they cannot design anything better:[37] that is an absurd reason for reaching the stated conclusion, and one that they cannot, perforce, acknowledge.

I do not think that anyone in their right mind could say that market socialism fully satisfies socialist standards of distributive justice, though they can rightly say that it scores better by those standards than market capitalism does. Notwithstanding that relative superiority, market socialism remains deficient from a socialist point of view, because, by socialist standards, there is injustice in a system that confers high rewards on people who happen to be unusually talented and who form highly productive cooperatives, and because market socialism's market exchange contradicts the value of community.

I do not say that we should aim to achieve, in this era of ideologically rejuvenated capitalism, a form of socialism more radically socialist than market socialism. As far as immediate political programs are concerned, market socialism is undoubtedly a good idea. But market socialist enthusiasts make grander claims for it, claims that should be resisted.

VI. Coda

The difficulties facing achievement of the socialist ideal are awesome, but the negative epithets hurled at the socialist ideal by erstwhile 'democratic Socialists,' such as those in Britain who gather under the banner of 'New Labour,' epithets like 'mechanical equality,' or 'sameness of outcome,' represent a failure to think through what the ideal implies and/or a semi-deliberate attempt to replace argument by rhetoric.[38] The epithets are inappropriate because the socialist ideal does not enforce sameness of outcome in the relevant sense of a deadly uniformity in which everybody is wearing a Mao jacket.

Any attempt to realize the socialist ideal runs up against entrenched power and individual selfishness. Politically serious people must take those obstacles seriously. But they are not reasons to disparage the ideal itself. Disparaging the ideal because it faces those obstacles leads to confusion, and confusion generates disoriented practice: there are contexts in which the ideal can be advanced, but is pushed forward less resolutely than it might be because of a lack of clarity about what the ideal is.

The socialist aspiration is to extend community to the whole of our economic life. As I have acknowledged, we now know that we do not now know how to do that, and many think that we now know that it is impossible to do that. But community conquests in certain domains, such as health care and education, have sustained viable forms of production and distribution in the past, and it is imperative, now, to defend community, since it is a value currently under aggressive threat from the market principle, and also because there is often immediate political mileage to be got from reasserting community in the mentioned particular domains, and calling for its extension beyond them, when that is possible.

I agree with Albert Einstein that socialism is humanity's attempt 'to overcome and advance beyond the predatory phase of human development.'[39] Every market, even a socialist market, is a system of predation. Our attempt to get beyond predation has thus far failed. But I do not think the right conclusion is to give up.

NOTES

1 I thank Sam Bowles, Miriam Cohen Christofidis, Cécile Fabre, Keith Graham, Lorraine Holmes, John McMurtry, John Roemer, Hillel Steiner, and Arnold Zuboff, all of whom provided excellent comments on an earlier draft of this piece.

2 You could also, of course, base a camping trip partly on collective and partly on private ownership: I shall not address that significant complication here.

3 But also, be it noted, on grounds of efficiency: think of the inordinate transaction costs that would attend a market-style camping trip.

4 Jean-Jacques Rousseau commented on the relevant claim in his myth about the origin of private property: 'The first man who, having enclosed a piece of land, took it into his head to say, "This is mine", and found people simple enough to believe him, was the true founder of civil society. The

human race would have been spared endless crimes, wars, murders, and horrors if someone had pulled up the stakes or filled in the ditch and cried out to his fellow men, "Do not listen to this impostor! You are lost if you forget that the fruits of the earth belong to everyone, and the earth to no one!"' (*Discourse on Inequality*, in Lowell Blair, ed., *The Essential Rousseau* [New York: New American Library, 1974], 173).

5 Two that come immediately to mind, beyond the one that I shall articulate in detail, are equality of outcome, and John Rawls's difference principle.

6 One may favour equality of opportunity on grounds other than ones of justice, on, for example, the utilitarian ground that it increases productivity, or on the perfectionist ground that it promotes the fulfilment of human potential. I am, however, concerned here only with the justice recommendation of the various forms of equality of opportunity that enter the taxonomy developed below.

7 An example of a prejudicial social perception which is not necessarily bigoted, as I would understand that term, is the belief of many teachers that most working-class children are unable to do well academically, a belief which is readily transmitted to the children themselves, with devastating effects on their life prospects.

The inclusion of opposition to informal status restrictions within bourgeois equality of opportunity means that it is a principle that can be very hard to realize, because of the limited purchase of law on social consciousness. That was my main reason for adding the phrase 'at least in aspiration' in the first sentence of the foregoing paragraph.

8 The distinction I have tried to draw here between status and other social deprivation obtains despite the fact that, where both types of deprivation exist, they interact in myriad ways.

9 What I call 'left-liberal equality of opportunity' is, therefore, what John Rawls calls 'fair equality of opportunity,' at page 73 of *A Theory of Justice* (Cambridge, Mass.: Harvard University Press, 1971). (Neither of us is committed to the entirely implausible claim that such equality of opportunity can be fully achieved.)

10 Save to the extent that capacities influence tastes and choices (as opposed to the scope of choice, which socialist equality of opportunity does not permit capacities to affect.) (There is, once again (see notes 7 and 9 above), no commitment here to the claim that socialist equality of opportunity can be fully achieved.)

11 Of course, some people love working, and some hate it, and that could be thought to (and I think it does) induce an injustice in the contemplated scheme, since those who love work will relish their lives more than those

who hate work do, but the same goes for people who enjoy each of apples and oranges more than others do. Even so, the apple/orange regime is a giant step towards equality, and so, too, is equal pay for every hour worked, with each choosing the number of hours that she works.

12 Accordingly, I designate the three forms of inequality as (i), (ii-a), and (ii-b).

13 See note 14, below.

14 That is so, because I am not convinced both that all choices are causally determined and that causal determination obliterates responsibility. If you are indeed so convinced, then do not blame me for thinking otherwise, do not blame right-wing politicians for dismantling welfare support (since, in your view, they cannot help doing so), do not, indeed, blame, or praise, anyone for choosing to do anything (and therefore live your life, henceforth, differently from the way we both know that you have lived it up to now).

15 I have treated the concept of community in general terms in section 5 of my 'Incentives, Inequality, and Community,' in Grethe B. Peterson, ed., *The Tanner Lectures on Human Values*, vol. 13 (Salt Lake City: University of Utah Press, 1992), and reprinted in Stephen Darwall, ed., *Equal Freedom* (Ann Arbour: University of Michigan Press, 1995).

16 My claim lapses when, for example, everyone is either a millionaire or a billionaire. The claim applies only so long as the lives of those with smaller incomes are challenging and/or difficult.

17 I say, then, that certain transactions that cannot be forbidden in the name of justice should nevertheless be forbidden (in the name of community). But is it an *in*justice to forbid the relevant transactions? Do the prohibitions merely define the terms within which justice will operate, or do they (justifiably?) contradict justice? The question needs more thought than I have had the opportunity to give to it. (It would, of course, be a considerable pity if community and justice were incompatible.)

18 Or another who serves you and thus enables you to serve me, or who serves another who serves you and thus enables you to serve me, and so on. I use the 'I-you' device for economy of exposition, but the relationships at issue here are, of course, multilateral.

19 I speak of the 'immediate' motive because a more ultimate motive can be to use market gains philanthropically (the motive for which use can in turn be philanthropy as such, or social recognition, or something else). In Amartya Sen's apt language, the marketeer is governed by a 'self-welfare-goal,' even if her welfare is not 'self-centered-welfare'; see 'Goals, Commitment and Identity,' *Journal of Law, Economics, and Organization*, 1 (2), (Fall

1985), 341–55. But while self-centred welfare is, unlike a self-welfare goal, not essential to marketeering, it is, of course, as a matter of contingent fact, the dominant form of welfare served by the market.

20 People can operate under a sense of service even in a market society, but, insofar as they do so, what makes the market work is not what makes them work. Their discipline is not market discipline. See, further, note 25 below.

21 Capitalism did not, of course, invent greed and fear: they are deep in human nature, related as they are to elementary infantile structures. But, unlike its predecessor feudal civilization, which had the (Christian) grace to condemn greed, capitalism celebrates it.

22 If you do not serve me, if you do not meet the expectation embodied in communal reciprocity, then I may be justified in ceasing to serve you, even if that induces an inequality between us: the ideal of communal reciprocity can justify inequality in circumstances that fall short of full compliance with it.

23 Cf. Karl Marx, *Comments on James Mill, 'Éléments d'économie politique,'* in Karl Marx and Frederick Engels, *Collected Works*, vol. 3 (London: Lawrence and Wishart, 1975), 227–8.

24 They do, of course, care about that instrumentally, if, for example, they have reasons of greed to want their trading partner to stay in business.

25 You may, of course, indeed want the other person to flourish, for non-instrumental reasons, but that desire does not affect what is strictly speaking, your market choice. (See, further, note 19 above.) If you drive less hard a bargain than you could because you have some affection for your opposite number, then an element of the gift relationship enters (and detracts from) the market relationship: the much vaunted efficiency of the market would be threatened if that generosity were common.

26 Cf. my 'Illusions about Private Property and Freedom,' in John Mepham and David-Hillel Ruben, eds., *Issues in Marxist Philosophy*, vol. 4, (Brighton: Harvester Press, 1981), 233–5.

27 Permit me to recall, here, two episodes that were critical to the development of my own realization that we socialists lack a convincing answer to the problem of how to design a non-market socialism.

The first episode occurred in Germany, in 1976, during a conference at Schloss Reisensberg, which is not far from Günzburg, which is not far from Ulm. I was strolling on the castle's grounds with the distinguished non-reactionary economist Leonid Hurwicz, and I had occasion to profess my commitment to socialism. Hurwicz responded in roughly these terms: 'Look, I have nothing against socialism, as an idea. But I'm a designer, I need to know how it's supposed to work. Tell me what design you have in mind.' Hurwicz rightly did not find my reply – 'democratic planning' – specific enough, and his intelligent scepticism gave me pause.

More decisive was what happened one day in London, in 1981, when I read David Schweickart's proof of the infeasibility of a democratic planning design sketched by Michael Albert and Robin Hahnel. From that day forth, I reluctantly settled for a socialist market, at least for the time being. The proof appeared at pages 217–18 of Schweickart's fine book, *Capitalism or Worker Control?* (New York: Praeger, 1980). He was commenting on pages 257–80 of Albert and Hahnel's *Unorthodox Marxism* (Boston: South End Press, 1979). I should add that Schweickart's *Against Capitalism* (Cambridge: Cambridge University Press, 1993) is a rewritten and expanded version of his 1980 book).

28 A merit good is a good 'the consumption of which is regarded as socially desirable irrespective of consumers' preference' (Graham Bannock, R.E. Baxter and Evan Davis, *Dictionary of Economics* [Harmondsworth: Penguin, 1998], 272).

29 In the rest of this section, and in section V, I reproduce material from Chapter 11 ('The Future of a Disillusion') of my *Self-Ownership, Freedom, and Equality* (Cambridge: Cambridge University Press, 1995).

30 Chicago: Chicago University Press, 1981.

31 See his 'Rights and Duties in an Egalitarian Society,' *Political Theory*, 14 (1986), Parts III and IV.

32 See page 68 above.

33 See my 'Future of a Disillusion,' section 8, for elaboration of that complex claim.

34 As the first two indeed were by Bernard Mandeville, whose market-praising *Fable of the Bees* is subtitled: *Private Vices, Publick Benefits*. Many contemporary celebrants of the market play down the truth in the first part of that subtitle.

35 It is not, as it is in the Carensian economy, only superficially market exchange: see page 70 above.

36 See page 67 above.

37 For more on this, see pages 253–7 of my 'Future of a Disillusion.'

38 For more on this, see my 'Back to Socialist Basics,' *New Left Review* 207 (Sept./Oct. 1994), and reprinted in Jane Franklin, ed., *Equality* (London: IPPR, 1997).

39 'Why Socialism?' *Monthly Review* 1 (1949), 1.

5

Welfare States and Democratic Citizenship

DIETRICH RUESCHEMEYER

The Question: Democratic Citizenship and Equality

Democratic citizenship – autonomous and active membership in the political community – is inherently a matter of equality, of equality in the political realm.[1] How are different approximations to political equality related to inequality in other spheres of life? Are these interrelations enhanced or undercut by collective systems of social provision? These are the main questions addressed in this essay.

Democratic welfare states revise the liberal conception of the good society: the triad of free markets, limited states, and universalist law. They enlarge the responsibility of the state and limit, but do not eliminate the role of the market. The goals of welfare states include guaranteed provisions for the elementary needs of education and health care, protection against the financial hazards of illness and disability, unemployment, and old age, and – in the more comprehensive cases – income redistribution and a compression of material inequality. One influential monograph formulates the tension between welfare states and a free market economy in its title: *Politics against Markets* (Esping-Andersen 1985).

Public policy shapes and contains markets to some extent in all modern states. The model of classic liberalism – of free market, limited state, and impersonal law – was, as Polanyi (1944) has taught us, just that: a model. It was a program that defied thorough and stable implementation.

The more comprehensive welfare states limit market forces more strongly than other advanced capitalist societies, especially in regard to the labour market. They create large areas of productive activity (and stable employment) that are not subjected to the success criterion of profit on the invested capital but rather are judged by broader, politically defined criteria of usefulness. In the technical, Marx-derived terminology these are known as areas of 'decommodification.'[2]

My central claim is that social welfare policies are of critical importance for enabling and invigorating democratic citizenship and that the more comprehensive welfare states give the strongest support to broad-based and autonomous participation in the democratic process.[3] After developing this argument I will consider liberal and neo-liberal claims to the contrary. I close with some reflections on the future prospects of welfare states.

Democracy Requires a Measure of Social Equality

Democracy is a matter of power. It is an approximation of equality in the political sphere of collective decision making, however imperfect in reality.

A certain balance of power in society is a necessary precondition for democracy. In particular, democracy comes about and gains in quality if previously weak groups and classes gain in power (Rueschemeyer, Stephens, and Stephens 1992). Even though state-society relations – the primary concern of liberal democratic theory – and international power relations played their part too, this empirically grounded proposition establishes the central importance of social inequality for the emergence and reproduction of democracy.

Individual engagement in democratic citizenship is also – like democracy at the level of society – a matter of power. As a form of political power, it rests on social power. At the same time, it is conditioned and influenced by inequalities in economic resources and social status.

Democracy relies on the active participation of citizens and atrophies without such participation (Tocqueville 1835–40/1966, Rueschemeyer 1998). The forceful participation of subordinate classes is of special importance for the quality of democracy (Huber, Rueschemeyer, and Stephens 1997).

Welfare states do not create democracy. History knows of authoritarian welfare states as well.[4] But democratic welfare policies strengthen democratic citizenship by giving material and organizational support to subordinate interests and by reducing differences in social status and social power. The neo-liberal claim that the security of comprehensive welfare provisions takes the spur of need out of popular political participation is not borne out by the facts (Huber, Rueschemeyer, and Stephens 1997; Rueschemeyer, Rueschemeyer, and Wittrock 1998).

Welfare State Policies Support Democratic Citizenship, Its Incidence and Quality

Material and Social-Structural Supports for Participation

Poverty inhibits participation. Georg Simmel (1958) saw the inability to participate meaningfully in social life as the mark of poverty beyond the physical survival level. The more comprehensive welfare states virtually eliminate this kind of poverty.

Democratic participation presupposes the expectation that one can make a difference. That explains the class differences in participation found in most societies. It also explains why active and successful social welfare policies stimulate more political participation than is found in political systems that are less responsive to popular interests, less 'substantively democratic.' Democratic participation is more even across class differences in the more comprehensive welfare states because of this 'it-does-matter' effect. This conclusion is supported by the fact that subordinate class organizations are more strongly developed in these countries (Huber, Rueschemeyer, and Stephens 1997).

Participation in and of itself is not sufficient for democratic citizenship. Many authoritarian political systems encourage or even mandate people's participation in centrally controlled associations. In order to advance the cause of democracy, social and political participation has to express divergent interests with a high degree of autonomy. This is of particular importance for those interests that do not command substantial power resources other than those of collective organization – that is, the groups and strata that possess little or no power grounded in wealth, religion, high status, or the cultural heritage. If these groups and strata are economically, socially, and/or culturally dominated by others, they are likely to replicate dominant interests in their forms of social participation.

The more comprehensive democratic welfare states enhance the autonomy of subordinate class interests since greater social security reduces economic and social dependencies. The stronger development of subordinate class organizations associated with more comprehensive welfare state development, since their mobilization typically made those policies possible in the first place, similarly enhances the autonomy of subordinate interests.

The Scandinavian welfare states have absorbed some of the caring work done previously in families. This has freed women for more civic engagement and political participation. The greater representation of women in Scandinavian parliaments is likely to have one of its roots in this effect of welfare state policy.[5]

Reducing Differences in Social Status and Social Power

Reducing large differences in social status is as important for democratic citizenship as offering material security. Social status is more than one's place in a rank order of 'prestige,' occupational or otherwise; it represents one's position in social life that shapes respect and self-respect and gives or denies 'voice,' the chance to gain a hearing and influence others. Once this aspect of status is recognized, it is obvious how important social status is for democratic citizenship.

The factors relevant here include the historical background of status orders, facilitating or hindering egalitarian participation,[6] the status implications of material security and equalization, egalitarian education, evenhanded administration of law, and administrative practices open to the demands and initiatives of popular organizations. I will not elaborate this further.

Social power, finally, must be added to material well-being and status. Social power is contained indirectly by reducing material inequality, by egalitarian systems of education, and by evenhanded judicial and administrative practices. It is limited most directly by social regulations affecting property rights. These regulations are of special importance because they shape social relations in the workplace, softening the profoundly undemocratic character of that central place in most people's lives. They can, and often do, also limit the impact of private power concentrations based on capital.

Social welfare policies, then – this is my claim – encourage and nurture democratic citizenship. They do much more than offering some support for the worst off, as is suggested by the American meaning of 'welfare.' Rather, they nurture democratic citizenship much more broadly, by reducing inequalities (1) in wealth and income, (2) in status and prestige, and (3) in power and influence. The more comprehensive welfare states do so most effectively.

There is evidence to support the claim that this matters. Edward

Broadbent has convincingly argued that the welfare states of the North Atlantic community have stabilized democratic regimes after the Second World War (Broadbent 1998). The development of civic participation in the more comprehensive welfare states of northwestern Europe has in recent decades fared better than social and political participation in the United States. At the same time, the Scandinavian societies seem to display in their civil societies, when compared for instance to Germany, the advantages of a more egalitarian status order as well as of a state more open to the demands and initiatives of civil society. Yet all the northwestern European welfare states protect their democratic systems better than the United States against the direct impact of material inequality, which removes much political decision making from democratic determination and stunts participatory citizenship (Rueschemeyer, Rueschemeyer, and Wittrock 1998).

Liberal Objections

I. Why is the Triad of Market, Universalistic Law, and Limited State Not Enough?

The liberal program in its strong form saw an egalitarian and liberating promise in a market economy protected by universal law but untrammelled by state 'intervention.'

Limiting state action, differentiating the economy from the political sphere, and protecting the steady pursuit of individual interests in the market were the core elements of a larger project of reshaping society: to liberate it from the burden of aristocratic rule and to create large spaces for individual liberty.

Liberal ideas are constitutive of the living constitutions of virtually all modern societies. Yet, the economic claims for free market economies as well as the broader liberal political project are problematic, especially in their strong form. Both the continued relevance of liberal ideas and the critical responses to the shortcomings of the liberal project are embodied in the modern welfare states.

To begin with the broader political project, the fundamental problem of the liberal position is that it commingles arguments about protecting individual liberty and arguments about protecting unequal privilege. The classic liberal claim that equality is incompatible with freedom is one expression of this. (It is a claim that has validity only under special conditions and fails to hold where approximations towards equality are achieved through democratic politics.) Focusing on the state as the main threat to individual freedom overlooks that the individual freedom of people in subordinate positions – and equally or more their participation in democratic rule – is threatened by social and economic dependencies within society, while a more active role of the state can serve as an effective and needed counterbalance to such dependencies.

Markets are indeed great coordination mechanisms, indispensable in any complex economy. They make the best use of widely dispersed economic intelligence and join in the same process signals about relative scarcity, incentives for efficient responses to changing scarcities, and the allocation of economic resources to the most efficient actors.

Many of the darker aspects of market exchange when it functions as the main or only mechanism of steering the economy are well known and need not detain us here at length. Such a market exchange may ignore

- needs and wants that are not backed up by income;
- the fact that income and wealth are co-determined by historical factors unrelated to economic efficiency, not to mention other reasonable criteria of distribution;
- 'externalities' – social costs (and sometimes benefits) that do not enter the price/cost calculus of self-interested economic actors; and
- the self-destructive tendencies of competitive markets – based in part on economies of scale, in part on the desire of powerful economic actors to be free of competition – that favour monopolistic and quasi-monopolistic tendencies and thus create large concentrations of private power.

There are, however, a number of other problematic aspects of market exchange that are less often acknowledged. A pervasive rule of the market principle of self-interest, which it presupposes, leaves little room for people, convictions, and patterns of behaviour that do not fit well with the market. Yet these seem to be a part of most people's conception of a good society – in the arts, in caring occupations. This has broader implications: social solidarities, such as family and community, as well as moral orientations that any society needs are likely to be undermined by a full-blown hegemony of the market principle. This was one of the founding insights of the continental European 'ordo liberalism' in the 1940s and 1950s, which drove the German policies of a 'social market economy' after 1949.[7]

It is worthwhile to note that unions and other associations representing shared interests, which are an indispensable underpinning of a functioning democracy, are at odds with strong versions of the free market principle. Unions used to be prohibited as unlawful 'combinations.' A noted neo-liberal theorist recently condemned strong coalitions of interests as a major cause of economic stagnation (Olson 1982). And it is no accident that neo-liberal politicians such as Vaclav Klaus and Margaret Thatcher have been explicitly hostile towards intermediary groups and associations.[8]

If competitive market exchange dominates a political economy, it not only makes certain collective goods – such as a strong solidarity in a society – unattainable; if pervasive and taken for granted, market functioning even undercuts the legitimacy of striving and working for these collective goods. Where neo-liberal economic ideas predominate, market exchange is conceived as setting the standard for all collective goals. In its strongest form, the neo-liberal creed denies any legitimate goals beside those that are confirmed by the market.

By contrast, it is possible to conceive of the functioning of the market as a means, an instrument that serves purposes set outside itself. The market in this view is subordinate to collective purposes, open to democratic determination. This instrumental conception of markets underlies – implicitly or explicitly – any argumentation for more or less comprehensive social welfare policies.[9]

Modern democratic welfare states embrace important core principles of liberalism, but they do so with a realistic appreciation of the inequalities in economy and society and their consequences for individual freedom. The legal protection of the participatory rights of expression and association is common to all democracies. And while individual liberties are at some risk of corporate as well as public bureaucratic intrusions, they, too, enjoy vigorous protective efforts across a variety of free market and welfare state regimes. The more developed welfare states differ from other political economies in how the relationship between public policy and the market is structured. The market is appreciated in an instrumental way, but it is subordinated to public policy, limited in its impact on people's lives, and transformed in significant outcomes. These differences hold both in public conception and in economic and political reality, though their full realization remains a matter of the balance power in society, as well as of favourable or unfavourable conditions in the historical background and in the international environment of a country.

II. The Welfare State Tends to Become an Illiberal Imposition on Its Clients

Welfare states, and especially the more comprehensive welfare states, have – so it is claimed – inherent illiberal tendencies. Whether they grew out of a pacification calculus of dominant classes, the initiatives of partially autonomous state elites, or the demands of subordinate classes, they tend towards paternalist impositions and insist on subordinating individual interests to collective solidarities. They thus infringe on the autonomy of democratic citizenship. They may do so in a different, more benevolently intended way than a political authoritarianism that just seeks to keep a regime in power, but the reduction of autonomy is real nevertheless.

This is a serious charge, and it is a claim that plays a certain role in current discussions in Scandinavia and Germany.[10] It is in my opinion based on real problems but mistaken in its causal analysis. At the same time, the current discussions themselves may be taken as a significant part of self-correcting tendencies.

Some of these problems are no doubt due to increased specialization of services and the difficulties of bureaucratic (or for that matter market) forms of coordination. Bureaucracy, that paragon of administrative efficiency, is also known for its bent towards conveniencing the organization and its administrators at the expense of the clientele. Much like market exchange, however, it is an unavoidable ingredient of any modern society. But bureaucratic rigidities and one-sided orientations are not invariant features of bureaucratic administration. Among the factors that may make a difference are precisely civic engagement and social participation.

Paternalist policies were often developed when the educational level of a good part of the clientele made them more reasonable. This was also a time when differences in the status order were far steeper than they are now. Inscribed into administrative practice and professional cultures, they persisted later, even though the material and intellectual resources, the mentality of the different strata, and the status order as a whole have changed profoundly. As a result, they not only are less appropriate even by the old standards, but clash now with demands for self-determination and recognition of idiosyncrasies that are the result of increased levels of material well-being and sophistication as well as a decline in invidious status distinctions.

A good deal of the arguments about inherent authoritarian tendencies in welfare states appear, then, at least potentially as consequences of the material, cultural, and status improvements that social welfare policies brought about. Many of the problems at stake seem to derive from a lack of synchronization between policies and administrative practices and different groups' changing resources, demands, and self-interpretations. I see no strong reason to doubt that over time processes of self-correction can straighten many of these problems out.

There is, however, a sense in which the liberal critique is on target, though not all will agree that it is right. Welfare state regimes do presuppose

- that problems and interests are structured socially rather than being simply due to individual choice and behaviour,
- that they can be represented collectively,
- that they can be analysed and responded to as social problems, and
- that adequate responses require social solidarity.

In other words, comprehensive welfare states are indeed premised on a certain subordination of individual to collective interests. This less individualist conception of the good society should in principle be acceptable even to moderate liberals, provided that no serious questions of repression and neglect are involved. Yet there are problems that emerge from such subordination even in a more socially oriented conception of good societies. I comment on two.

The various collective definitions of problems as well as of solidarity obligations are social constructions that involve leadership and organizational fixation as well as responses by the rank and file. These understandings and norms are likely to change over time. In this process, quite serious disjunctures may develop between the understandings and moral assumptions of different groups – of political leaders, administrators, professionals, well-off citizens, and the more needy clients of the welfare state. This first problem is really a broader version of the interpretation I offered above for the sense of imposition articulated in recent critiques.

A second problem is potentially more serious. It derives from the imperfect nature of collective representation of interests, which in a different context we identified as the 'inherent ambiguity of collective action' (Rueschemeyer, Stephens, and Stephens 1992). Robert Michels (1949) has pointed to a pervasive tendency in collective organizations towards a self-perpetuating oligarchy at their core. This acquires far greater importance than mere consolidation of power and perquisites for the few once we realize that collective interests are not simply given but are constructed in the process of organization and are then subject to disproportionate influence by 'the oligarchy.' In the extreme, the oligarchic leadership not only becomes autonomous vis-à-vis the rank and file but is able to collude with other elites at the expense of the followers.

Both Michels' 'iron law of oligarchy' and the possibility of elite collusion at the expense of the rank and file are, however, tendencies subject to varying albeit only incompletely understood conditions. It is a good theoretical guess that the conditions that favour broad-based autonomous civic engagement will counterbalance both tendencies in significant ways.

Our discussion, then, suggests two propositions of considerable weight. First, welfare states are under continuous pressure to change partly because of their own success (for instance in raising the level of education). Second, and even more important, the democratic citizenship supported by egalitarian social welfare policies at the same time reduces the chance that welfare states will pursue policies that violate individual liberty and dignity.

Current and Future Problems: Do Comprehensive Welfare States Undercut Their Own Viability?

Welfare states are today facing a number of profound challenges. This is not only because 'politics against markets' is an endless struggle, even in the most comprehensive welfare states. Some analysts have in fact diagnosed a worldwide crisis of welfare states. I will leave aside two major issues, the financial problems of welfare states that derive from an aging population and the effects of economic globalization. Instead, I will comment on issues that may have been created by the welfare state policies themselves.

There is no question that welfare state policies are a major cause of social change. The claim of this article that democratic welfare states deepen democracy and strongly support democratic citizenship is one such major change. Massive interventions in the life of societies are, however, very likely to have multiple consequences, not all of them desirable and some perhaps counterproductive of the social policy goals. What are some candidates for such counterproductive outcomes due to 'perverse incentives,' and how do we evaluate them?

First is the question whether social security in the broad sense of the word undercuts the commitment to work and to work efficiently. The most radical neo-liberal answer is a simple and resounding yes: social security undercuts efficiency to the point where welfare states simply become unviable. A more moderate claim holds that labour commitment will be whittled away in the long run.

Several considerations cast doubt on these hypotheses:

- The commitment of people to work is deeply grounded – in personality, social reciprocity, and institutional arrangements.
- Labour commitment was not destroyed even in the East European state socialist countries that went much further than any democratic welfare state in removing employment from market forces. Immediately after the fall of Communism, work turned out to be more often a central life concern of interview respondents in East Germany than in West Germany (Mau 1996, 62–4). The dramatic and growing inefficiencies of the East European economies seem to have had quite different causes, among them the radical non-use of the market.
- The history of the northwestern European welfare states, of Sweden, Norway, Denmark, the Netherlands, Austria, and Germany, does not accord well with the decline-of-work-commitment hypothesis either. Surely their success in international markets and their economic growth rates over long periods of time indicate that welfare states are quite able to hold their own economically.
- Finally, the history of these welfare states makes it clear that they have often been able to deal with more specific undesirable consequences of social policies, such as particularly high rates of absenteeism in special sectors of employment, by adjusting and restructuring policy measures.

This last observation entails again the important principle, already formulated, that precisely because social policy interventions have multiple and often unforeseen consequences, welfare states have to continually reproduce themselves, even partially reinvent themselves in order to stay viable. A major challenge for the future may well be to join policies designed to strengthen individual empowerment as well as responsibility with measures that maintain a high level of social security.

A second instance of claimed 'perverse incentives' are the changes in the family structure, in particular the rise in single parenthood, which creates new and financially significant welfare problems. This claim is well advertised politically but it, too, raises considerable doubts:

- Some of these claims give too much weight to limited financial 'incentives.' Neither the decision not to marry, nor the decision to get divorced, nor the decision to have a child while unmarried is likely to be influenced by money grants that lie well below the poverty level.
- More generous welfare supports for women do indeed set women free to live singly or in single-parent households. But so does the rise in individual incomes in much less generous welfare states. The difference lies in a different class distribution of this new-won freedom of women.
- Finally, here, too, there are differences across countries. Some of the northwestern European welfare states, such as Germany, pursue policies that shield traditional family structures more and offer less socioeconomic empowerment of women than the Scandinavian countries.

A third possible instance of 'perverse incentives' are changes in the patterns of civic engagement. There seems to be a shift in the concerns of associations of various kinds, both in the United States and in the Scandinavian countries (Putnam, Rothstein, and Selle in Rueschemeyer, Rueschemeyer, and Wittrock 1998) away from political and social reform and towards more inward oriented activities, from unions and parties to self-help and mutual support groups. Is such a privatization of concerns as expressed in social participation perhaps a consequence of increased levels of well-being and security and, while also found in rich societies with weak social provisions, a result of comprehensive welfare state policies as well? If a threat to more participatory citizenship, does it also put into question the very functioning of systems of social provision, which as we have seen also depends on active civic engagement?

We know as yet too little about such developments. However, one should not extrapolate trends too easily into the future. For one thing, the very need to restructure and even to reinvent welfare state policies may reactivate social concerns and political conflicts and thus remobilize popular participation. Furthermore, there are new concerns that mobilize people in ways different from the old forms. I think here of the recent waves of the women's movement, of environmental concerns, and so forth.

Finally, if in a rich society a majority is well off, this may well undercut the political chances of gaining a strong coalition for social policies that deal with the problems of the weaker minority. German political discourse labelled this condition the 'two-thirds society.' In established welfare states, this condition may become a threat to the successful reproduction and restructuring of social welfare policies. Once large shares of the national product are committed to a set of programs, their beneficiaries come to represent powerful constituencies that may prevent successful restructuring.

While this may become indeed a serious problem, it should not be forgotten that issues of restructuring and proportional reallocation are much harder to solve politically in situations of economic stagnation than in a context of economic growth. Furthermore, growing affluence may do something more than lift a majority out of immediate concerns with social welfare provisions, leaving the rest to fend for themselves. Growing affluence may make people more generous towards the suffering of those less fortunate. There is anecdotal evidence to suggest that that is the case on the individual level, even though it is a well-known fact that people of moderate means give a higher proportion of their income to charities that the affluent. Whether this translates into politics as well, probably depends on a number of conditions that are more favourable in societies that offer strong social security and limit the sense of competitiveness between groups. Greater solidarity across divisions in society may well be enhanced by secure well-being.

Given that the *Communist Manifesto* recently had its 150th anniversary, one might relate this problem to a grand issue expressed in Karl Marx's hope that capitalist productivity would in the society of the future surpass human needs and wants and eliminate scarcity. Marx was, of course, not naive enough to assume that there would simply be an upper ceiling to the proliferation of wants. Rather, he theorized about changes in needs and wants as contingent on social conditions. This suggests the question whether comprehensive welfare states are able to contain needs, wants, and consumptive ambitions better than more liberal and individualist political economies. It is at least a question worth examining if it makes a difference for the development of actually pursued wants and desires whether a society is characterized by unequal private affluence and public poverty or by egalitarian private austerity and public wealth. The assumption that an endless and rapid expansion of needs and wants is built into the human condition and thus independent of social and political construction is surely not as self-evident as we often tacitly assume.

Coda

Democratic welfare states maintain and deepen democracy and support democratic citizenship as they enhance material security, equalize social status, and mitigate differences in social and economic power. Even the most comprehensive democratic welfare states embrace a good part of the liberal heritage, appreciating the market as an instrument as well as the value of individual liberty. They are at odds, however, with the more radical forms of the old and the new liberalism.

If we examine current and future problems of the humane functioning of welfare states, it turns out that their support for civic engagement and democratic citizenship is also a major means for self-correcting tendencies. Yet it is important to realize that the future is an open field with many challenges. As in the past, today's welfare states have to innovate in order to maintain themselves.

NOTES

1 Equality is, of course, an extreme concept that defines a dimension of closer or more distant approximations. It also raises immediately the question: equality of what? (see Sen 1992).

2 See Esping-Andersen (1990) for an empirical typology of different established systems of social welfare provisions. I should note that in this article I neglect many of the important differences between welfare states that the work of Esping-Andersen and many others has highlighted.

3 Much of what follows is based on earlier collaborative work, in particular Rueschemeyer, Stephens, and Stephens (1992); Huber, Rueschemeyer, and Stephens (1997); and Rueschemeyer, Rueschemeyer, and Wittrock (1998). I wish to thank Miguel Glatzer and James Mahoney as well as Marilyn Rueschemeyer for valuable comments on an earlier draft.

4 This article deals only with democratic welfare states. Authoritarian welfare states may well stabilize authoritarian regimes and social policy may be used as an alternative to democratization. In fact, one comparative statistical study (Cutright and Wiley 1969) found that the existence of significant social security provisions was associated with stability in the constitutional status quo, whether democratic or authoritarian. Authoritarian welfare states typically arrange their social provision in such a way as to limit the autonomy of groups and associations in civil society.

5 I wish to thank one of the anonymous reviewers for reminding me of this point.

6 Repairing a historical background of stark inequality becomes one of the central issues of a pro-democratic social policy. This is of particular importance in the dimension of status because status orders seem to have a special tendency to persist historically.

7 One neglected monograph of the time formulates these ideas under the ironic title of 'marginal morality' (Schöllgen 1946).

8 On Margaret Thatcher see Michael Burrage (1997); on Vaclav Klaus Michal Illner (1998).

9 Ironically, market outcomes can and must then be analysed and evaluated in a logic similar to that is used in the principal-agent analyses of neo-liberal property rights theory.

10 See, for example, Jensen (in preparation) on Norway; more generally see the claims of Habermas (1987) about a 'colonization of the life world' by the modern state. In regard to the particular case of Norway one may want to keep in mind that Norwegians report the highest level of satisfaction with the workings of democratic government as reported in international survey studies, and the ranking of Germany and Denmark is not far behind (Fuchs, Guidorossi, and Svensson 1995).

REFERENCES

Broadbent, Edward. 1998. 'Six Steps to Save the Welfare State.' *Canadian Forum* 76, n. 866 (Jan./Feb.), 11–15.

Burrage, Michael. 1997. 'Mrs. Thatcher against the "Little Republics": Ideology, Precedents, and Reactions.' In Terence C. Halliday and Lucien Karpik, eds., *Lawyers and the Rise of Western Political Liberalism*. Oxford: Oxford University Press, 125–65.

Cutright, Phillips, and James A. Wiley. 1969. 'Modernization and Political Representation: 1927–1966.' *Studies in Comparative International Development*.

Esping-Andersen, Gosta. 1985. *Politics against Markets*. Princeton, N.J.: Princeton University Press.

– 1950. *Three Worlds of Welfare Capitalism*. Princeton, N.J.: Princeton University Press.

– 1996. *Welfare States in Transition: National Adaptations in Global Economies*. Thousand Oaks, Cal.: Sage.

Fuchs, Dieter, Giovanna Guidorossi, and Palle Svensson. 1995. 'Support for the Democratic System.' In H.-D. Klingemann and D. Fuchs, eds., *Citizens and the State*. Oxford: Oxford University Press, 323–53.

Habermas, Jürgen. 1987. *The Philosophical Discourse of Modernity*. Cambridge, Mass.: MIT Press.

Huber, Evelyne, Dietrich Rueschemeyer, and John D. Stephens. 1997. 'The Paradoxes of Contemporary Democracy: Formal, Participatory, and Social Dimensions.' In *Comparative Politics* (April), 323–42.

Jensen, Thor Øivind. Forthcoming. 'The Rise and Fall of the Modernist Health Project.' In Jan Froestad, Thorvald Gran, Tor Halvorsen, and Thor Ø. Jensen, eds., *Modern Norway: State, Experts, and Society*.

Illner, Michal. 1998. 'Local Democratization in the Czech Republic after 1989.' In D. Rueschemeyer, M. Rueschemeyer, and B. Wittrock, eds., *Participation and Democracy East and West: Comparisons and Interpretations*. Armonk, N.Y.: M.E. Sharpe, 51–82.

Mau, Steffen. 1996. 'Objektive Lebensbedingungen und subjektives Wohlbefinden.' In Wolfgang Zapf and Roland Habich, eds., *Wohlfahrtsentwicklung im Vereinten Deutschland: Sozialstruktur, sozialer Wandel und Lebensqualität*. Berlin: R. Bohn, 51–77.

Michels, Robert. 1949. *Political Parties*. Glencoe, Ill.: Free Press, first German ed. 1908.

Olson, Mancur. 1982. *The Rise and Decline of Nations: Economic Growth, Stagflation and Social Rigidities*. New Haven, Conn.: Yale University Press.

Polanyi, Karl. 1994. *The Great Transformation*. New York: Rinehart.

Putnam, Robert. 1978. 'Democracy in America at the End of the Twentieth Century.' In D. Rueschemeyer, M. Rueschemeyer, and B. Wittrock, eds., *Participation and Democracy East and West: Comparisons and Interpretations*. Armonk, N.Y.: M.E. Sharpe, 233–65.

Rothstein, Bo. 1998. 'The State, Associations, and the Transition to Democracy: Early Corporatism in Sweden.' In D. Rueschemeyer, M. Rueschemeyer, and B. Wittrock, eds., *Participation and Democracy East and West: Comparisons and Interpretations*. Armonk, N.Y.: M.E. Sharpe, 132–56.

Rueschemeyer, Dietrich, Evelyne Huber Stephens, and John D. Stephens. 1992. *Capitalist Development and Democracy*. Cambridge: Polity Press, and Chicago: Chicago University Press.

Rueschemeyer, Dietrich, Marilyn Rueschemeyer, and Björn Wittrock, eds. 1998. *Participation and Democracy East and West: Comparisons and Interpretations*. Armonk, N.Y.: M.E. Sharpe.

Schöllgen, Werner. 1946. *Grenzmoral. Soziale Krisis und neuer Aufbau*. Düsseldorf: Bastion Verlag.

Selle, Per. 1998. The Norwegian Voluntary Sector and Civil Society in Transition: Women as Catalysts for Deep-Seated Change.' In D. Rueschemeyer, M. Rueschemeyer, and B. Wittrock, eds., *Participation and Democracy East and West: Comparisons and Interpretations*. Armonk, N.Y.: M.E. Sharpe, 157–202.

Sen, Amartya. 1992. *Inequality Reexamined.* Cambridge, Mass.: Harvard University Press.

Simmel, Georg. 1958. 'Der Arme.' In G. Simmel, *Soziologie: Untersuchungen über die Formen der Vergesellschaftung*. Berlin: Duncker & Humblot, first ed. 1908.

Tocqueville, Alexis de. 1967. *Democracy in America.* New York: Harper & Row.

6

Equality, Community, and Sustainability

IAN ANGUS

In the period from the end of the Second World War until its dismantling in recent years, the welfare state achieved a degree of equality and social justice that was unprecedented in North Atlantic capitalist societies. By balancing the endemic inequalities caused by a capitalist economy with redistributive and social security programs enacted through the nation-state, the welfare state managed to bring the working class into the mainstream of capitalist society. The idea of social rights – rights to employment, good working conditions, unemployment insurance, education, health care, pensions, etc. – that underlay the practice of the welfare state gained the acceptance of a majority of the working class, such that they could see themselves as full citizens of capitalist society. In return for this inclusion, they accepted the necessity to work and to contribute socially, through taxes, to the maintenance of the society that guaranteed those social rights. T.H. Marshall, the major theorist of the welfare state, explained social rights as 'the whole range from the right to a modicum of economic welfare and security to the right to share to the full in the social heritage and to live the life of a civilized being according to the standards prevailing in the society.'[1] It is important to emphasize in the contemporary context that social rights were universal rights – they applied to everyone equally – and not simply a 'social safety net' for the poor, unfortunate, or unworthy.

Social rights reformed the capitalist conception of property understood as the unrestricted right to exclude all others from the use of a good. Such an exclusive property right had become dominant by displacing an earlier, pre-capitalist conception of property in which various persons and groups could have different property rights in the same thing. Each thing used to be criss-crossed, as it were, by a net of overlapping uses that were recognized in the notion of common property. Common property is the right not to be excluded from the use of a thing, whereas the capitalist conception of property is the right to exclude all others. C.B. Macpherson was referring to this history when he argued that 'the rise of the welfare state has created new forms of property and distributed them widely – all of them being rights to a revenue.'[2] If one has the right not be excluded from a revenue, one gains the right to exercise one's abilities in the production of that revenue. This right may then be called a right in a common property. The welfare state made an important incursion into capitalist property by asserting that everyone has a right to make a living and thus that the necessary means for work are common property. This did not mean, of course, that capitalist private property was abolished as such, rather, the nation-state asserted the right of workers not to be excluded from the provision of jobs by private industry. In short, the state was committed to policies aimed at securing full employment. In Macpherson's words, 'that right amounts to a right of access to the means of labour which they do not own.'[3] A common property in the means to work as enforced by the nation-state was a key component in ending the social marginalization of the working class.

The recognition of social rights and common property in the welfare state forged a new and compelling identity for most members of the working class. These new rights were not simply new elements of their situation; in identifying strongly with them, the identity of the working class was transformed. They became citizens with rights that extended into the workplace and family. This new identity displaced the us-versus-them mentality that had previously prevailed and allowed the majority of citizens to identify with the goals of society as a whole, to create a national moral community that mitigated the competitive individualism and class antagonism of market society.

The resurrection of thinking about the welfare state is thus an important task in the contemporary context, where social programs are castigated as simply 'free lunches' for the poor; where national politics has been reduced to a battle of interest groups without ethical content; where individualism runs rampant and moral feelings are derided as sentimental and unrealistic; where multinational capitalist firms put pressure on governments to reduce taxes; where the fabric of everyday life is increasingly degraded by the stress of intensifying work, unemployment, and homelessness; where marginalization of individuals, groups, and regions threatens to become permanent; and where many citizens retreat into cynicism or private life. Many concerned citizens today fear that the capitalism of the future will look more like the capitalism of a hundred years ago than the apparently anomalous episode of the welfare state. It is no wonder that we live in a time in which us-versus-them thinking is on the rise throughout all arenas of social life.

The welfare state, as a key moment in the history of socialism in which workers became citizens, was characterized by an expanding post-war industrial economy, with its emphasis on Fordist production and mass consumption. Expenditures on social rights could thus be combined with an expectation of general employment and a rising standard of living. For this reason, the ideas and practice of the welfare state continued the dominant emphasis in the socialist tradition on the idea of progress.[4] Since the eighteenth century Enlightenment, the idea of progress has been associated with the domination of nature by science and technology such that material wealth for greater general abundance could be created. Such general abundance was believed to provide the essential conditions for a society of greater equality, political participation, and both individual and social development. The socialist tradition differed from the liberal one in arguing that this ideal could only be realized if class inequality was eliminated or, at least, decreased, but the attachment to the idea of moral-political progress through the domination of nature was a common heritage from the Enlightenment.

In our time the idea of continuous progress has come under serious criticism, largely due to the nightmarish experiences of the twentieth century in the use of science and technology to intensify the destructiveness of war, repression, and genocide. But it is also apparent that the huge increases in material production during this century have failed to translate into general equality and social participation. The welfare state, in holding to the idea of progress through industrial growth, has thus been out of step with the major criticism of the idea of progress that has emerged in our time. Moreover, even in the hey-day of the welfare state there were factors that suggested that the translation of industrial growth into social equality through national programs entailed some negative effects on social participation and individual development. The institutionalization of social rights through national bureaucracies produced a 'clientism' and de-politicization that reinforced the channeling of expectations into private life defined on a consumerist model. The new citizen-identity as it emerged in the welfare state was thus subject to endemic forces undermining its efficacy from the outset. A contemporary renewal of social rights, and a renewed citizen-identity, must take its departure from the evident reality of our time that the expanding Fordist economy on which the welfare state was based cannot be recovered and that national bureaucracies have a corrosive effect on political life.[5] For these reasons, I will suggest that contemporary socialism must take up the minority tradition that attempted to harmonize humanity with nature and sought human equality and individual development outside of industrial growth. It is not a question of rejecting scientific and technological development, but of rejecting the ideology that such development should be conceptualized as a continuous 'advance,' such that critics are always charged with trying to 'retard' technology or 'return' to an earlier time. The issue is to assert human equality, individual development, and community as the criteria for what counts as an 'advance' or progress, rather than expecting human goals to simply adjust to developments in science and technology. It is a question of what type of development and for what purposes.

In order to pose the question of how social rights and common property might be re-invented in our time, I want to begin by considering the relationship of the market to the whole range of human activities. Whereas revolutionary socialism attempted to abolish the market, and social democracy has accepted it in its present form, I think that our present task is how to displace, or push aside, the market from its domination of social life through its monopoly over the social representation of value. While the market may be expected to continue to exist, a central goal of democratic socialism must be that fewer and fewer subsistence needs be obtained through the market and, in general, that the market be subordinated to subsistence needs as defined through a community. A subsistence-oriented economy, unlike a market-driven one, has a decent chance at a sustainable relation to nature. This implies that the legislative activities of national and provincial states should be oriented towards enabling relatively independent, sustainable communities.

The commodities exchanged on the market are defined through their prices. Only by having a price does a thing, being, or activity become a commodity. And, through the relation between prices, it becomes essentially comparable to any other commodity. The market is the total system of relative prices and, as such, embodies within itself a system of universal comparability and relative value. In market-intensive capitalist societies, the market is the central form of the social representation of value. You and I as individuals often regard a thing (such as a photograph of a dead friend or relative), a being (such as a human being, a household pet, or a wild goose), or an activity (such as running, growing vegetables, or making love) as having inherent, or intrinsic value – that is to say, a value good in itself. But such values are not socially effective, they are 'private' or 'subjective' we say, because they do not enter into the effective social representation of value through the market. If they were to enter into the market by being assigned a price, their value would become socially recognized by becoming a relative value in comparison to other things, beings, or activities. It would also raise the issue of how its social value, as represented by its price, has transformed its intrinsic value, the value that inheres in a thing, being, or activity itself.

This poses a problem for environmental issues. If clean water, or wild geese, do not have a price, then their value is regarded as only a private or subjective affair. Thus, environmental issues are often posed in terms of an opposition between objective market value and non-market subjective or emotional values such that environmental concerns are seen as always interfering with, and retarding, the market. They are seen as entirely non-market goods whose only possible effectivity is through state regulation. On the other hand, if environmental goods are given prices, they become relative values defined by their price and, given enough time, one can expect that they will be reckoned less valuable than something else. If a park's value is determined by a price, then the condos are not far away.

The monopoly of the social representation of value through the market is thus a general problem for environmental issues. But it is not only environmental issues that are affected in this way. We all perform work that is not valued through a price, or wage. One of the primary examples of unpaid labour is domestic work, mainly performed by women, but yard work, fixing the car or children's toys, volunteer community work, shopping, and so forth also constitute unpaid labour. While the market system of relative prices is universal in the sense that any thing, being, or activity can be assigned a price, it is in another sense partial. The market abstracts from the whole complex of things, beings, and activities that define our practical life. It lifts one aspect out of its practical context and, after considering it in isolation, sets it into the systemic relation with other aspects that constitutes relative value.

The point is that the market system does not, and cannot, represent the whole of practical life. It necessarily leaves out many things, beings, and activities. More can always be added in, but the process can never be complete. While the market is not extensionally limited – in principle, it can be extended to cover any new commodity – it is limited by the process of abstraction from which it begins. In abstracting from the whole complex of practical life, the market system thus continually raises the question of its applicability and effects in social life as a whole. It is this question that is encapsulated in the distinction between intrinsic value and relative value.

Even in high-intensity market societies, the market relies upon and affects a multiplicity of other things, beings, and activities which constitute the fabric of our social lives. The limitations of the social representation of value by the market is thus an important political issue in such societies. One way in which this issue has been posed is in terms of the relation between the market economy and the household in which the situation of women is crucial. Another, as I have already suggested, is in the environmental movement where the relation between the market economy and natural beings and cycles is crucial. There are, necessarily, many other examples. The argument that I am making in abstract terms refers to all situations in which the relative prices reckoned on the market intersect with the concrete, specific intrinsic values that constitute the quality of our everyday lives.

The project of democratic socialism thus requires that the market system be dislodged from its monopoly of the social representation of value. Social economists and critics have coined a number of terms – such as the informal economy, shadow work, or subsistence economy – to refer to transactions that are not represented as prices.[6] I will use the term 'subsistence' to refer in the widest sense to all things, beings, and activities in high-intensity market societies that are presupposed by, ignored by, or outside the market but that are nevertheless important to the lives of people within such societies. The term subsistence economy is thus a way of formulating the surrounding context within which the market operates and which it continually affects and reorganizes. While the market functions to reorganize subsistence around that which can be given a price, the goal of socialism is to subordinate price, or relative market value, to subsistence.[7]

Subsistence has three main components. First, there are those things, beings, and activities necessary to the useful functioning of market-represented values but which are not themselves assigned prices. For example, the vegetables that I buy at the corner store have a price, but my buying activity does not, nor does the walk home or the cooking or the eating of those vegetables. Second, there are those things, beings, and activities that remain outside the market system. Traditional subsistence, such as growing and eating my own vegetables, would fall into this category, as would inherent natural values such as wild geese and clean air. Third, there are those transactions that simply take place outside the market through barter or other informal exchanges. Subsistence represents the practical world defined by the intrinsic values of things, beings, and activities which constitute the actually experienced form of life, or the qualitative standard of living, of people in high-intensity market societies. The goal of democratic socialism is to increase the qualitative standard of living, or, in the widest sense, the 'real wealth' of people as experienced in their subsistence.

There are several advantages to thinking in terms of subsistence economy, or practical use-value. It brings into consideration those activities important to the qualitative standard of living – such as cooking, housework, or home repairs and improvements – that are usually invisible. Also, it allows us to reckon what is lost through market exchanges in relation to what is gained. For many people, for example, taking a job to receive a wage requires enduring a long commute to work, frustration in traffic jams, and maintaining a expensive car. Some of these costs can be given a price and some cannot, but all must be reckoned against what is gained as a wage. Time lost in a commute that cannot be spent with one's children will never find a price on the market, but I think that it is not hard to understand that it has to do with their quality of life.

Because of the difference between market values and intrinsic values, market societies have always contained an opposing tendency to the reduction of values to the market. Following Karl Polanyi at this point, I will call such tendencies the 'self-protective response of society.'[8] Such a response comes from those sectors of society which are threatened by market forces. Initially, it was primarily the aristocracy and the working class who enacted measures to limit and contain the market. The vehicle of this response was never confined to the nation-state – the working class's first response, for example, was to form unions – but was mainly institutionalized through regulation of the market by the nation-state. Despite the near-monopoly of the social representation of value by the market, the nation-state became an arena for the articulation and representation of non-market values.

Actually existing market societies are thus torn between two conflicting tendencies. The dominant one tends to reduce all value to relative value represented by a price such that, to put it quickly, if it is not represented by a dollar value, it is not a real, or efficacious, need. A secondary, responsive tendency asserts intrinsic values against the market and looks for alternative forms in which they can be socially represented. The welfare state reflected relative equilibrium between these two tendencies, in which the intrinsic values represented as social rights were effectively asserted through the regulative power of the nation-state. Actually existing market societies are thus riven by a tension between market and community. I mean the term 'community' to refer to those collectivities which have sufficiently asserted intrinsic values against the market to constitute themselves as effective actors in the society. My claim is thus that community versus the market, not class versus class, is the main tension of contemporary market societies. And communities assert themselves as identities, that is to say, as actors which constitute themselves in social spaces where market forces are slack, or have been pushed aside. While the tendency of the market is towards uniformity, the protective response is of necessity plural, as plural as the threatened intrinsic values.

With the decline of the welfare state, the main community actors have become social movements. Their activism constitutes social identities which resist the relative values promoted by consumer society. The environmental movement, feminism, First Nations movements, urban reform, national and regional movements, gay and lesbian movements, and many more have been the main forces whereby the market has been held back from entirely dominating society. Their assertion of intrinsic values, subsistence, and concrete experience has forged senses of community that have sustained us and which hold out the promise of renewing the project of democratic socialism. They have done so, by and large, without being able to count on the nation-state for social protection from the market.[9]

The assertion of community by social movements thus provides the basis for assessing the qualitative standard of living of people as experienced in their subsistence that is the goal of democratic socialism. Communities propose new forms of the social representation of value that displace the monopoly of the market. It is in social movements that identities that become countervailing powers to consumerism and clientism are constructed. However, contemporary social movements have been considered primarily as forces that occur outside work and economic production. The main tendency of capitalism has been to reduce necessary work through the introduction of technology and increasingly capital-intensive enterprises; thus it raises the spectre of increasing marginalization for many sectors of the population. And work, in the narrow sense of wage labour, or activity with a price, has become less central to the identity of citizens. But no more now than in the past can socialists consider work that gains a wage on the labour market the criterion of useful activity. If we bear in mind the argument that I have made for displacing the market, and consider work in the wide sense as all useful activity, it can be understood as the crucial link between human beings and nature, as that which transforms nature into a human environment.

It is through human activity that our identities are constructed. Activity undertaken in a community brings forth a social representation of its value that makes identity social – that puts it into relation with other actors and their activities. When we understand human activitity as that which produces subsistence, or concrete well-being, its connection to sustainability becomes clear. Unsustainable practices are tolerated because those who initiate them do not have to live with their consequences. Resources are depleted, natural cycles are violated, for reasons defined outside of a given community. If the profit goes out of the community, the sustainability of the enterprise ceases to be an issue. But communities must live with the consequences of their actions; they have nowhere else to go, unless they simply cease to exist. Economic activity and markets become destructive when they cease to be local, that is, based in a community which both reaps the rewards and lives with the consequences.

There is thus an important link between the emphasis on locality in sustainable economics and the idea of work as useful activity oriented to subsistence, rather than wage labour. In this way, one can break down the apparent opposition between human action and nature that often appears in environmentalists and anti-environmentalists alike. The prior condition for this synthesis is a critique of the social representation of value by the market and an opening up to new social representations of value in the communities asserted by social movements. The principles and practicality of a sustainable society have been much debated in recent years. Without entering into the details of that debate here, there are two main respects in which the idea of a sustainable society makes an important contribution to contemporary socialism. First, while the idea that human activity can ever be entirely in 'harmony' with nature may well be an over-simplification, it is a definitive break with the Enlightenment idea that greater domination of nature is the vehicle of greater human equality. Posing the issue in terms of a form of human production that is sustainable in the long term in relation to natural cycles and processes entails a break from the ideology of progress that assumes a linear advance or retreat in the domination of nature by science and technology. Second, the question then becomes what forms and kinds of human productive use of nature do not destroy their natural basis. Thinking in this way means that both the types of productive relation to nature and their human purposes become amenable to ethical-political evaluation. The idea of sustainable society thus necessarily asserts the priority of ethical-political evaluation over material progress and in this respect returns us to the deeply ethical impulse of socialism from its infatuation with industry.

While it is an important ideal, the idea of a sustainable society as a steady-state relationship between humans and nature has one crucial drawback: to decide that a policy or social arrangement is sustainable in this sense would require extensive knowledge of natural systems and the impact of social organizations on them; it would seem to imply that decisions be taken by an army of natural and social scientists. Such a requirement would undermine democratic participation in decision making. Moreover, even in the apparently optimal case of highly informed decision making by a scientific and technical elite, knowledge is necessarily limited to those studies that have already been done. New impacts on nature by technical innovations, by accumulation of isolated impacts, and by new forms of social organization would still necessarily introduce imbalances into the human-nature relationship. Scientific knowledge of problems necessarily lags behind the identification of those problems themselves: the knowledge requirement of steady-state sustainability is too high to be realistic and contains an unfortunate undemocratic implication.

But it is not necessary to interpret sustainability in terms of a positive steady-state relationship between humans and nature. The idea of sustainable society arose in the context of an environmentalist critique of many of the practices of industrial society as being unsustainable. While sustainability is hard to define, unsustainability is much easier to spot and demands remedial action, if not an ultimate remedy. We should therefore understand sustainability as not-unsustainability, as based in a criticism of unsustainable practices (for which we do have compelling evidence) and as proposing new practices which are, at minimum, less unsustainable than current ones. Such practices will need to be worked out in local contexts in relation to the subsistence of the local population. For this, democratic participation is essential since subsistence wealth, unlike prices, can only be defined by participants.

Human activity in making useful things can thus be made sustainable in relation to nature if the market is displaced from its monopoly on the social representation of value. Democratic participation in local, subsistence activities oriented to sustainable practices can provide another form for the social representation of value that might vie with the market to generate new forms of the self-protective response of society. This perspective does not imply that the market need be abolished, nor that it need be accepted in its current form; it implies that the market be displaced from its monopoly and re-embedded in sustainable, subsistence-oriented practices. In many cases, community and government intervention is necessary to protect local and regional markets from global ones. The right to a revenue, the right to make a living, means the right to participate in the social representation of value. This would be a new form of common property. On this basis, workers, as citizens, could participate fully in the rights and responsibilities of society in a new form by creating spaces for independent community action within the nation-state.

The route to realizing such an environmental socialism is itself diverse. Socialism has tended to limit itself to solutions either through the socialization of industry or redistribution by the nation-state. But the diversity of subsistence, articulated through democratic processes that socially represent value, suggests that there is no single solution to the domination of human activity by the market and its siphoning off of locally produced value by international money circuits. The goal is to promote and rely upon diverse and interconnected forms of economic activity which promote the development of subsistence wealth and useful human activity, maximize their travel through local circuits, and therefore maintain community employment.[10] Community control of investment through credit unions, if possible combined with legislation forcing banks towards the devolution of investment decisions, would be an important component. Diverse forms of ownership of local enterprises is also important. Social ownership through municipal and community boards, worker control, small business, and many other forms can all promote a diverse and sustainable local economy.[11] It is not likely within the forseeable future that the global market will subside. It is the task of an environmental socialism to build alongside it sustainable, subsistence-oriented local economies that hold out the possibility of withdrawing from dependence on global capital. The transition period will likely be very long, but the task is to build within the shell of the old society the incipient forms of the new, and to await the moment when it is demonstrated in the daily lives of citizens that their survival requires a break with the global market.[12]

There will remain a role for the welfare state – and the assertion of social rights, common property, and community through the nation-state – but the dynamic has now moved elsewhere. It is only by reconstituting them in new forms, from the ground up, within cooperative forms of self-organization that we can form the social relations that might sustain us in the moment when we are abandoned to environmental ruin and social marginalization by the shiny forces of globalization. These forces will indeed abandon us in the moment when it becomes more profitable to do so. At that time, we need to be prepared with an alternative conception of property, wealth, and citizenship that could extend the achievements of the welfare state into a new stage. In my view, subsistence and sustainability must be the watchwords of this new socialist ideal. We will be engaged in many struggles aimed at realizing them in specific communities.

NOTES

1 T.H. Marshall, 'Citizenship and Social Class,' in *Class, Citizenship and Social Development* (Garden City: Doubleday, 1965), 78.
2 C.B. Macpherson, 'A Political Theory of Property,' in *Democratic Theory: Essays in Retrieval* (Oxford: Clarendon Press, 1973), 131, cf. 12, 91, 134, 181.
3 Ibid. 132.
4 It is important to note, however, that there was always an important minority tradition that advocated the reconciliation, or harmony, of humanity with nature. The utopian socialists, the early Marx, and the anarchist tradition are the main examples of this. Kropotkin perhaps put this ideal of local self-reliance most clearly when he argued for 'a society where each individual is a producer of both manual and intellectual work; where each able-bodied human being is a worker, and where each worker works in both the field and the industrial workshop; where every aggregation of individuals, large enough to dispose of a certain variety of natural resources – it may be a nation, or rather a region – produces and itself consumes most of its own agricultural and manufactured produce.' Peter Kropotkin, *Fields, Factories and Workshops of Tomorrow* (New York: Harper, 1974), 26.

5 This statement requires a crucial qualification. While bureaucracies, when they seek to handle public problems, produce a depoliticizing, and thus undemocratic, clientism, nevertheless, there is a necessary task for public welfare, and that in practice probably means bureaucracy, in assuring the preconditions – such as health, nutrition, and education – for social and political participation.

6 See, for example, Ivan Illich, *Shadow Work* (Boston and London: Marion Boyars, 1981); Alejandro Portes, Manuel Castells, and Lauren A. Benton, *The Informal Economy* (Baltimore and London: Johns Hopkins University Press, 1989); and Claus Offe and Rolf G. Heinze, *Beyond Employment*, trans. Alan Braley (Cambridge: Polity Press, 1992).

7 I hope that this phrasing avoids a possible misunderstanding of the perspective that I am advocating. Unwaged labour has often been, for that very reason, a source of dependence and exploitation and, in many cases, access to wage labour has been a liberating experience. Similarly, giving environmental goods a price would give them some standing in the market. Nevertheless, I am arguing that the real locus of wealth is in subsistence and that the transformation of work into wage labour has intrinsic limitations.

8 Karl Polanyi, *The Great Transformation* (Boston: Beacon Press, 1971).

9 In my view, social movements need a political party to carry their intrinsic values into a common field and, indeed, to the nation-state. But they cannot be confined to a party. Indeed, the party of democratic socialism must largely take its impulse from such movements and become the arena in which the plurality of intrinsic values are debated and reconciled. The moral community that was asserted at the national level by the welfare state needs to be built up from other communities. It does not work if it is asserted directly and exclusively at the level of the nation-state, which is too large and impersonal a form of association.

10 This perspective is often called 'community economic development.' See, for example, Burt Galaway and Joe Hudson, eds., *Community Economic Development: Perspectives on Research and Policy* (Toronto: Thompson, 1994) and David P. Ross and Peter J. Usher, *From the Roots Up: Economic Development as if Community Mattered* (Toronto: James Lorimer, 1986).

11 See Diane Elson, 'Market Socialism or Socialization of the Market,' in *New Left Review* 172 (Nov.–Dec. 1988), 2–44, and 'The Economics of a Socialized Market,' in Robin Blackburn, ed., *After the Fall: The Failure of Communism and the Future of Socialism* (London and New York: Verso, 1991).

12 A global market is, in a certain sense, still compatible with the perspective outlined here. But it should be a market in non-necessities, a market from which subsistence is gradually withdrawn.

PART THREE

INEQUALITY IN THREE DEMOCRACIES

7

Rethinking Equality and Equity: Canadian Children and the Social Union

JANE JENSON

Equality and inequality are political constructions; both their conditions and their definitions vary across space, time, and philosophical families. Concepts of equality and inequality as well as of fairness are thus historically rooted, taking shape and shifting as economic and social conditions restructure and as the balance of political forces alters. Inequalities and inequities are named as such when the structural conditions and the ideas we use to identify them create space for such meanings. Otherwise they remain veiled in the realm of the private or hidden by other visions.

This said, it is useful to address the following question: have everyday political definitions of equality and equity recently changed in Canada? If so, what are the consequences for democratic citizenship?

In the present article I argue that the answer to the first is affirmative. The definitions of equality and equity have definitely altered of late and there are clear consequences for the discourse and practices of equality in Canada. The goals inscribed in social and employment policy, indeed in most policy domains, reflect these definitions. In recent years, Canadian governments, and particularly the federal government, have reinforced, indeed virtually confined, the use of social policy to fighting poverty, via a flowering of selective and tax delivered programs.[1] In doing so they have weakened any promise of equality while intensifying the commitment to equity as the basic principle of social policy.

This is a perspective that envisions 'social safety nets' rather than equality of condition, active labour market policy, or social and economic rights of citizenship.[2] Thus, if Canadians have proudly believed that their welfare state was more universal than that of their southern neighbours, the reality of current program design does not match the belief. Since the late 1970s there has been a significant shift from universal programs to selectivity.[3] Secondly, governments have engaged in a reassignment of the responsibilities of the state, markets, and families.[4] They now put greater emphasis on individuals' (and therefore their family's), responsibility for their own well-being, their own life chances, and their own income security, as well on the market as the mechanism for delivery of life chances and conditions.

The result is a redefinition of collective responsibility and social justice anchored by a liberal version of equality of opportunity.[5] On the one hand, the burden for 'Canada's well-being' has supposedly been shifted away from the state towards the private sector, communities, and families. This shift essentially involves a dual decentralization, towards markets and towards provincial governments. On the other hand, to the extent that the state retains a role for public institutions and posits some collective responsibility for the well-being of vulnerable Canadians, it has refocused its policy efforts towards children.

The new focus is expressed in the 'children's agenda' now traversing federal policy communities and in the redesign of federalism and intergovernmental relations via the social union agreement. There are a new set of tax-based transfers and credits as well as a focus on children's health and social development in the early years. In all of this, the 'citizen' has been reconstructed with reference to a central image, that of the 'child,' while the state's responsibility for fostering equality of opportunity is limited to this child, or at most young people. Adults are left to fend to themselves 'responsibly' in the neo-liberal world of individualization and market relations.

The new emphasis on equality of opportunity for children in the social union discussions and agreement – while clearly benefitting some children and their families – has come with a cost. It has made other dimensions of equality, such as equal access to democratic institutions or fostering gender equality in the economy, the society, and the family somewhat more difficult to pursue.

A Liberal Welfare State

Along with United States and the United Kingdom, Canada has always been one of the liberal welfare states.[6] In the first three post-war decades it was a 'low-end' welfare state of mixed construction. Some social programs (for example, health care, pensions, and unemployment insurance) did deliver universal social rights. But others have been of the 'safety net' variety, targeted at the poorest and leaving other Canadians to fend for themselves. Canada thus possessed a classically liberal welfare state regime. As O'Connor et al., write, 'Typically, liberalism's broader social policy content has been evoked with general references to Titmuss's ... model of residual social policy, in which public policy has a role only when market and family fail.'[7]

In addition, since the 1970s there has been a major shift in the form and delivery of income security. Selective – that is, targeted – benefits have risen from 21 per cent to 52 per cent of income transfers since the mid-1970s, and governments now spend more on selective income transfers than they do on universal social insurance programs.[8]

Yet, through the early 1990s, the Canadian welfare state had not been unsuccessful in meeting the limited goals it set for itself. As numerous cross-national analyses have shown, in the 1980s net incomes in Canada were distributed more equally than in the United States, despite the strong similarities in economic structures, corporate forms, cultural preferences, and self-described neo-liberal governments.[9] In particular, in the 1980s when the Luxembourg Income Study tracked mounting income inequalities in the United States, it did not observe the same in Canada. While inequalities in market incomes – that is, gross earnings and income from property – rose in Canada as in the United States, the disposable income gap was not as wide. In other words, the fight against poverty, especially among the elderly, has been more effective in Canada than in the United States.[10]

Studies have attributed the maintenance of a narrower disposable income gap to two factors. The first involves in particular the use of tax rates and tax credits to redistribute income from high to lower income earners as well as from the employed to the unemployed and other individuals not in the labour force. The second factor reflects the less severe decline of unionization rates and minimum wage laws in Canada than in the United States. This second difference accounts for two-thirds of differential growth in wage inequality.[11] Such patterns reflect, then, the power of formal institutions such as the state, via fiscal and social policy, and unions, via collective bargaining, to shape income distribution in the direction of greater equality.

The lesson to draw from such observations is not that Canada's record is superior to that of the United States, however. Indeed, these patterns have not necessarily held up in the decade of the 1990s, marked by the 'fight to get the deficit under control' and the politics of tax cuts in provinces such as Alberta and Ontario. Poverty among children has risen over the 1990s, despite formal governmental commitments to eliminating it by 2000. Discussions about equity in Canada are, for the most part, conducted with governments and parties in power that do not claim the social democratic tradition as their own. Indeed, in at least two provinces, including the largest, there are quite proudly neo-liberal governments. The federal government is also again in the hands of the Liberals, who took a neo-liberal 'cure' in the 1980s.

Therefore, the lessons to be drawn about any existing differences between Canada and the United States on dimensions of income equality are that these numbers are the lingering result of the continued influence of the post-war Canadian citizenship regime, with its values of equity, among individuals and across regions. Future directions of these trends will depend upon choices now being made about how to alter that citizenship regime, choices about its principles, the place it grants to formal institutions, and especially democratic collective choices – whether in public institutions or those of the private sectors, such as unions and social movement organizations, particularly the anti-poverty movement – located at the intersection of state and civil society.[12]

The post-war years were marked by discursive coherence and practices in a wide range of institutional connections between state and citizens. However, states and citizens' responses to the economic and political conditions of the last years of the twentieth century dismantled that regime and reconstituted citizenship, so that the post-war regime exists no more. If neo-liberalism has dismantled the old, the shape of the future is not yet completely clear, however.

Challenges to Canada's Post-War Citizenship Regime

A citizenship regime denotes the institutional arrangements, rules, and understandings that guide and shape concurrent policy decisions and expenditures of states, problem definitions by states and citizens, and claims-making by citizens.[13] A citizenship regime encodes within it a paradigmatic representation of identities, of the 'model citizen,' as well as who can carry a passport, and of the 'second-class citizen' who can make claims for full citizenship. The regime also encodes representations of the proper and legitimate social relations among and within these categories, as well as the borders of 'public' and 'private.'

We can identify Canada's choices about such representations in the construction of the citizenship regime after the Second World War. At the time, the Liberal government had to look to its left; social democrats were making electoral threats and a first-stage construction process of the post-war citizenship regime took off.

The social policy decisions made in the 1940s and again in the 1960s can be 'deconstructed' for their understandings of equality. The values were basically liberal, to be sure, but principles of equity were similarly strong. As a result of the fiscal crises that struck the provinces in the 1930s and the needs of wartime mobilization, Ottawa could accumulate much more authority to direct the Canadian economy and society than it had previously enjoyed. The federal government shaped the new welfare state and extended the citizenship regime by incorporating new social rights in two waves, one in the 1940s, the other in the 1960s. In particular, the federal government assumed the responsibility for public policies that would foster a pan-Canadian identity based upon broadly similar access to income security and social protection. The notion was that all Canadians should have more or less the same life chances, whether they lived in wealthy Toronto or poverty-stricken Newfoundland.

A discourse of equity and social development supplemented the liberal grounding of social rights in previous decades and in these years social rights of Canadian citizens became even more distinct from those available in the United States. The discourse of equity and social justice was pervasive, shaping proposals for everything from reforming party financing to health care. A wide variety of institutions also shared a conceptualization of how citizens should gain access to the state. Organizations rather than individuals were the primary actors in this vision. In the 1940s and again in the 1960s, trade unions increased in size and gained collective bargaining rights to represent their members to employers and to the state. Parties changed shape, developing more elaborate internal machinery for selection of leaders and policy discussion. Indeed, the New Democratic Party organized itself finally to provide representation to workers' organizations as well as to individuals. The Québécois nationalist movement spawned parties and associations beginning in the early 1960s and was soon joined by organizations of the English-Canadian nationalist movement and then by the Aboriginal nationalist movement, all struggling to represent their political position to the state as well as citizens more generally.

Concerns about 'Canadian' identity flowered. In part, but only in part, this was because of the challenge of Québécois nationalists. The issue was not simply one of competing national identities, however. The strategy of nationalists in Quebec was to use the state to realize their development project, in particular to build a sophisticated, secular, and above all an activist state with the capacity to catapult Quebec society into modernity. The completion of the Canadian welfare state became both a response to the initiatives coming from Quebec and a reflection of the reinforcement of a discourse of social justice overlaid with nation-building motives. Matters of equity were now also matters of national identity.

A similar blending of the themes of fairness, national identity, and a role for the state was provided by the English-Canadian nationalist movement. Only a state actively pursuing an economic strategy to promote Canadian culture and Canadian ownership and to sustain Canadian distinctiveness could fend off the threat to its cultural, economic, and political autonomy.

The discourse of social justice was accompanied by a boom in state support for intermediary organizations to assure representation of citizens to and in the state.[14] Reform of the electoral system and party financing was prompted by the goal of assuring equitable treatment of parties by the media and by the recognition that resources were not evenly distributed among social groups. The electoral regime established in 1974 thus recognized political parties for the first time, then proceeded to regulate their access to the media, limit their campaign expenditures so that the richest parties and candidates would not overwhelm the less well-endowed, and provide public funding for their campaigns. The logic of these actions was that equitable access and fair competition were integral to the well-being of democracy. Realization of the political rights of citizenship required both regulation and state support for these basic institutions that guaranteed access to citizens.

The citizenship regime promoted three different dimensions of equality: social, political, and gender.

In terms of social equality, the citizenship regime gave the federal government the lead in employment and social policy design, while it sought to induce provincial governments to follow its initiatives. The key programs of the 1940s were a national unemployment insurance system and family allowances, followed in the 1960s by the Canada Assistance Plan (CAP), Canada Pension Plan, Medicare, and so on. These programs were divided into two types. Some, such as health care, old age pensions, and family allowances, sought a certain socioeconomic equality, being available to all Canadians as a right of citizenship. They were designed to smooth over the unequal risks of poor health, old age, raising a family, or unemployment. Others, and here the CAP is the classic example, were designed to provide for the 'needy,' those who had fallen out of the structures supposed to maintain income security. Social assistance was for the lone parents who had 'fallen out' of the protection of marriage, or the long-term unemployed who had 'fallen out' of unemployment insurance. These were anti-poverty programs, designed to protect against being poor, but not to equalize conditions. Thus, the goal was social equity more than real equality.

The post-war citizenship regime had a second important equality dimension, one that touches directly on democracy. In particular, by the 1960s and 1970s there was a strong commitment by the federal government and several provinces to fostering more equitable access to political voice and representation for disadvantaged groups in the population. In concrete terms this meant, as well as a new electoral law, financial support for advocacy groups and others representing women, Aboriginal peoples, the poor, the disabled, and others claiming 'categorical equity.' The basic idea was that a well-functioning democracy required more than formal political equality; there was a public responsibility for making available the means to act, and to make claims.[15] As Bernard Ostry, a former assistant under secretary, said about the Citizenship Branch he directed, its goal was to 'develop and strengthen a sense of Canadian citizenship, chiefly through programs that would aid participation and assuage feelings of social injustice.'[16]

The third dimension of equality that we can identify in the post-war citizenship regime was that of gender equality. By the late 1960s the Canadian women's movement had taken form and was mounting claims for gender equality. The Fédération des femmes du Québec (FFQ) and numerous women's groups in the rest of the country lobbied for the creation of the Royal Commission on the Status of Women. This quasi-public body firmly installed a language of gender equality as well as equity in the universe of political discourse. Its recommendations, as well as the claims mounted by feminist groups subsequent to its 1970 Report, altered many laws, policies, and understandings of the relationships between women and men, moving them towards more egalitarian positions. Indeed, these groups were sufficiently strong to extract the equal rights and anti-discrimination guarantees embedded in the 1982 constitution and pay equity policies in several jurisdictions, as well as legislation on equal treatment for Aboriginal women and other civil rights victories.

To say that gender equality was a dimension of the citizenship regime does not imply that gender inequalities were eliminated, of course, any more than anti-poverty social policies eliminated the risk of being poor. Nonetheless, it did become legitimate – and meaningful in political discourse – to make claims in the name of equal rights for women, and thereby to expose the structures of discrimination and other impediments to achieving equality. In a similar way, it became legitimate and meaningful to support groups advocating for the less powerful, whether workers, the poor, women, Aboriginal peoples, the disabled, or whatever.

If we examine these principles more closely, we can conclude that the central figure of the citizenship regime, the 'citizen' who was imagined as the object of state action as well as the bearer of political and social rights, was clearly an adult. This citizen was a worker, a retired person, or a parent. This was not a citizenship regime focused primarily on the male breadwinner, as so many social democratic or Christian democratic regimes were.[17] Just as single mothers were important to the imaginary of social policy discussion, so too were working women, and especially working mothers. Above all else, however, the regime assumed that the risks to be confronted were those of adult life, whether they were from unemployment, sickness, old age, or child-raising.

In recent years the imagined 'model citizen' has altered in the face of a rising tide of neo-liberalism, with its preferences for privileging market relations, reducing the role of the state, and thrusting more responsibility onto communities. Thus far in Canada, the direction of movement in changing the citizenship regime has been from equality towards marketization. This has involved a replacement of equality as a principal value by 'choice' and 'responsibility' as well as fairness for the poorest. Not only has the growing support for neo-liberalism's definition of the relations among markets, states, and citizens been central to this transformation, but the analogy of the market has been superimposed directly on the concept and practice of citizenship. There has also been an important shift in the territorial dimensions of citizenship. The national state is no longer the relevant territory, with the shift and decentralization of power and decision making to the provinces. Thirdly, under the market analogy, the representation of identities and interests is seen to be a competitive market, and ideally a free market, whose appropriate players are individuals. A role for intermediary associations in narrowing the gap between formal rights of citizenship and actual access to them is assumed to be unnecessary and, indeed, undesirable.

The trajectory of this transition may very well mark a reduction of the space in which citizens can act together as social and political citizens. Nonetheless, in this ongoing reconfiguration of the citizenship regime positions still remain fluid, interestingly enough because the rights of democratic citizenship remain a powerful mobilizing concept within civil society. If the neo-liberal tide is finally being held at bay, although by no means turned back, it is because there have been adaptations in the ways that democracy and equality have come to be defined in the Canadian citizenship regime for the twenty-first century. Some gains have been made, but it remains important to interrogate the threats that remain or the new ones created as the post-war citizenship regime gives way in the face of new thinking and new initiatives.

The New Model Citizen in Citizenship Discourse

Thinking about equality and democracy has been effected by the struggles with neo-liberalism. One of the clear legacies of triumphant neo-liberalism is its major tenant that individuals must take responsibility for their own lives. They must assume responsibility for their life choices and also for representing themselves. There has been a sustained assault on the collective institutions which provide representation for the economically and socially weak and disadvantaged. There has even been an assault on advocacy groups speaking in the name of middle-class interests.[18] Unions have been tagged as 'special interests,' along with advocacy groups representing women and other categorical interests. Their right to make claims, as we have seen recently in the pay equity challenges, has been disputed.

At issue here is not only the question whether one can imagine equal political participation without collective organization, a lesson taught as long ago as the nineteenth century by political movements of the left as they struggled to gain representation for workers. Also threatened are the distributional outcomes referred to previously, such as the narrower gap in disposable income in Canada as compared to the United States. Recall that this difference was in large part attributed to the presence of unions in collective bargaining, and progressive coalitions.[19]

With neo-liberal ideology thinning out the political landscape and removing 'bulky objects' such as collective actors representing the force of numbers, we also see another change: the juvenilization of the 'model citizen.'

Increasingly, neo-liberalism's preference for equality of opportunity has come to influence policy makers and social reformers, even those speaking the language of social justice. The latter recognize, of course, that real equality of opportunity must be fostered and supported. Some form of redistribution is often necessary if the promise is to be more than formal. As a consequence, social policy in Canada has returned to a theme present in classic texts of 1940s social liberals such as Lord Beveridge and Richard Titmuss in Britain, or Leonard Marsh and others in Canada. This is the recognition that many jobs do not generate sufficient income for working fathers (and mothers) to feed their families. For example, wartime analysis of income and nutrition revealed that even in the midst of the booming wartime economy with full employment, only 44 per cent of families of wage earners (except in agriculture) had sufficient income to guarantee a nutritionally satisfactory diet. Therefore, the government proposed what was in 1940s terms a huge redistribution of income to parents. Family allowances supplementing income from wages would consume $200 million of the national income, then only $12 billion.[20]

This same problem of the working poor has re-emerged and become exceedingly pressing in recent years. The restructuring of employment is generating a polarization of the wage system. The 'hollowing out of the middle' means that it is becoming harder to earn a wage sufficient to raise a family.[21] Campaign 2000 found that in the 1990s, while the unemployment rate fell, the rate of child poverty rose, because it was often part-time jobs that were being created.[22] In 1998, the United Nations Human Development Index ranked Canada tenth out of seventeen developed countries for its level of income disparity.

Labour market restructuring has eliminated more and more full-time, well-paid, permanent jobs, while creating more and more part-time, low-paid, and temporary jobs. It has also generated more non-employment, both among youth and the long-term unemployed. Such labour market restructuring has elicited a similar response in many countries. They have sought to increase their participation rates, especially among women, whether single mothers or in two-earner couples. At the same time, however, because of the predominance of low-income jobs being created, governments faced a challenge to the mantra that promoting economic growth, and even job expansion, would solve the poverty problem.

This dilemma has produced movement on two fronts. The interface of labour force participation and social assistance has become a focus. In other words, we have seen the rise of the 'employability' discourse and policies. Canada has its own policies of workfare, representing the punitive side of this policy response. But at the same time, there has been the invention of what the Caledon Institute calls the first truly national social policy since Medicare and the Canada Pension Plan in the 1960s,[23] the National Child Benefit System (NCB), and in particular the federal government's portion, the Canada Child Tax Benefit (CCTB) and its supplements. It is the major success of post-1995 intergovernmental battles and negotiations that eventually also resulted in the social union agreement (SUFA) of 1999.[24]

The Child Tax benefit is available to any family with children, whether the parents are employed or not. It is income tested, and so can be claimed by families on social assistance as well as those whose income comes from non-custodial parents or employment insurance. The benefit is a classic negative income tax (NIT) measure, available to medium-income families in declining amounts until the ceiling is reached.[25]

My purpose here is not to go into the details of the Canada Child Tax Benefit. Nor is it to adjudicate between supporters of the benefit in progressive milieux (such as the Caledon Institute) and its progressive critics, found among advocates for welfare recipients angry about the decision of eight provinces to tax back any increase going to social assistance families, as part of their 'reinvestment plans.' Rather, I will take the Caledon Institute at its word – that this is a major structural change – and ask what implementation of the benefit teaches us about shifts in the citizenship regime and the definitions of equality inscribed within it.

The goal of the Canada Child Tax Benefit, as well as reforms proposed by the commission headed by Camil Bouchard in Quebec, is 'to get children off welfare.'[26] This catchy phrase means that children should be removed from the stigmatized welfare system into a more universal one. The Canada Child Tax Benefit is the flagship of the new era. It was prefigured, however, by several provinces which had already redesigned their income security programs around child benefits. Others did so at the same time that the NCB was being created.[27] It is interesting to note, moreover, that all these new programs are called 'children's benefits.' Only Quebec diverged from this discursive practice, calling its program a 'family allowance.' Thus, policies targeted to low-income adults are available to them because they have children, rather than directly because of their own income situation.

British Columbia and Quebec were early reformers. The B.C. Family Bonus (which in some ways served as the prototype for the CCTB) was put into place in 1996. The bonus is an income-source neutral payment to families with dependent children. In its 1997 major reform of family policy, Quebec also developed a new family allowance payment targeted to low-income families, so as to mesh with its general reform of social assistance and employability.[28] The family allowance replaced social assistance payments to families with children. To create the new benefit, the government combined three existing payments, including the generous baby bonuses that had been intended to promote a higher birth rate. The only separate allowance retained was for disabled children.

A number of other provinces reformed their social assistance and family benefits as the NCB came into being. For example, the Saskatchewan Child Benefit provides for children outside of the province's social assistance regime. As in Quebec, the provincial government saw the benefit as a substitute for the portion of social assistance paid to families on behalf of children. Three of the four Atlantic provinces also created 'children's benefits' as part of their reinvestment plans, or otherwise to complement the CCTB. These are the New Brunswick Child Tax Benefit, the Nova Scotia Child Benefit, and the Newfoundland and Labrador Child Benefit.

Most provinces diverged from the CCTB model, however, by maintaining working income supplements, paid only to parents with some earned income and thereby rewarding labour force participation. The longest running of these programs is Manitoba's Child Related Income Support Program (CRISP), created in 1981. Quebec has also had APPORT (Parental Wage Assistance) since 1988. More recently Ontario created its misleadingly named Child Care Supplement for Working Families (1998). This is an earned income supplement available to low- and middle-income families with children under seven. Because it covers families with one stay-at-home parent, it is less a 'child care supplement' than a working income supplement. Seven of ten provinces have such working income supplements, while three (Alberta, Ontario, Manitoba) provide only this form of benefit and no income-source neutral benefit

Why should these developments matter? The shift matters because it makes children the 'model citizens.' Equality defined as equality of opportunity really only makes sense when one is thinking of children. All of the notions we associate with equality of opportunity, such as investments in human capital, social investment, training, and so on are most relevant for the young. Survey the most popular and politically legitimate social spending in Canada as well as that associated with the children's agenda, and you find children at their centre. In addition, as Helen Penn[29] puts it while quoting Jerome Kagan, a focus on the child, especially the young child, fits well with neo-liberalism, indeed liberalism in general: '... so many people believe in infant determinism (because) it ignores the power of social class membership. Though a child's social class is the best predictor of future vocation, academic accomplishments and psychiatric health, Americans wish to believe that their society is open, egalitarian, without rigid class boundaries. To acknowledge the power of class is to question this ethical canon.'[30]

Policy thinking emerging in the last years focuses on schools, on population health, and the importance of the 'early years,' on childcare, child development and 'healthy starts,' on enforcing the financial responsibilities of 'deadbeat dads.' A veritable explosion of interest in the health and developmental needs of young children is sweeping Canada. Camil Bouchard's 1991 report, *Un Québec fou de ses enfants*, was the underpinning of the major 1997 restructuring of family policy.[31] In spring 1999 Margaret McCain and Fraser Mustard delivered to the government of Ontario their report entitled *The Early Years Study: Reversing the Real Brain Drain* recommending a major new investment in public spending and responsibility for early childhood, including childcare centres. As long-time advocate for childcare – and thus someone who has lived through the many disappointments of previous shelved initiatives – Martha Friendly wrote recently, 'Research and policy analysts in diverse fields – economics, health and medicine, education, and human rights – have come to support traditional advocates in feminist, social justice and trade union circles to insist that action on child care is imperative. There is broad recognition that a strategy for developing early childhood services that offer both early childhood education to strengthen healthy development for all children ... is in the public interest.'[32]

Even employment policy focuses on the youngest of the workers – unemployed youth. It seeks to manage their transition to labour force participation. The purpose in all this is to prepare the next generation to take its place as responsible adults. In addition, part of the 1996 reform of employment insurance also instituted a family income supplement for unemployed parents with an income under $25,291.[33] Their earning replacement rate would thus rise to 80 per cent whereas other low-income earners received only 60 per cent replacement.

The goal of these public interventions is to ensure that children are not made to suffer for the conditions which their parents' lives – their choices, their actions, and their life difficulties – impose on them. In other words, equality is redefined as equality of opportunity for future life chances.

My general point is, then, that the redesign of Canada's citizenship regime is doing more than cutting some social programs and redesigning others, more than reducing universality and increasing targeting. As we come out of the dark years of pure neo-liberalism and seek new ways to reknit social bonds, new values of social justice and equality are being constructed. The debates about the social union are where this is happening,[34] and these debates are constructed in large part around the figure of the child. He or she is the focus of collective as well as private responsibility.

What are the consequences of this juvenilization of the citizen meriting support from the collectivity? Here I will simply list a set of concerns, about the new silences that such child-focused definitions of equality might involve. Let me start by saying, however, that I share with many others the concern about the future of Canadian children and about reducing the appalling rates of poverty. My point is not to argue against the National Child Benefit, the National Children's Agenda, or strategies of intervention in the early years. Nor is it to dismiss the real difficulties of intergenerational sharing of work, which problems of youth unemployment express. My purpose is simply to point out that restricting the definition of equality to one of equality of opportunity, and then making children the primary focus, may reinforce or foster other forms of inequality in any new citizenship regime.

There are several areas of concern. The first is the issue of outcomes. Promoting equality of opportunity is perhaps the most limited definition of social justice. The language of substantive equality and of universal social and economic rights has been significantly reduced in Canadian public discourse. Much of this reduction has occurred by 'stealth.' The time has arrived for real public debate about the need to reknit the bonds of social cohesion via universal programs and equality more than equity.

In addition, most provinces as well as the federal government now focus their policy on achieving 'responsibility,' by moving parents into employment. The popular slogan is now that 'any job is a good job,' no matter how low paying.[35] In order to mitigate the financial difficulties of those adults charged with raising children, the new child benefits kick in. This vision provides little guarantee, however, that the gap between gross income and disposable income will continue to be narrowed.

The second issue is that of adults. Such a redesign of welfare and income redistribution does nothing to address the income security needs, assure equity, or promote equality for adults whose children are grown or who have no children. In particular, employment policies focused on the youngest cohorts render virtually invisible the needs of older workers, whether they are women returning to the workforce or male workers who have lost their employment in traditional industries. For example, welfare to work programs focus almost exclusively on families with children. Quebec's APPORT (parental work assistance program) provides an income supplement if any income at all (a monthly minimum of $100) is earned. The target of NB Works, a six-year experimental program mounted with the federal government, was overwhelming single parents. An adult without a dependent child has little support even for efforts to get into the labour force or recognition for doing so.

Childless adults have become virtually invisible in social policy as well as having very few forms of support available to them. The shunting of the disabled, adults as well as children, from social assistance regimes to their own programs, as well as the 'removal' of children from social assistance has meant that those adults who need income supports are at risk of simply being classified as 'undeserving' and without any claim on collective resources.

Third, there is the issue of gender equality. It is true that much of the focus on children has had the happy consequence of bringing the need for childcare to the fore. However, beyond the mantra that women or families must be able to reconcile work and family life, we are actually experiencing a decline in attention to matters of gender equality. Rights to unpaid parental leaves remain unchanged since the 1970s, except in Quebec. As for those with a right to paid leave, the transition from unemployment to employment insurance (EI) substantially reduced eligibility. Thus, the recent extension from six months to one year, while welcomed by those parents who are still eligible for EI paid leave, does nothing for the more than 50 per cent of new mothers who are not. Questions of gender power in the workplace, in politics, and even in everyday life are more and more difficult to raise, as adults are left to take responsibility for their own lives.

Finally, there is the matter of democracy. Children may be symbolically citizens in my analysis, but they are not full citizens in fact. They remain minors. They cannot, as real citizens must, employ the force of democratic politics to insist on social reform in the name of equality. A child-centred definition of equality is, then, also one which renders less visible the need for collective action by citizens mobilized to make claims and thereby to use the state against all forms of unequal power, particularly the power of market forces.

NOTES

1 On the history of Ottawa's social interventions as an anti-poverty policy see Ronald Haddow, *Poverty Reform in Canada, 1958–78: State and Class Influences on Policy-Making* (Montreal: McGill-Queen's University Press, 1993).

2 The first was obviously the position of most revolutionary leftists as well as some democratic socialists in the post-war years, the second can be associated with Nordic-style social democracy, while the third is a Marshallian position, most recently seen in Canada in debates about the 'social charter' during the Charlottetown constitutional debate.

3 John Myles and Paul Pierson, 'Friedman's Revenge: The Reform of "liberal" Welfare States in Canada and the United States,' *Politics and Society*, 25 (4) (December 1997), 443–72

4 While feminists and others have always understood the importance of the 'triangle' of state, market, and family to the distribution of welfare, mainstream theorists have taken longer to incorporate the third dimension. Recently, however, prominent theorists have begun to analyse welfare capitalism in terms of these three major structures and to ask questions about distribution and redistribution among all three. For example, see Gøsta Esping-Andersen, *Social Foundations of Postindustrial Economies* (Oxford: Oxford University Press, 1999).

5 This notion of equality of opportunity is part of the Policy Research Group on Social Cohesion's definition of social cohesion. See Jane Jenson, *Mapping Social Cohesion: The State of the Literature in Canada* (Ottawa: CPRN F-03, 1998).

6 For a recent discussion of these liberal welfare states, including Australia, see Julia S. O'Connor, Ann S. Orloff, and Sheila Shaver, *States, Markets and Families: Gender, Liberalism and Social Policy in Australia, Canada, Great Britain and the United States* (Cambridge: Cambridge University Press 1999).

7 Ibid., 43.

8 Keith Banting, 'The Social Policy Divide: The Welfare State in Canada and the United States,' in Keith Banting, George Hoberg, and Richard Simeon,

eds., *Degrees of Freedom: Canada and the United States in a Changing World* (Montreal: McGill-Queen's University Press, 1997), 267–309.

9 Rebecca Blank and Maria Hanratty, 'Responding to Need: A Comparison of Social Safety Nets in Canada and the United States,' in David Card and Richard Freeman, eds., *Small Differences That Matter: Labor Markets and Income Maintenance in Canada and the United States* (Chicago: University of Chicago Press, 1993).

10 This is the general point made by Myles and Pierson, 'Friedman's Revenge.'

11 These data are from Frank Vandenbroucke, *Globalisation, Inequality and Democracy* (London: IPPR March 1998).

12 Haddow, *Poverty Reform*, analyses the development of enthusiasm for the guaranteed-income approach to policy, beginning in the 1960s with old age pensions, describing the actors involved. Parties and unions were not the main activists. Advocacy groups and bureaucrats played a more important role, although at certain points unions did reluctantly accept the GI approach.

13 For a presentation of the concept of citizenship regime see Jane Jenson and Susan Phillips, 'Regime Shift: New Citizenship Practices in Canada,' *International Journal of Canadian Studies* 14 (Fall 1996).

14 For the details of these actions see Leslie Pal, *Interests of State* (Montreal: McGill-Queen's University Press, 1993) and Jenson and Phillips, 'Regime Shift.'

15 This commitment went far beyond social policy. Electoral law, for example, was instituted in the 1970s to improve equitable access to candidacy and to the electronic media.

16 Pal, *Interests of State*, 109.

17 O'Connor et al., 26ff.

18 The discussion of this assault is described in detail in Jenson and Phillips, 'Regime Shift.'

19 Myles and Pierson, 'Friedman's Revenge,' attribute the greater poverty-fighting power of Canada's tax-delivered social programs to a sort of 'silent coalition' of support for the benefits accruing to low-income Canadians from a neo-liberal anti-universalist ideology. Low-income families tended to see their benefits rise (or at least be protected) when they were 'clawed back' from high-income earners.

20 Dennis Guest, *The Emergence of Social Security in Canada* (Vancouver: UBC Press, 1980), 129–30.

21 John Myles, 'Post-Industrialism and the Service Economy,' in Daniel

Drache and Meric S. Gertler, eds., *The New Era of Global Competition: State Policy and Market Power* (Montreal: McGill-Queen's University Press, 1991), 356.

22 Campaign 2000, *The 1998 Federal Report Card*, on www.campaign2000.org. This shift was hinted at in Garnett Picot and John Myles, 'Social Transfers, Changing Family Structure and Low Income among Children,' *Canadian Public Policy* 22 (1996).

23 See Ken Battle, 'The National Child Benefit: Another Hiccup or Fundamental Structural Reform?,' presented to the Conference on the State of Living Standards, CSLS, 30–31 Oct. 1998. Available at www.caledoninst.org.

24 See Gérard Boismenu and Jane Jenson, 'A Social Union or a Federal State?: Intergovernmental Relations in the New Liberal Era,' in Leslie Pal, ed., *How Ottawa Spends 1998–99: Balancing Act: The Post-Deficit Mandate* (Ottawa: Carleton University Press, 1998), 57–80.

25 It is, therefore, substantially different from the strategy of the U.S. government, which has systematically widened the distinction between 'deserving' and 'undeserving' by investing more and more in the earned income tax credit while eliminating 'welfare as we know it.' The working income supplement (WIS) which mimicked the U.S. earned income tax credit, was eliminated (or rolled into) the CCTB along with the Child Tax Benefit, created in 1993.

26 For a presentation of this report, by one of its authors, as well as of the controversy surrounding it, see Alain Noël, 'La contrepartie dans l'aide sociale au Québec,' *Revue française des Affaires sociales* 50 (4) (oct.–déc. 1996), 99–122.

27 For the details of these programs see Jane Jenson with Sherry Thompson, *Comparative Family Policy: Six Provincial Stories* (Ottawa: CPRN F-08, 1999).

28 Jane Jenson, 'Les réformes des services de garde pour jeunes enfants en France et au Québec vues de l'institutionnalisme historique,' *Politique et Sociétés* 17 (1–2) (1998), 139–51.

29 Helen Penn, 'Getting Good Childcare for Families: What Canada Can Learn from Other Countries?' a paper prepared for 'Good Child Care in Canada in the 21st Century: Preparing the Policy Map,' Toronto, May 1999.

30 Jerome Kagan, *Three Seductive Ideas* (Cambridge; Mass.: Harvard University Press, 1998), 147.

31 Ministère de la Santé et des Services sociaux, *Un Québec fou de ses enfants: Rapport du Groupe de travail pour les jeunes* (Québec: Ministère de la Santé et des Services sociaux, 1991). Known as the Bouchard Report.

32 Martha Friendly, 'Child Care and Canadian federalism in the 1990s: Canary in a Coal Mine,' working version of a paper prepared for 'Good Child Care in Canada in the 21st Century: Preparing the Policy Map,' Toronto, May 1999.

33 It also lowered the family income threshold for full access to benefits from $63,570 to $48,750 and the replacement level to 55 per cent from 57 per cent.

34 The details of this debate, including the implications for federalism, are discussed in Boismenu and Jenson, 'A Social Union or a Federal State?'

35 Both the Alberta government of Ralph Klein and New Brunswick's Department of Human Resource Development (HRD-NB) make this slogan their own.

8

How Growing Income Inequality Affects Us All

ARMINE YALNIZYAN

The federal government's 1989 declaration to eliminate child poverty by the year 2000 passed its tenth anniversary with 50 per cent more of Canada's children living in poverty. Around the same time, late in 1999, the federal finance minister announced with conviction that the next budget would finally deal with the discomforting issue of 'child' poverty, which is really the poverty of families, including adults.

After ten years of intense lobbying of a parliament that had unanimously proclaimed child poverty a national disgrace, this is what we got: a promise that something would appear in the budget of 2000 to begin to address the issue.

As it turned out, that budget could not be described as one that would significantly effect the level of general poverty let alone eliminate child poverty. Concerns about poverty were sidetracked by a proliferation of opinion columns, politicians, and business leaders who touted tax cuts as the key intervention by government for improving the standard of living of all Canadians.

Even in a period of economic growth, the fact remains that, as a society, we have not reduced poverty. The repeated chanting that all the economic fundamentals are right – fundamentals like inflation rates, interest rates, growth of the economy – rings hollow in the face of evidence that the real human fundamentals, like adequate food and shelter, are increasingly tenuous for a growing number in our midst. As poverty has grown, many of those who could do something about it simply averted their eyes.

Some of the people with the power to influence action in Canada have ignored the issue of poverty because they dismiss the measure of poverty that is used. They insist poverty should be redefined, that what is lacking is a proper measure of the scale of genuine despair.

It might come as something of a shock to them that, while the size of the economic pie doubled in size over the last generation, the bar for measuring poverty dropped. Choose a measure, any measure, and hold it constant over time: the number of people who are poor has grown, and the depth of their poverty has increased. Not only do they have less income, that income buys them less. Housing costs much more today than it did five years ago and the costs of other basics, such as public transportation and prescriptions, have also gone up.

More families are struggling with cutbacks in health and education by doing more fundraising and spending more time caring for people at home and in institutions, whether nursing homes, hospitals, or schools. And the things that add to the lives of families with children – libraries, skating rinks, drop-in centres, and swimming pools – have been subject to more cutbacks or increases in fees.

Poverty is often seen as something that does not really affect the vast majority of Canadians and can thus be largely ignored. But a trend that does affect us all has been overshadowed by the poverty debate: growing inequality.

Trends in growing inequality arise foremost from changes in how people make a living. However, most people do not live by themselves: 85 per cent of Canadians live in some kind of a family formation. Daily reality for most people is about making choices, balancing household needs – including the needs of those who do not work – with household resources.

At any point in history, the households that raise dependent children are the sites where the next generation of citizens – both leaders and followers – learn more than how to balance the ever-scarce resources of time and money. This is where they are taught what and whom to value. These are the building blocks of future society, the liquid from which the river of life is made. So it is of more than passing interest to know how the economic circumstances of families raising children have changed over the last generation.

Can You Hear Me Now? The Growing Gap in Incomes

Picture this. Two people stand together in a room. One represents an average family from the richest 10 per cent of families raising dependent children. One represents the poorest 10 per cent.

In 1973, the richest families in Canada earned twenty-two times as much as the poorest. Average income from the market for the top 10 per cent was just over $108,000. The average market income of the poorest 10 per cent was just over $5,000.[1]

Let us imagine this as a physical – not just economic – distance. This puts them about twenty-two steps away from each other. Not close, but it is still possible for both parties to overhear the problems the other is coping with, to be well aware of each other's existence.

By 1984, as the recovery from the 1981–2 recession begins, they stand sixty-five steps apart. The average rich family is now pulling in about $125,000 a year, while the average poor family is earning just under $2,000 over the course of the year. You would have to raise your voice to be heard – very unCanadian.

The next peak of the market was in 1989. In that year more Canadians were working, and they were putting in longer hours than at any other point in post-war history. Despite boom times, however, representatives from our two families are standing thirty-nine steps apart. This is almost twice the social and economic distance of sixteen years earlier. The average earned income of the richest families has risen to about $145,000 while that of the poorest families is now $3,700.

By 1997 – at the top of the next business cycle and very much like business conditions during 1973 – these two families are standing 109 steps apart. This is almost five times the distance of a generation ago, and further apart than during the worst recession in the post-war period. The two neighbours are not in the same room anymore. In fact, they almost certainly are not even in the same building. The average rich family is now earning $137,000. The average poor family earnings are down to $1,255.

This distance has grown during a period of economic growth, not decline. It is unlikely that they can hear each other. Not only do these two families not talk to one another, they virtually do not exist for one another in any meaningful day-to-day sense.

It is no coincidence that government approaches to poverty have hardened during a period in which poverty has become worse and the economy bubbles along. As the gap grows larger, people who find themselves with little or no market income are actually falling further and further out of the line of sight of the people who make the decisions. They are invisible, irrelevant to the choices that must be made to get the 'economic fundamentals' right.

What is wrenching about inequality in Canada, as everywhere around the world, is less what is happening at the top than what is happening at the bottom of the distribution. And the major trend at the bottom is that it has become increasingly difficult to gain access to a sustaining amount of paid work. In 1973 only about one-third of the poorest 10 per cent of families had no earned income over the course of the entire year. By 1997, almost two-thirds (63 per cent) of these families had no source of earned income throughout the year. Among families that had paid work, the number of weeks of work during the year had also fallen to twenty-seven weeks in 1997, compared to forty-three weeks in 1973.[2]

In today's world, if you are not working you do not count. And the majority of those at the bottom are not working. When a group of people becomes invisible to the decision makers, is it because they can be politically ignored? Or is it because the decision makers have simply forgotten they are leaving something important out of the calculus of what matters?

Who Belongs in the Middle Class?

Adjusted for inflation, the Canadian economy is twice as big as it was a generation ago. The value of our output now weighs in at more than $880 billion. With a bigger economic pie to share, are there now more families in the modest 'middle class,' as it was defined a generation ago? With an economy so much more productive and efficient, are there fewer poor families? The answer to both questions is no.

There are fewer families in the middle of the income spectrum. In 1973, 60 per cent of families raising children earned roughly between $24,500 and $65,000. By 1996 the proportion earning that amount had dropped to 44 per cent. (Remember these are not the same families. They are a new generation of adults and children, muddling their way through parenting as best as they can, given economic and social circumstances.)

And there are more poor families: in 1973 only 10 per cent of Canadian families earned less than $14,000 a year; by 1996, almost 17 per cent of all Canadian families raising dependent children fell below that threshold. For the poor, it is not about failing to keep up with the Joneses. More of our fellow and sister citizens, in both absolute and relative terms, find themselves without enough income to provide adequate shelter or enough to eat. These numbers have risen most dramatically among the young.

At the same time, there are also many more 'rich' families compared to a generation ago. In 1973 only 10 per cent of Canadian families with children earned more than $80,000 a year. By 1996, about 18 per cent did.

Perhaps, over time, it has become easier for people to dismiss the phenomenon of a growing number of people at the bottom of the income spectrum since there is also a growing number of people at the top. A kind of confused lottery mentality seems to have taken hold of a growing number: if it is true that there are more people getting 'rich,' then I am determined to become one of the lucky ones, so get out of my way. If you are not getting ahead, it is probably your fault.

The Nasty Nineties

What is alarming is how much of this change in opportunity and attitude has happened over the course of the 1990s. During the previous decades, in the wake of the worst post-war recession the country had seen, Canadians were cursed with double digit unemployment and double digit inflation. Free trade, privatization of government services, and deregulation of the private sector were promised as the best way to spur economic growth. And economic growth for the 1990s was supposed to mean prosperity for all. Indisputably, the level of prosperity did rise, as measured strictly by dollars and cents. Over the course of the decade, total Canadian assets grew by about $1.5 trillion.[3]

But this form of prosperity did not mean improved pay cheques for the vast majority. In fact, average incomes were lower in 1997 than in 1989.[4] Income inequality grew over the nineties just as it did over the course of the previous period. However, for most of the period since 1973, the hallmark of inequality was not just that the poor got poorer and the rich got richer; there were also both more poor families and more rich ones. The developments of the 1990s, however, took us in one direction only. Instead of pulling us in two opposite directions – towards greater affluence or towards greater poverty – the vast majority of families raising children saw their incomes slide downwards, towards the bottom of the income ladder.

Canada's growing gap has become a slippery slope. A growing number of middle-income families lost economic ground, sliding towards the lower income categories. Whereas over the course of a generation the proportion of families at the top of the income spectrum grew, during the 1990s that proportion actually shrank. Income inequality grew, just as before, but this time because incomes at the bottom fell more rapidly than those at the top.

It may come as a surprise that there were fewer, not more, families at the top of the income heap. It helps to remember that these statistics are about people's ability to earn a living from the fruits of their labour (market incomes) and the results of actions that governments take to redistribute that income through transfers and taxation (after-tax incomes). They do not include the growth or decline in value that is not attributed to paid work – assets like pension funds, RRSPs, bonds, equities, and real estate.[5]

Between 1989 and 1997, the slide to the bottom could be measured in two ways: the dramatic surge at the bottom of the income spectrum (with the consequent erosion of the middle), and the deterioration of incomes among the very poorest families.

A Rapid Slide to the Bottom End of the Income Ladder Was the Dominant Trend of the Nineties

In 1989, 30 per cent of families earned less than $35,388. By 1997, 35.4 per cent of families fell into this category, an 18 per cent increase in the proportion of the population who found themselves at the bottom of the income ladder. It bears mentioning that both 1989 and1997 were also at the top of their respective business cycles.

In terms of after-tax incomes,[6] 30 per cent of families were living on less than $35,038 in 1989. By 1997, the proportion of families living under that threshold had grown by 23 per cent, accounting for 37 per cent of all families raising children.

There Are More Poor Families among Us ...

In 1989, the poorest 10 per cent of families earned no more than $11,567. By 1997, the proportion of families with market incomes less than $11,567 had grown to 13.7 per cent. In after-tax income terms, the poorest 10 per cent of families were living on less than $19,320 in 1989. By 1997, 13 per cent of Canadian families raising children had less than $19,320. Not only are there more families in the lowest income category but they have also become poorer over time: the threshold for belonging to the poorest 10 per cent of the population meant earning less than $11,567 in 1989. By 1997, 10 per cent of the population did not earn more than $6,591. The threshold defining poverty had dropped.

And the Poor are Significantly Poorer ...

Average market income for the poorest 10 per cent of families was $3,741 in 1989, falling to $1,255 in 1997. Again, these are both strong performance years, at the top of their respective business cycles. In after-tax terms, average incomes for the poorest 10 per cent of families fell from $15,396 in 1989 to $13,806 by 1997.

But There Are Not More Rich ...

In terms of market incomes, the trigger income for crossing the threshold into the 'top ten' category was $100,500 in 1989. By 1997, 10 per cent of families raising children still made this much or more. But by then, the average income of the richest 10 per cent of families had fallen, from $144,699 in 1989 to $136,394.

In after-tax terms, the circle of affluence actually grew smaller. In 1989, the richest 10 per cent of families lived on $79,557 or more. By 1997, only 9 per cent of families fell into this circle of affluence. Average after-tax incomes of this group fell from $106,963 in 1989 to $98,746 in 1997.

The greatest erosion was among the families that used to be in the upper end of the distribution, but not the very top. In 1989, 20 per cent of Canadian households raising children had after-tax incomes ranging between $57,000 and $79,557. By 1997, only 17.6 per cent of households found themselves in this category of income.

By any measure, the vast majority of Canadian families raising children saw their incomes fall in the 1990s, despite a booming economy and despite a trend that shows these families were putting in longer hours in the labour market. Inequality remained pervasive.

What's Growth Got to Do With It?

The downward slide is creating a growing divide between the haves and have-nots – a divide made more intractable as the odds of crossing over to greater affluence or even getting to the middle becomes a longer shot. At the same time, public services are being cut back for everyone, rich and poor.

The rising tide of prosperity of the mid- to late 1990s did not raise the general standard of living, as defined by incomes (though some individuals have benefited from the growth and increased concentration of assets). Nor did it raise the collective standard of living by enhancing public provisions available to all.

For most of the post-war period, a growing economy was expected to increase both private and public forms of wealth – such as better health and education facilities; more recreation centres, libraries, and parks; and improved efficiencies in transportation and other urban and rural infrastructure. Economic growth in the 1990s, however, has been accompanied by a falling standard of living, at both the private and public levels.

Indeed, the path to greater economic growth in the 1990s has been predicated on a model of stripping expectations at both the private and public level. At a recent 'think-tank' session on productivity, a young man reported on the latest 'buzz' in management circles: 'denominator management.' Denominator management? If you want to boost your productivity in sourcing, production, marketing, sales, he explained, you have to bring down the costs of the denominator. The denominator in every case turned out to be people. Shaving those costs could mean having fewer people doing these functions, or paying them less. Put quite simply, that is the current preferred method to attract and keep the attention of investors.

The dominant theme of the 1990s has been downsizing, whether within the private or the public sector. One of the more striking examples occurred in October 1998, when Canadian National Railways announced a further lay-off of 3,000 workers, having thereby reduced their workforce by 50 per cent (from 36,000 to 18,000 people) in just over four years. Share values soared. The financial press tripped over itself with accolades and the front cover of the *Financial Post Magazine* proclaimed Paul Tellier, the head of CN, as 'CEO of the Year.'

Shortly after this round of lay-offs, a business report exposed the uncaring side of the new growth mentality. The reporter asked a stock market analyst if CN had cut too many people in its 'drive for efficiency.' The chilling answer offered by Terrence Fisher of HSBC Securities (Canada) was that it did not matter if Tellier had made a mistake or not: 'I would have expected the cuts [of 3,000 workers] over three or four years, not over one year. But those people aren't going anywhere. They can always call these guys back if traffic goes up.'

These cuts were not ultimately about becoming more competitive in order to grow. In 1992 CN trains hauled goods over 19,5000 miles of track; now it has only 14,100 miles.[7] In today's world, growth is not primarily about doing more of something. It's about doing it cheaper so that shareholders get ever-increasing value for money.

We can now see why that the relationship between growth and prosperity is gradually shifting. Growth within a corporation used to be the way in which increased prosperity found its way into the homes of more and more of its workers, not just those of its shareholders and top executives. Today 'growth' of a company can just as easily mean that workers have been declared surplus to the operation or – if lucky enough to keep their jobs – will have to work harder for the same dollar.

While there was overall job growth at the end of the 1990s, this growth was not matched with wage increases. The trend was crisply depicted in the opening paragraphs of a front-page story early in 1999: 'Financial markets were dizzy with relief yesterday, racking up huge gains on several fronts after the release of a jobs report showing the U.S. economy is in no danger of overheating. The report, which showed a surprise mix of strong jobs growth with a drop in wage gains in February, sent bond prices soaring and lifted the Dow Jones industrial average to a record high.'[8]

That story consistently repeated itself in the United States and Canada during the remainder of 1999. While job growth was robust, wages languished. The Dow Jones continued to break records.

This situation defies what is taught in Economics 101, where tight labour markets are supposed to lead to rising wages. The only inflationary trends had been among executive compensation packages, which routinely yielded double-digit rates – as compared to average workers' pay packages, which finally increased above the rate of inflation in 1998, although worker productivity had also surged.[9] As in the United States, market signals in Canada were dancing to the same tune: growth was seen to be good, as long as workers' pay cheques were held in check.

What can account for this? While it is good that unemployment rates have dropped to those of a decade ago, the employment rate remains below that of 1989 and the degree of job insecurity remains very high. The proportion of jobs that is contractual, casual, seasonal, or based on self-employment is at an all-time high. A worker may be fully employed today, but her job prospects in a month or six months may be completely uncertain. In this context, individual or collective bargaining pressure to improve wages or benefits has remained slight.

A New Role for the Government

For more than a decade, Canadians were promised that less government and greater reliance on market forces would unleash unparalleled economic expansion in which all would benefit – a rising tide raises all boats. But as we have seen the results worked only for those with speed boats. Poor families became more numerous and poorer, the middle class made no progress, and the gap between the rich and poor increased even further. This is not supposed to happen in a democracy.

In his powerful analysis in The Great Transformation, the economist Karl Polanyi asserts the primacy of society, arguing that an economy is imbedded in society. Society is the given. The economy is the consequence. Canadian governments in the post-war period had assumed a responsibility for nation-building, for fostering greater equality within and between regions. We have recently witnessed the inversion of this thinking. The economy is accepted as the given, and individuals and society are expected to struggle to adapt to its exigencies. Not only is this seen as a more realistic lens through which to judge development; it is even portrayed as a more neutral and, hence, a morally superior arbiter of human enterprise.

The evidence from the 1990s demonstrates an important truth: from the point of view of equality, we overvalued markets and undervalued the importance good government policies can have. During the recessionary period of 1989 to 1993, the gap between rich and poor grew in market terms, but government actions helped close the after-tax gap despite tough economic times. The opposite trend occurred during the recovery period of 1994 to 1997.[10] Average market incomes improved for all income groups, including the poorest, closing the market gap, but in after-tax terms the gap grew at the most rapid rate since the 1970s, when we first started tracking trends in income inequality. Let us look at each phase separately.

During the period of economic recession, from 1989 to 1993, the gap in market incomes between rich and poor grew rapidly. This was an era of permanent, not temporary, lay-off of workers. Record numbers of public and private sector enterprises were cutting back, spinning off, or merging their activities with others. Others were relocating in the United States or simply folding in the face of heightened competition.

Yet between 1989 and 1993, the after-tax income gap between rich and poor actually decreased in Canada. The three largest provinces – Ontario, British Columbia, and Quebec – introduced improvements to their welfare rates and/or minimum wages during this period. The income floor was raised in all three provinces just before the recession took its toll on incomes throughout the spectrum, including those at the upper end. The 'war on the deficit,' unilateral changes in federal financing of social programs, and the devolution of responsibilities also generated the conditions for the introduction of temporary federal and provincial income surtaxes on upper- and middle-income earners. These changes combined to tilt the national experience in the direction of closing the income gap, placing Canada among a handful of nations around the world that were cited as examples where the inexorable processes of globalization did not automatically lead to a deteriorating distribution of incomes.[11]

In terms of market incomes, the gap shot up and down on a wild, volatile ride between 1994 and 1997, demonstrating the unpredictability of finding steady work for those at the bottom, even while the economy was growing. The largest source of new employment in this period was self-employment, accounting for 77 per cent of all new jobs in 1996 and 84 per cent of all new jobs in 1997. Still, in comparison to the recession, average earned incomes improved for all income groups, including the poorest, and disparities in market incomes shrank.

However, the gap between rich and poor in after-tax incomes grew more rapidly between 1993 and 1997 than at any time since the early 1970s. The mid-1990s was a period of government cutbacks, especially for transfer programs like Unemployment Insurance, social assistance, and workers' compensation. Unemployment insurance benefits covered 74 per cent of the unemployed in 1989, but only 36 per cent by 1997, turning the fund into a deep pocket for financing deficit reduction at the federal level. No provinces improved social assistance after 1993, and eight provinces actually cut welfare benefits or eligibility for social assistance since the mid- 1990s. Some jurisdictions, notably Alberta and Ontario, also introduced tax cuts in this period.

The net effects of these changes benefitted the richest 10 per cent of families and no one else. The richest 10 per cent was the only group of families with a lower effective rate of income tax in 1997 than in 1993, and thus posted healthy increases in their average after-tax incomes, rising from $131,412 to $136,394.

Meanwhile, the poorest 10 per cent of families paid more taxes and received fewer income supports. Their net loss of 11 per cent in average after-tax incomes was by far the biggest loss of any income group in this period. Though their earned income improved (from an average of $511 a year to $1,255 a year),[12] after the inclusion of government supports and taxation, average after-tax incomes of the poorest 10 per cent of Canadian families raising children fell from $15,581 to $13,806.

Overall, the impact on equality of what governments did, or chose not to do, far outweighed the impact of the market, both in times of recession and in times of recovery. Sadly, the story of the 1990s was that while governments were helpful to Canada's poorest citizens during the most difficult economic times, when they could actually afford to do more they produced anti-egalitarian policies. This general trend has important exceptions, however.

Provincial Results Vary

The growing gap was not a one-size-fits-all proposition. Ontario, the richest province, fostered an exploding gap in incomes when prosperity overall was growing. Newfoundland, the poorest province, made exceptional efforts to reduce the results of market-driven disparities.

Another group of provinces–both rich and poor – have a recent track record of keeping the gap between rich and poor small despite recession or recovery. Manitoba, Saskatchewan, and Quebec are notable cases.

There were significant differences in rates of economic growth and decline across the country, but as the evidence below shows, in the final analysis, the state of inequality was more likely to correspond to choices of the governments in power than economic circumstance.

For those wedded to the prevailing neo-liberal ideology this can be upsetting, because for them economic growth is both the necessary and sufficient prerequisite for reducing income inequality. Such economic thinking makes the following links: economic growth gets more people working, higher employment rates lead to higher earned incomes, more total income leads to a better distribution of income. This ideology adds another link in the chain: tax cuts generate economic growth and get the whole system functioning as it should, creating prosperity for everyone.

The data presented in Table 8.1 reveals the limitations of economic growth per se in reducing inequality.

The provincial data prove that economic growth does not necessarily lead to reduced inequality. Ontario and Alberta, the two strongest performing economies in Canada, have alarming levels of inequality. Nor do sluggish or even declining economies inevitably result in growing income inequality. Newfoundland, Quebec, and Manitoba are testament to this reality. There is simply no rule that explains the relationship between market performance and the distribution of incomes.

TABLE 8.1
Making the links: changes from 1994 to 1997, by province

Province	GDP growth (%)	Employment rate (%)	Total market income (%)	Market income gap* (%)	After-tax income gap* (%)
British Columbia	+4.2	−0.2	+3.9	−15.9	+11.1
Alberta	+10.9	+0.8	+11.2	−10.7	+3.6
Saskatchewan	+11.7	+1.2	+2.2	−31.7	−3.8
Manitoba	+9.5	+0.2	+6.7	−9.7	+1.0
Ontario	+8.7	+0.3	+7.7	−71.7	+23.7
Quebec	+4.5	+3.3	+1.7	+33.9	+9.5
New Brunswick	+4.4	+1.8	−4.4	−47.0	+4.3
Nova Scotia	+3.3	+2.9	−7.7	+53.3	−5.6
Newfoundland	−0.2	−1.8	−14.8	+1315.2	−17.3

Source: *Canada's Great Divide*, Centre for Social Justice, p. 39. Calculations based on Statistics Canada data.
*Change in the relationship between the richest and poorest deciles (10 per cent of the population of families raising children).
A negative sign in front of the number means that the gap between rich and poor shrank.
A positive sign means that the gap grew.

Nor do the individual theoretical links in the chain of the theory hold up to empirical analysis. Table 8.1 shows that

- Provinces with the highest rate of economic growth were not the provinces with the fastest increase in employment rates (the proportion of the population who had a job);
- Provinces with the biggest increase in employment rates did not have the biggest increase in total earnings;
- Provinces with increases in total market incomes did not always see reductions in income inequality;
- Provinces with decreases in market income inequalities, even strong decreases, did not always end up with less after-tax income inequality;
- Provinces that introduced tax cuts were not necessarily the provinces that grew the fastest.

While the role of the market in ensuring a greater degree of prosperity for everyone has clearly been overestimated, the role of government, on the other hand, both positively and negatively, has been vastly underestimated.

Prosperous economic times in the 1990s failed to produce consistently better earnings opportunities. Record profits coincided with using less or cheaper labour. More austerity at the bottom of the organization drove the profit machine, which paid for bigger bonuses for executives and higher stock values for shareholders. The market reality is that economic growth on its own leads neither to more equality nor to more stability. Government action made the critical difference.

The 1990s presented Canada's various levels of government with a crucial political choice: (1) Continue the tradition of providing more equality and social stability – a job complicated by increasingly volatile market forces; or (2) Bow to new pressures to back off from a democratic government's role as the 'great equalizer.'

Throughout the decade, and especially after 1994, the federal government increasingly opted for political choice number two. It adopted a 'less is more' approach to social supports and took the lead in changing the role other levels of government play in Canadians' lives.

The federal government cut back on transfer payments to individuals and the provinces, and it also privatized or downloaded many of its traditional responsibilities. This put pressure on provincial and municipal governments to make new political choices of their own.

Governments clearly did an about-face in the social priorities over the course of the 1990s. From a long-standing role of stabilizing or improving the distribution of incomes among families raising children, governments have systematically withdrawn vital income and other supports, perhaps most importantly social housing.

The current vogue for tax cuts is just one aspect of changing political choices. Shrinking disposable incomes and growing income inequality are two others. All three are inextricably linked.

Tax cuts have been cast as the latest 'solution' to increase economic prosperity. But they fail to address the problem on two fronts: they do nothing for the poorest families who have no income to register a tax cut and they erode the funding needed for the public services and supports people rely on in their communities. In 1996, 32 per cent of tax filers had no taxable incomes. They had no taxes to cut. Twenty-three per cent of all tax filers had incomes of less than $10,000.[13]

Tax cuts are not the solution because high taxes are not the problem: good jobs and reliable public goods are the key variables for the vast majority who want to improve their standard of living.

As we have seen, despite tax cuts and economic growth, the gap between rich and poor grew between 1994 and 1997. In fact, it could be argued that both the current recipes for tax cuts and economic growth lead to, rather than mitigate, income inequality. The proliferation of tax cuts as the latest solution to increase economic prosperity raises the following question: what are the elements of a public policy that will help narrow the gap? The solution lies in four things: even distribution of job growth; better wages; services to help families meet their basic needs; and supports for the poorest families. This is how to ensure everyone is better off – not just a privileged few.

Defining Ourselves

'I'd always assumed I was the central character in my own story, but now it occurred to me I might in fact be only a minor character in someone else's.'

Russell Hoban from *Turtle Diary*

It is a truism that how a community treats its most vulnerable members speaks volumes about that society. For thousands of years, spiritual leaders of all religious beliefs have urged us to remember 'There, but for the grace of God, go I' and to create a society that recognizes the essential humanity in each of us. This way of thinking is not much of a stretch for those who lived through the Depression and war years, when relying on community made all the difference in the world. But after years of 'rugged individualism' notions of equal citizenship and compassion are losing ground to the notion of deservedness: 'I am where I am because I worked hard. I was smart. I earned my place in the world. Others are where they are because of choices they have made.'

Luck and chance have no place in this philosophy, nor do larger social and economic forces. Only personal virtue counts in today's lottery of life.

We are madly dashing to ensure that we do not fall out of the circle of affluence, or that we inch closer to it. Do the recipes for success – tax cuts, productivity enhancements, economic growth at all costs – make those around us increasingly peripheral to our lives? If other people and communities can be considered 'surplus,' expendable to the concerns of the bottom line, then so too could we.

The daily diet of crises we are fed includes fears of what a spike in interest rates will do to the economy, fears of a potential stock market 'correction' fears that high taxes are threatening future growth. Meanwhile, alongside sizzling growth rates in the economy, a growing number of households are dealing with far more immediate crises: whether they will have a home at the end of the month, whether they can feed their family and themselves every day of the week.

These crises are not seen or acknowledged by the decision makers who live outside these households, outside these neighbourhoods. The fact is that most people do not believe they will ever have to confront these issues. Denial and avoidance shrink the circle of what gets defined as important.

What happens when those who have been pushed outside the circle press to get our attention again? Right here, in our polite quintessentially middle-class Canadian communities, pepper spray has been used to dispel the protesting homeless, laws have been passed to make it illegal for beggars to talk to us on the street.

This is the story of growing inequality: it implicates us all. In the pursuit of prosperity, the importance of simply earning a living is being lost. In the process of getting the 'economic fundamentals' right, many fundamental human rights have been brushed aside. The definition of progress is increasingly about personal material gain, rather than the full development of individual capacities and the social context required to make this result possible for everyone.

We are encouraged to think that we grow our way to a better world, that we can better share the wealth by creating more wealth, that being a millionaire is the ultimate form of human satisfaction. Can a nation build its future by creating more millionaires? Is all that is missing is more 'more'?

Of course it is easier to reduce inequalities if the whole system is growing. But we *have* been growing and income inequalities are worse. For society to enjoy the fruits of a better distribution of income – as recent history has clearly shown – we must actively seek that specific result. Unfortunately, today's definition of 'better' looks more like 'more rich' than 'more just.'

With such a mindset, for everybody to taste a better life, the 'required' rate of growth is unaffordable and unsustainable, both for economic and ecological reasons. Imbedded in what is 'required' for the system to function for the majority of people today is an ever-accelerating rate of busyness – ever more production and ever more consumption.

Even if we were to achieve this frenzied 'optimal' state for a brief time, the promise of a better life for most may not be kept. In an era when a nation's gross domestic product can increase due to the use of labour-replacing technological change, corporate mergers, or environmental disasters, economic growth will not automatically mean everybody is better off, even in strictly economic terms. For that to occur, there has to be a political expectation that it is supposed to occur; that growth will translate into more paid work; that these jobs will pay living wages; that those at the top will not siphon off the gains. The issue is less how fast the economy grows than how that growth is achieved and how its benefits are shared.

During the 1990s we witnessed a palpable shift of money, shift of power, shift of heart. This shift has made it harder to collectively focus on the central problem of our era, which is less about economics than about value, less about private 'goods' than about the public good, less about just deserts than about a just society.

We are out of balance. The desire to be viewed and treated as an equal is as fundamental a human longing as the desire to win and have that success mean something. The trick is to put in balance these two impulses in our dealings with others.

When we fail to find the right balance within our households, the result is described as a dysfunctional family. No such label is applied when we fail to find that balance between equality and power at the collective level. But the result is perhaps more devastating.

NOTES

1 Market income comes primarily from earnings from employment and self-employment, but also includes income from investments (such as interest and sales of stocks, but not the gains in assets from rising share values, or stock options). These figures are provided by Statistics Canada, from the Survey of Consumer Finances, the only consistent source of income distribution data in Canada since the 1970s. All figures are in constant 1997 dollars, so are adjusted for inflation.

2 Based on unpublished data from Statistics Canada, Survey of Consumer Finances. Figures calculated by the Canada Council on Social Development from micro-data sources supplied by Statistics Canada for Armine Yalnizyan, *The Growing Gap: A Report on Growing Inequality Between the Rich and Poor in Canada* (Toronto: Centre for Social Justice, 1998), 41 and

Armine Yalnizyan, *Canada's Great Divide* (Toronto: Centre for Social Justice, 2000), 61.

3 Statistics Canada, National Balance Sheet Accounts.

4 At the time of writing, 1997 was the most recent year for which Statistics Canada provided data on the distribution of incomes in Canada.

5 Statistics Canada has not published information on the net wealth of Canadians since 1984. Their most recent survey of assets and debts of Canadians, completed in the summer of 1999, should be available by the time this book is published. At that time we will be able to reflect on changes in the distribution of net wealth in this country.

6 All incomes are measured in constant 1997 dollars. The definition of market income is found in note 1. After-tax income refers to market income plus transfers (UI, welfare, family allowance/children tax benefit primarily for this group) minus federal and provincial income taxes.

7 Oliver Bertin, 'Investors Applaud CN Cuts,' *Globe and Mail Report on Business*, 22 Oct. 1998, B1.

8 David Thomas, 'Stock Prices Soar on U.S. Jobs Report,' *National Post*, 6 Mar. 1999, A1.

9 'Productivity Growth Surges to Three Times 1998's Rate,' *Toronto Star*, 2 May 2000, C2.

10 The recovery period is capped in 1997 for the purposes of this analysis, since there is no more recent data on the distribution of income than in that year. Changes to per capita income show an upward trend in 1998 but tell us nothing about the distribution of those gains to all groups in society, and do not disaggregate the income into market and after-tax components.

11 United Nations conference on Trade and Development, *Trade and Development Report*, 1997, 109; and more generally, the database from the Luxembourg Income Survey.

12 This growth in average earned incomes of the poorest 10 per cent of families in a period of economic recovery raises these families from a level roughly comparable to the gross domestic product per capita in the Democratic Republic of the Congo up to the average standard of living in Bangladesh. (Calculated from figures in the United Nations Human Development Report, 1999.) While an improvement, it is hardly a victory of the market. Average after-tax incomes provide just over $1,150 a month to roughly 400,000 families for raising their dependent children and saving for their future.

13 Revenue Canada, *Income Statistics: 1996 Tax Year* (Ottawa: Revenue Canada, 1998). At the time of writing, this was the latest available data for taxation statistics.

9

American Style Welfare Reform: Inequality in the Clinton Era

BARBARA EHRENREICH

Many people in the United States think welfare reform is a rather exotic issue pertaining solely to a mythical underclass of derelicts and layabouts. But it's not just their fate that is at stake with the recent drastic cuts in social services for the poor. What happened to welfare is important because it's what's going to happen next to Social Security, Medicare, and the public schools. In fact, welfare reform is symptomatic of a much larger policy trend today: the transformation of our government from a source of help to people to what is primarily a mechanism for law enforcement and incarceration.

The subject of this article is the Clinton administration's welfare reform:[1] First, what it is supposed to accomplish, and what its real effects are likely to be – not only for the 14 million women and children on what used to be known as Aid to Families with Dependent Children (AFDC, now known as TANF or Temporary Aid to Needy Families), but for the millions of other women (and men) who make up the working poor. I also want to address the big question of how we got to this pass, focusing on how Americans came to distrust the government and the very idea of government services. Finally, I want to examine the implications of these policy changes for the quality of American life.

The main feature of American welfare reform is that welfare recipients – meaning poor single women raising children on their own – are being hustled into the workforce as quickly as possible. So let's start by taking a quick look at the work world that welfare recipients are about to enter. The single overriding fact about today's work world is that blue-collar wages have not caught up to the levels of the 1970s, while health benefits and pensions have actually declined.

Thus millions of people have been discovering that hard work does not necessarily pay any more. Over one-fourth of Americans now work full-time but are unable to lift themselves out of poverty. As a result, according to *Second Harvest*, the Chicago-based hunger-relief organization, more and more of the people lining up at food pantries today are working people, often from double-income families, because their jobs – even two jobs per family – do not pay enough to put food on the table.[2]

The major claims for welfare reform were that (1) it would help the poor themselves, both economically and morally, and (2) that it would somehow improve the economy and society overall by reducing the role of government.

I will begin with the first argument, that welfare reform will help the poor. For sixteen years, since the publication of Charles Murray's book *Losing Ground,* the line from the right has been that 'welfare causes poverty.'[3] To put it another way, if you give people money, they turn into degenerate, promiscuous, substance-addicted parasites. That may be true in the case of many of our elected officials; in general, however, the statement 'welfare causes poverty' is at the same logical level as saying 'Social Security causes baldness.' Welfare was never a very satisfactory program, of course, especially for those who have had to rely on it. But it does not cause poverty. Low wages cause poverty – in fact, let me restate that since it is an important economic discovery that seems to have been entirely forgotten. Low wages cause poverty, along, with other factors like chronic illness, disability, and $600 rents for studio apartments.

Let's look at the claim that ending welfare will have a morally uplifting effect on poor women. In many ways, the campaign for welfare reform was conducted as a moral crusade against the presumed promiscuity of low-income women and what was seen as the resulting epidemic of 'illegitimacy.' In fact, the Clinton administration's welfare reform bill contains the offer of $20–25 million 'bounty' to states that decrease their out-of-wedlock births while also decreasing their abortion rates![4] This is for all women, not just women on welfare, which suggests that the moral crusade that welfare reform represents is a crusade ultimately aimed at 'reforming' the behaviour of women of all social classes.

I saw how much of a moral crusade welfare reform was at a conference in the spring of 1997 in Washington, D.C., featuring speakers from the right-wing Heritage Foundation and the Cato Institute. Listening to Heritage's Robert Rector,[5] who wrote the welfare reform plank for the

Republicans' 1994 *Contract with America*, it would have been easy to conclude that welfare benefits function, more or less like semen, to impregnate the poor (singlehandedly). Welfare, he told us, 'rewards dysfunctional behavior' like out-of-wedlock childbearing, while welfare reform will somehow 'encourage marriage' by withdrawing the fertilizing flow of benefits. Later, the conference's other ideological heavy-hitter, the Cato Institute's Michael Tanner,[6] went even further with the sexual imagery, telling us that black men have been 'cuckolded' by the welfare state.

We might meditate, for a moment, on the interesting spectacle of President Clinton signing a bill – the welfare reform bill of 1996 – designed to curb promiscuity. The welfare reform bill provides approximately $50 million per year to be used to bring 'abstinence education' to unmarried poor women. But why, you might wonder, should we waste it on them?

This emphasis on illegitimacy as the 'real' problem with welfare has gone along with the idea that the solution to female poverty is marriage. In early 1998,[7] Arizona State Representative Mark Anderson introduced a bill that would appropriate $2 million to train welfare recipients how to find a husband – by, for example, teaching 'positive thinking and attitude adjustment techniques' – which sounds to a lot of Arizona women, Republicans included, like a plan to teach women how to put up with any kind of behaviour their men have to offer.

Our conservative pundits and elected officials continually argue that there would be very little poverty if the nation's single mothers would simply get married. But, as I said, workers' real wages have not reached where they were thirty years ago. A working-class woman would have to marry approximately 2.3 men of her own class to escape poverty. Which strangely enough is illegal.

Furthermore, we should question the use of the word 'illegitimacy,' which the political right has brought back as part of their campaign to 're-stigmatize,' as they put it, the bearing of children out of wedlock. How can any child be 'illegitimate'? And think about the implication of that word for women. The implication is that a mother can give birth, but only a father can confer full membership in the human community, that is, 'legitimacy.' In English common law, an out-of-wedlock child was described as 'filius nullius,' the Latin for 'child of no one,' which is a way of saying that unmarried women do not count, and their children are, to use the vernacular, bastards.

There is a further problem with the emphasis on welfare reform as a way of ending promiscuity and illegitimacy: it has no basis in empirical reality. There is no evidence, for example, that welfare has served as an incentive to have out of wedlock babies. And why should it? Would anyone have a baby if someone offered her two hundred dollars a month to support it? Three hundred dollars? Whoever imagined that the answer might be 'yes' has not checked the price of Pampers recently. In fact, the evidence against any link between out-of-wedlock birth and welfare is overwhelming, as many within the Clinton administration have known all along. States with higher-than-average welfare benefit levels do not have higher-than-average rates of out-of-wedlock births or higher teen pregnancy rates than states with lower-than-average benefits. In fact, some studies show that women receiving welfare actually have lower birth rates than poor women who are not receiving welfare.[8]

What about the other major claim for welfare reform: that it will improve the lives of poor women economically? So far, no one knows what is happening in general to people who are deprived of welfare – there are no nationwide statistics, nor was there any provision, within the Clinton welfare reform legislation, for tracking the fate of former welfare recipients.[9] There is one 1998 study[10] from the University of Wisconsin in Milwaukee on the fate of former welfare recipients in that city, the results of which are very disturbing. Three months after being dropped from welfare, only 34 per cent of 25,000 Milwaukee residents had found full-time work. Another 34 per cent reported zero earnings for that period. And only one in six of the former welfare recipients was earning enough to put them above the poverty level for a family of four. On the bright side, the media occasionally feature glowing reports about individual women who are overjoyed to be off of welfare and earning six to seven dollars an hour in a factory or fast food outlet, which is, after all, more money than they got on welfare. But most of those women who assert they are better off working are still receiving state subsidies for childcare and transportation. Like welfare itself, according to the reform legislation's requirements these subsidies can only last for a maximum of five years per individual, after which the former welfare recipients will have to try to make do on their wages. In addition, this is a time of nearly full employment. It should be easy enough to find a job. Nevertheless, there are already millions of Americans working part-time who would prefer to find full time work and cannot. What happens when the business cycle enters a downturn and even low-wage jobs become hard to find?

The major problem is that, even with nearly full employment, wages have not been rising to a point where a relatively unskilled person can expect to support herself and her children on her earnings alone. Recent work by Diana Pearce at the University of Washington shows that a single person needs to earn approximately $11 an hour to support a single child. Most former welfare recipients will be earning six to seven dollars per hour.[11] According to Kathryn Edin and Laura Lein's recent book, *Making Ends Meet*,[12] women working at low-wage jobs actually end up being worse off than welfare recipients, because of their transportation and childcare expenses. Edin and Lein conclude that low-wage jobs, not welfare, condemn women to a lifetime of poverty. The answer to the question of whether work ends poverty is no. And that answer is not derived from ideology, but from arithmetic.

Not surprisingly, there is already evidence of deepening poverty among the working poor. The Centre on Budget and Policy Priorities reports a 50 per cent increase in the poverty rate of low wage workers during the past two decades.[13] And this, remember, is a time when jobs were becoming plentiful and fewer than half of welfare recipients had been pushed off the rolls.

What will happen as welfare reform kicks in the next few years, and more and more of the poor are cut off or will not be eligible for welfare in the first place? Already, we can predict – and begin to see – three disturbing outcomes.

First, the new drastic limitations on welfare will have a negative effect on millions of women, including middle-class women, who are not currently on welfare. A stunning amount of data has emerged in just the last two years showing that the biggest single factor leading a woman to go on welfare is the need to escape an abusive husband or boyfriend. A recent study from the University of Massachusetts,[14] for example, finds that a majority of AFDC recipients were victims of abuse, and many of them had experienced abuse within the previous twelve months. Now the escape hatch has been cut off: many battered women will decide to endure domestic violence rather than plunge their children into sudden destitution and possible homelessness.

Second, there is no question but that welfare reform is going to have an economic impact that goes way beyond the approximately four million adult women who have been on AFDC: it will also affect millions of working women (and men) who were never on welfare. In part, this is because welfare recipients are being hired, in many places, to take the jobs held by regular workers, but at much lower pay. It is also due to the fact that an influx of poor and often desperate people into the workforce inevitably pulls down wages. As the chairman of a temp staffing services company in Salt Lake City put it: 'Without the welfare people ... we would have had to raise [the] wage[s].' In fact, the effect has already been felt nationwide. On 15 September 1998, the Bureau of Labor Statistics announced that for the first time in twenty years the wage gap between men and women has begun to widen. And the most likely reason for this, according to experts, is welfare reform: thousands of welfare recipients are being dumped into the low-wage end of the workforce, pulling down the average wage for women.

But here's the surprise: welfare reform is going to be great for business, and not just in the obvious sense that it will have the effect of lowering wages. It is beginning to look as if the real agenda of welfare reform is 'privatization' – turning the administration of state and county welfare programs over to private corporations – such as, for example, Lockheed-Martin, IBM, Unisys, and EDS. Lockheed and EDS want to do the fingerprinting (or 'finger-imaging,' as the euphemism goes) of welfare recipients, as well as run entire welfare departments. Other companies, like America Works and Maximus, are rushing in to take over counties' 'job readiness' programs. There are two reasons for this rush to privatize what is left of welfare. First, one of the things federal welfare reform does – and this has not received much attention so far – is remove the requirement that welfare programs must be run by governments. Second, one of the key provisions of the bill is its five-year lifetime limit on welfare, the enforcement of which will require a vast investment in technology to track individuals through name changes and geographical moves, for decades on end, creating a huge apparatus of surveillance and a growth industry for the 'finger-images' and information technologists.

That conference on welfare reform that I mentioned, for example, which was organized by something called the World Research Group, was really on how business can profit from welfare reform by taking over state and county programs. The brochure for the conference urged businesses to 'capitalize on the massive growth potential of the new world of welfare reform/Gain a leading edge in the market while it is in its early stage!' Even more explicit was the brochure for the World Research Group's December 1996 conference on prison privatization, which said 'While arrests and convictions are steadily on the rise, profits are to be made – profits from crime. Get in on the ground floor of this booming industry now!'[15]

You may wonder what these corporations know about welfare. The answer is, more than you might think. Take Lockheed. When it merged with another defence contractor, Martin Marietta, in 1996, the U.S. government gave it a $1 billion subsidy for carrying out this merger. The point is, Lockheed has first-hand experience with welfare – as a recipient. What has happened is not welfare 'reform' or even welfare 'repeal,' but the transformation of social welfare into corporate welfare. The advocates of welfare privatization are promising to cut state and county welfare expenditures by as much as 40 per cent, while at the same time making healthy profits for the private companies involved. Where will these saving and profits come from if not out of the pockets of the poor? I should mention here that the rush to privatize is supported by no evidence that the private companies can do the job of welfare administration any better than the public sector. And there is legitimate concern about conflict of interest resulting from the privatization of welfare.

The shift from social welfare to corporate welfare parallels the general trend in all parts of our economy: the upward redistribution of wealth (and along with it of course, power) to those who already have more than they know what to do with. In fact, this should be counted as the third likely effect of welfare reform: to accelerate the redistribution of wealth that has been going on since the late 1970s, and which has led to a dramatic increase in inequality. The richest 1 per cent of Americans now own 40 per cent of the wealth, while the bottom 20 per cent of Americans can claim only negative assets. Chief executive officers now earn over 419 times more than entry-level workers in their firms,[16] compared to about 15 times more in the early 1960s. At Christmas time, we read about $1 million bonuses on Wall Street, while poor women in American cities stand in line for hours to get free toys for their children provided by charity. The latest mark of status among the rich in New York is to order $2,000 bottles of wine with dinner, while poor families worry about the price of a carton of milk.

After welfare the next targets for elimination and/or privatization are likely to be the big middle-class entitlements offered by the American welfare state: Social Security, Medicare, and the public schools. At the Heritage Foundation and Cato Institute, the point-men on welfare have already shifted their attention to Social Security, and they are very clear that their agenda is to both curtail and privatize it. Welfare was small potatoes compared to Social Security and Medicare, just a warm-up for the coming all-out attack on middle-class entitlements.

Why have we been going in this direction? Why cut social programs at a time when the private sector is still not generating enough jobs that low-skilled people can support themselves on, or affordable childcare, health insurance, or housing. This is a time to be expanding social programs – not just welfare – not eliminating them. The standard answer has been that these programs must be cut or privatized because of the need to shrink 'big government.' Many people say they ardently support programs to help the poor, as well as programs, like universal health insurance, to help everyone. But they do not want the government doing these things. Hatred of government is now a majority political stance. Surveys show that the proportion of Americans who say they 'trust the government in Washington' only 'some of the time' or 'almost never' more than doubled between the 1960s and the 1990s.

The truth is, cuts in social spending have not caused the U.S. government to 'shrink,' as the conservative politicians have promised. Only the helping functions are shrinking. The intrusive and repressive function of government – as represented, for example, by the war on drugs and a proliferation of anti-terrorism measures that threaten individual rights – and more generally, all those functions that involve the use of force, have been expanding almost without check.[17]

At this point, the United States has the largest percentage of its citizens incarcerated of any country except Russia. The number of Americans under the control of the criminal justice system has reached five million. Most prisoners are male, but the female incarceration rate has been rising at twice the rate of male prisoners. Reasons for the exploding rate of female incarceration, according to experts, include mandatory drug sentencing laws and 'cutbacks in federal assistance programs.' We are evolving from what the right likes to call a 'nanny state' – meaning one that actually tries to offer a helping hand now and then – to one that far more resembles a police state. And the right itself must take a lot of the blame.

Who, after all, has been barking about 'law and order' for at least the last twenty-five years? Who has insisted on more police officers, more prisons, more executions? (not for white middle-class people, of course, always for 'the other guy'). The right-wing choice, over and over, has been for 'law and order' over social spending, police over jobs, prisons and Pentagon over schools and childcare. The result is that even before the present assault on the welfare state we did not have a soft, cuddly government, the kind that offers its people health insurance, help with higher education, and livable assistance for the unemployed. We had a huge and heavily armed police officer. The only mass jobs program our government offers is the military. And the biggest low-income housing program it runs is the penitentiary system.

To appreciate the social effects of the decision to spend on law enforcement and the military rather than on jobs and welfare, consider the career trajectory of one particular individual: Timothy McVeigh. Like thousands of young people he finished high school only to find that there were no jobs that pay enough to live on. Nor, of course, were there any government programs that would provide him with an education or job training. So, like so many other ill-educated, disadvantaged young people, he signed up for the military, where he was painstakingly drilled in the art of killing efficiently and without remorse. Then, after a while, the military did not need him either. McVeigh failed the psychological tests for the Special Forces, or Green Berets. He returned to civilian life and a job as a security guard, again, with no hope of earning enough to live on. He drifted for awhile, and the only explanation he could find for his predicament was in the kind of far-right literature that blames all our nation's problems on Jews, blacks, gays, and immigrants not to mention that other favourite scapegoat group, welfare mothers. Of course, you know the rest of the story.[18]

If you look at other paramilitary groups active in recent years, like the Montana Freemen or the Arizona Viper Militia, you find life histories very similar to McVeigh's: marginal and usually low-paying employment combined with some military experience, at least enough to provide training in the use of explosives.

But the truly alarming thing is that the process we have embarked on – cutting the caring functions of government while expanding the armed and intrusive functions – seems to have a self-reinforcing dynamic of its own. Cuts in social welfare, especially in social welfare for the poor, almost inevitably mean that government has to beef up its repressive functions, if only to control an increasingly economically desperate subpopulation. And of course the burden of these repressive measures – police and prisons – eventually calls for still more cuts in social welfare spending.

There are many twists to this vicious cycle. For example, there is the fact, as Robert Reich[19] has pointed out, that as public services deteriorate, the upper middle class simply withdraws into private alternatives:

private schools, individual retirement accounts, nannies instead of community day care. The upper middle class ceases to be an advocate for the wider community and the common good.

Or there's the fact that as social protections like Medicare, Social Security, and the social safety net are eroded, or vociferously threatened, by political leaders, a kind of panic mentality sets in: 25-year-olds are not encouraged to lobby for Social Security[20] but to obsess about their mutual funds and individual retirement accounts. Everyone starts scrambling for an individual solution as the ground gives way under us, as the huge fissure between rich and poor grows wider. Under these circumstances, old virtues like compassion and solidarity begin to seem like luxuries that few can afford to indulge in.

It does not take a Ph.D. in political science to see that if we continue on this path of cutting social programs while increasing the coercive functions of government we will descend into an ever more sharply divided society. Already, we see fortified islands of affluence in a sea of poverty, shanty-towns, and trailer parks, with of course, ever more prisons to house the dissidents, the 'criminals,' and the poor.

The State of Idaho provides a preview of this nightmare future, or at least a white, rural version of it: between 1993 and 1998 state cutbacks led to a 70 per cent reduction in the number of welfare recipients.[21] It has also cut funding for education and programs for children. Meanwhile, in the last twenty-five years, it has increased its prison population tenfold, in part by imprisoning people for offences like drug possession or writing bad cheques. At this point, the state cannot keep up with its expanding prison population. At the same time, reading levels among school children have fallen drastically and Idaho now leads the nation in its proportion of abused and neglected children.

Do we really want to live in a world like this, a world divided between fortified urban apartment towers and low-income hovels? Between lovely gated communities on the one hand, and desolate trailer parks on the other? Huge economic inequalities inevitably invite crime and a general brutalization of society. Look at Johannesburg, Mexico City, or Los Angeles, and you find an anxious upper middle class living in walled compounds, protected by private guards and personal security devices, afraid to move freely out of doors. No amount of law enforcement or prisons can protect the comfortable and well-fed in a world inhabited by so many who are hungry, under-employed, and desperate. No amount of personal wealth can buy security in a world in which so many people have none.

The point of describing the self-reinforcing downward spiral towards greater inequality and the frightening future it augurs for us all, is not to depress us but to reveal what we are up against. We are not condemned to an increasingly unequal and brutalized society. Stereotypes, falsehoods, and facile scapegoating can and must be challenged with facts. Hopelessness and pessimism can be countered with the growing number of examples of people responding militantly and constructively all over the United States. I am thinking of the campaigns in many cities for a livable wage, and of what seems to me to be a new surge of welfare rights organizing – in, for example, New York, California, Wisconsin, and my own home state of Montana. Finally, we need more international exchanges, where we can share and build on the experiences of people facing the same trends in different national settings.

NOTES

1 There is widespread agreement about the purpose of the welfare reform legislation passed by Congress (the Personal Responsibility and Work Opportunity Reconciliation Act of 1996). It was to decrease 'welfare dependence' and increase work among public assistance recipients. This legislation abolished AFDC (Aid to Families with Dependent Children) and replaced it with TANF (Temporary Assistance to Needy Families). Welfare benefits were made time limited and closely tied to work requirements were intended to move welfare recipients off welfare and into the labour force. See 'How Will We Know if Welfare Reform Is Successful?' www.ssc.wisc.edu/irp/faz9.htm

2 During the first quarter of 1997, 39 per cent of emergency food recipient households (those served in soup kitchens, food pantries, and emergency shelters) had at least one adult working. Of these with at least one person working, 49 per cent were employed and working full-time (forty hours or more per week). America's Second Harvest, 'Hunger 1997: The Faces and Facts,' America's Second Harvest National Research Study (1998). The study interviewed 28,000 low-income emergency food recipients at pantries, kitchens, and shelters January through March 1997.

According to the U.S. Conference of Mayors, 37 per cent of people requesting emergency food assistance in American cities are employed. United States Conference of Mayors, 'A Status Report on Hunger and Homelessness in American Cities 1998: A 30 City Study,' 1998. See also

Jared Bernstein, Chauna Brocht, and Maggie Space-Aguilar, 'How Much Is Enough?' May 2000. The report concludes that given the wages available to low-wage workers, and the costs of decent housing, suitable childcare, and other work-related expenses, many low-income working families will not be able to earn enough to meet their essential consumption needs, such as food, housing, childcare, health care, and transportation. www.epinet.org/books/howmuch.html

3 Charles Murray, *Losing Ground: American Social Policy, 1950–1980* (New York: Basic Books, 1984). *Losing Ground* attacked the welfare state, claiming that it was not only ineffectual, but actually left the poor worse off than ever before. Charles Murray is the Bradley Fellow at the American Enterprise Institute for Public Policy Research, Washington, D.C. His main research areas are welfare, crime, and bureaucracy.

4 The 1996 welfare reform bill contained three provisions intended to combat illegitimacy. First, it required each state to set numeric goals for reducing illegitimacy over ten years. Second, it provided bonus funding to states which reduce illegitimacy without increasing abortion. Third, the bill created a new program to provide abstinence education.

The laws established a bonus for states which demonstrate that the number of out-of-wedlock births and abortions that occurred in the state in the most recent two-year period decreased compared to the number of such births in the previous period. The top five states will receive a bonus of up to $20 million each, or $25 million if less than five states qualify. See Jodie Leven-Epstein, *Teen Parent Provisions in the New Law* (Washington D.C.: Center for Law and Social Policy, November 1996). http://epn.org/clasp/teens.html.

5 Robert Rector is a senior research fellow at the D.C.-based Heritage Foundation and author of *America's Failed $5.4 Trillion War on Poverty* (Washington, D.C. Heritage Foundation, 1995).

6 Michael Tanner is director of health and welfare studies at the Cato Institute.

7 For details of H.B. 2617 see Kathleen J. Ferraro, 'Women, Violence and Welfare Reform in Arizona.' Paper presented at the annual meeting of the Society for the Study of Social Programs, San Francisco, 20–23 Aug. 1998.

8 See Arlene T. Geronimus, 'Teenage Childbearing and Personal Responsibility: An Alternative View,' *Political Science Quarterly* 112 (3) (Fall 1997), 405–30.

9 The welfare caseload has fallen by 7.2 million recipients from 14.1 million recipients in January 1993 to 6.9 million in March 1999, a drop of 51 per cent since President Clinton took office. U.S. Department of Health and

Human Services Fact Sheet, 'The Personal Responsibility and Work Opportunity Reconciliation Act of 1996,' 4 Dec. 1999. www.hhs.gov/new/press/1999pres/991204a.html

Welfare reform cannot be evaluated simply by examining changes in the size of caseloads. Other outcomes may indicate changes in family and child well-being, such as changes in wages, employment and income, in housing and homelessness, and in levels of child maltreatment and foster care placement. See 'How Will We Know If Welfare Reform Is Successful?' www.ssc.wisc.edu/irp/faq9.htm

10 John Pawasarat, *Employment and Earnings of Milwaukee County Single Parent AFDC Families: Establishing Benchmarks for Measuring Employment Outcomes under 'W-2'*? (University of Wisconsin – Milwaukee Employment and Training Institute, 1998).

11 Diana Pearce, *Six Strategies for Self-Sufficiency* (Washington, D.C.: Wider Opportunities for Women, 1996). The minimum wage in the United States is $6.15 per hour. See U.S. Department of Labor, http://www.dol.gov/dol/esa/public/minwage/main.htm

12 Kathryn Edin and Laura Lein, *Making Ends Meet: How Single Mothers Survive Welfare and Low-Wage Work* (New York: Russell Sage Foundation, 1997).

13 The Center on Budget and Policy Priorities reports that over the past two decades, the poverty rate among working families has increased by nearly 50 per cent (1999).

14 Mary Ann Allard, Randy Albelda, Mary Ellen Colten, and Carol Cosenza, 'In Harm's Way? Domestic Violence, AFDC Receipt and Welfare Reform in Massachusetts' (Report from the University of Massachusetts; Boston: McCormack Institute, 1997). The Institute for Women's Policy Research found that between 60 and 90 per cent of recipients of AFDC have been or currently are victims of domestic violence ((1997) http://www.iwpr.org/). Idaho's domestic violence shelters estimate that of the 695 victims they sheltered in 1996/7, over 70 per cent left their programs as recipients of the AFDC in order to escape an abusive family situation. '"It Takes Time": A Study of Welfare Reform and Domestic Violence in Idaho.' www.nwafdev.org/paper/iddvreport.html. See also Jody Raphael and Richard M. Tolman, 'Trapped in Poverty: New Evidence Documenting the Relationship between Domestic Violence and Welfare,' Taylor Institute and University of Michigan, Apr. 1997, www.ssw.umich.edu/trapped.

15 See article at http://www.corpwatch.org/trac/feature/prisons/gulag.html.

16 Sarah Anderson et al., *A Decade of Executive Excess: The 1990s* (Washington, D.C.: Institute of Policy Studies and United for a Fair Economy, 1999).

17 The rate for most serious crimes has been dropping or stagnant for the past fifteen years, but during the same period severe repeat offender provisions and a 'get-tough' policy on drugs have helped push the U.S. prison population up from 300,000 to around 1.5 million during the same period. This has produced a corresponding boom in prison construction and costs, with the federal government's annual expenditures in the area now 17 billion dollars. In California, passage of the infamous 'three strikes' bill will result in the construction of an additional twenty prisons during the next few years. http://www.corpwatch.org/trac/feature/prisons/gulag.html.

18 On 19 Apr. 1995 a truck bomb tore down the north face of the Alfred P. Murray Federal Building in Oklahoma City, killing 168 people. Timothy J. McVeigh was sentenced to death for his role in the bombing.

19 Robert B. Reich, *The Work of Nations: Preparing Ourselves for the 21st Century* (New York: Alfred A. Knopf, 1992). Robert B. Reich, the former U.S. Secretary of Labor, is a university professor and the Hexter Professor of social and economic policy at Brandeis University.

20 Social Security is the public contributory old age pension in the United States. Social Security payments provide a nationwide, uniform floor of income protection for aged, blind, and disabled persons. The program makes monthly cash payments to people in these categories with limited income and resources. See www.ssa.gov for details.

21 www.deltast.edu/ccd/newsletters/articles/clarion.htm.

10

Equality and Welfare Reform in Blair's Britain[1]

RUTH LISTER

Introduction

The New Labour Government inherited a country scarred by a level of inequality exceptional by both post-war and international standards. Its response reflects the ideological legacy of eighteen years of New Right Conservative government, which has helped to shape New Labour's approach to social and economic policy and its emergent philosophical underpinnings. According to Driver and Martell, New Labour can be understood as 'an exercise in *post-Thatcherite* politics' (1998, 1, emphasis in original), shaped by Thatcherism, yet also representing a reaction against it.

Having briefly detailed the scale of inequality and poverty in the United Kingdom, the article will explore a number of key shifts in Labour thinking away from an equality agenda to one comprising the trinity of Responsibilities, Inclusion and Opportunity (RIO), each of which is expressed primarily through paid work. The chapter then looks at how this agenda has translated into New Labour's 'welfare' reform strategy, which Blair had signalled in the Election Manifesto was central to its overall project. Ever since becoming leader, Blair has been groping for the 'big idea' that would make sense of this project. After a number of false starts, he appears to have settled on the 'Third Way.' This article will look at the debate inspired by the Third Way before concluding with a very brief assessment of the likely implications for (in)equalities of New Labour's approach.

The Legacy of Poverty and Inequality

When Labour came to power in 1997, nearly a quarter of the population was living on an income below 50 per cent of the average after housing costs (generally used as an unofficial poverty line in the absence of an official one), compared with just under one in ten in 1979. For children, the proportion was just over a third compared with one in ten in 1979.

Over the same period, the real incomes of the bottom tenth of the population fell by 9 per cent in real terms compared with an increase of 70 per cent for the top tenth and 44 per cent overall. According to John Hills 'this inequality growth was exceptional internationally ... with inequality increasing further and faster in the 1980s than in any comparable country.' Thus, while the increase in inequality was a product, in part, of wider economic forces and demographic trends, the impact of these was aggravated by regressive tax-benefit and employment policies under the Conservatives. The result was that 'overall income inequality was greater in the mid-1990s than at any time in the forty years from the late 1940s' (Hills 1998a, 5).

Within these figures are hidden complex cross-cutting social divisions including those of gender, race, and disability. Overall, in 1996–7, women's gross average weekly income was 53 per cent of men's compared with 35 per cent in 1975. Over this period, the 'gender income gap' has 'narrowed for all age groups up to male state retirement age and particularly for younger age groups' (EOC 1997, 2). This partly reflects a narrowing of the hourly pay gap from 71 per cent in 1975 to 80 per cent in 1998, although the weekly pay gap is wider and the disparity between part-time female earnings and full-time male earnings 'has not altered significantly' (EOC 1999, 4). Thus, not all women are benefiting from the narrowing of the gender income gap, as inequalities widen within the female population between better-educated 'successful' women and those either in part-time low-paid work or living on benefit. Women are overrepresented in the bottom fifth of the income distribution (even without taking into account hidden inequalities within households). These inequalities interact, in turn, with other divisions of race, disability, and age. Members of minority ethnic groups, particularly Pakistanis and Bangladeshis, of whom nearly three-fifths are in the bottom quintile, are at greater risk of poverty than the rest of the population.

From Equality to Equality of Opportunity

In contrast to the Conservatives, New Labour does identify the overall increase in income inequality as a problem, although, significantly, it tends to bracket it with a qualifying phrase relating to welfare spending, as evidence that the latter is ineffective.[2] Thus, for instance, the Green [official consultation] Paper on Welfare Reform (discussed further below) identifies as one of three fundamental problems with the social security system 'increased inequality and social exclusion, despite more spending' (DSS 1998a, 9). Likewise, the government's First Annual Report (an innovation) pinpoints as part of its inheritance the growth in inequality 'despite ever-higher spending on welfare' (Prime Minister 1998, 52).

A more equal society has traditionally been at the heart of the Labour Party's political vision. Vestiges of that vision still surface from time to time. Thus, for instance, in 1996, Gordon Brown, now Chancellor of the Exchequer, used his John Smith Memorial Lecture to argue for the restoration of 'equality to its proper place' in Labour's trinity of values, and Blair told the *Independent on Sunday* 'I believe in greater equality. If the next Labour Government has not raised the living standards of the poorest by the end of its time in office, it will have failed' (28 July 1996), a sentiment repeated in *The Independent* (8 December 1997) once he was in office. Even the official Red Book, which accompanied the 1998 Budget, stated that the government is determined to create 'a more equal society' because of the social and economic consequences of inequality.

Despite these residual expressions of more traditional Labour sentiments, since the 1992 election defeat (which was widely, though the evidence suggests erroneously, blamed on Labour's tax and benefit policies) and more decisively the death of Labour leader John Smith, there has been a marked retreat from greater equality as a goal and from redistribution through the tax-benefit system as the primary mechanism for achieving it. Back in January 1997, Brown announced what was widely interpreted as a key symbolic step in 'the forward march of New Labour' (Lloyd 1996). Having a decade earlier denounced passionately the reduction in the top rate of income tax to 40 per cent (which is low by European standards), he promised that there would be no increase in income tax rates during the first term of a new Labour government.[3] In the words of Hugo Young, a prominent political commentator, 'we are on notice that it will be a government which has abandoned the fight against inequality by the standard method' (*The Guardian*, 21 January 1997).

'The standard method' of redistribution through the tax-benefit system has been rejected in favour of 'redistribution of opportunity' through education, training, and paid employment. Higher income tax, perceived to be a vote-loser, has become a taboo subject. Even after a series of progressive and redistributive budgets, when questioned on the radio, Brown could not bring himself to admit it. The talk is of 'quiet redistribution' or 'redistribution by stealth,' as redistribution has become the 'r' word, whose name the government dare not speak. The retreat from overt redistribution partly reflects a fear of frightening the voters of Middle Britain, whom the party wooed in order to win power, but also a belief that the constraints imposed by economic global forces mean that traditional 'tax and spend' policies are no longer sustainable.

The underlying philosophical shift in Labour's beliefs was crystallized in an exchange between Brown and Roy Hattersley, a former deputy leader of the party and traditionally seen as being on its right wing. Hattersley attacked what he sees as New Labour's 'reluctance to come to the aid of the disadvantaged' and its acceptance of 'gross inequalities ... as an unavoidable characteristic of developed economies' (*The Guardian*, 6 August 1997). Following an earlier intervention by Hattersley, Brown used the old anti-egalitarian argument to explain that New Labour rejects 'equality of outcome' (something of a caricature of the egalitarians' objective) as neither desirable nor feasible, imposing uniformity and stifling human potential; instead, it espouses a view of equality of opportunity that is 'recurrent, lifelong and comprehensive' (*The Guardian*, 2 August 1997). In response, Hattersley, in the tradition of R.H. Tawney, pointed out that 'true diversity is only possible in a society which avoids great discrepancies in wealth and income' (6 August 1997). (The issues now commonly treated as part of a 'diversity' agenda tend not to be addressed in these debates; see below).

Hattersley's position was further denounced by Peter Mandelson (then a key figure in the Blair government) as representing an artificially chosen 'limited definition of egalitarianism in the face of 'many different routes' to 'a more equal society' (Mandelson 1997, 7). At this point the academic community, in the form of fifty-four professors of social policy and sociology, entered the fray, with a much-publicized letter to the *Financial Times* during Labour Party Conference week. While accepting that redistribution is not the only route to a more equal society, the letter argued that the government appeared 'to have erased it from the map altogether despite evidence of the massive redistribution from poor to rich achieved by the Tories.' Even though marginalized as 'Old Labour,' the case for greater equality and redistribution continues to be made by those who believe that equality of opportunity, even as defined by Brown as the chance for 'everyone to realise their potential to the full' (Brown 1996), is likely to remain a chimera, as massively unequal starting points affect the ability to grasp the opportunities opened up. As David Marquand observed in an essay reviewing the government's first year in power, in the context of a growing fault line 'between the winners and losers in the global marketplace ... no project for social inclusion will work unless it captures some of the winners' gains and redirects them to the losers' (Marquand 1998, 24).

Social Exclusion/Inclusion

Social inclusion is one of New Labour's leitmotifs. The main focus of the speech by Mandelson, which had prompted the letter from the 'FT54,' was 'tackling social exclusion.' 'Our vision is to end social exclusion,' he declared; 'tackling the scourge and waste of social exclusion' represents the overriding challenge if the government is to 'deserve another historic victory' (Mandelson 1997, 6).

Although Labour rehabilitated the 'p' word, 'poverty,' expunged from the official lexicon under the Tories, initially it preferred to use the language of social exclusion. However, the language of poverty made something of a comeback in 1999, with a much publicized commitment by Blair to eradicate child poverty by the year 2020 and the publication of the first of what are to be annual monitoring reports on *Tackling Poverty and Social Exclusion* (DSS 1999).

The term 'social exclusion' originated in France and has been adopted by the European Commission, but it is only relatively recently that it has gained currency in the United Kingdom. Academics and campaigners are divided as to its value. Some dismiss it as merely a euphemism for poverty. Others believe that it encourages a more multi-dimensional, relational, and dynamic analysis than does poverty on its own (Room 1995). The danger is that, if deployed uncritically, the concept of exclusion can be used to obscure the associated poverty that stems from an unequal distribution of resources and the wider relations of inequality and polarization that frame it. As a number of commentators have observed, the key relationship tends to be a horizontal one of 'in' or 'out' rather than a vertical one of 'up' or 'down' (Duffy 1998).

The notion of exclusion can in fact be deployed in very different ways, depending on whether the primary objective is social cohesion or social justice. Ruth Levitas (1998) has summed up these different approaches in what she calls the three discourses of SID, MUD, and RED.

RED refers to a redistributive, egalitarian discourse that embraces notions of citizenship and social rights, which she associates with critical thinkers and activists but not with the mainstream stance adopted by the European Commission and the U.K. government. The primary objective here is social justice whereas other two discourses are activated by the primary objective of social cohesion and distinguished by a lack of concern about wider inequalities (see also Driver and Martell 1997). MUD is a moralistic discourse that deploys the divisive and stigmatizing language of the 'underclass' and 'dependency culture' to portray those excluded as culturally distinct from mainstream society. It emphasizes individual behaviour and values. SID, a 'social integrationist discourse,' increasingly dominant in both the United Kingdom and the wider European Union, is focused primarily, and sometimes exclusively, on exclusion from paid work. Levitas sums up the differences between the three discourses according to 'what the excluded are seen as lacking,' namely money (and we might add power) in RED, morals in MUD, and work in SID.

The government's approach to tackling social exclusion reflects an uneasy amalgam of SID, MUD, and RED. Its definition of social exclusion stands, perhaps surprisingly, in the RED tradition, as 'covering those people who do not have the means, material and otherwise, to participate in social, economic, political and cultural life' (*Hansard* 1997). Yet all too often it deploys the language of 'the dependency culture,' 'handouts,' and, albeit less frequently, 'the underclass,' redolent of MUD. The importance of such discourses in shaping the parameters of debates around social exclusion and policies to combat it is not to be underestimated (Naples 1997). Its policies are firmly rooted in SID, most notably in their identification of paid work, supported by education and training, as the key route to social inclusion.

SID also underpins the establishment of a Social Exclusion Unit, 'at the heart of government' (Blair 1997b), reporting directly to the prime minister.[4] Launching the unit, Blair described it as 'an experiment in policy-making that is vital to the country's future ... Its purpose is central to the values and ambitions of the new Government' (Blair 1997a). The remit given to the unit was to 'focus on some of the most difficult problems, where several Departments need to work together and where solutions have been very hard to find.' The emphasis is on prevention, clear targets for tackling discrete problems and 'joined up solutions for joined up problems' through the breaking down of interdepartmental and interorganizational boundaries at both national and local level (Mulgan 1998). The unit's initial task was to report speedily on the three problems of truancy and school exclusions; rough sleepers; and those living in 'deprived neighbourhoods,' initially described as 'worst estates,' an unfortunate stigmatizing label as the unit soon discovered (Wallace 1998). Subsequently it has looked at teenage parents, unemployed sixteen- to eighteen-year-olds and excluded young people more generally.

The unit's reports on its original brief have been generally well received. In particular, it has spearheaded an ambitious strategy of neighbourhood renewal. Nevertheless, support for the unit's work tends to be tempered by a degree of scepticism among those who have seen similar initiatives come and go in the past, both in the United Kingdom and the United States (Stewart 1997; Kleinman 1998; Plowden 1998); disappointment that once again, despite official acknowledgment of the failure of traditional 'top-down' approaches, 'the excluded' are not always sufficiently involved as active participants in developing policies (Thompson and Holman 1998); and a concern that a focus on discrete 'problem' groups or people could encourage the belief that these groups are themselves the problem (Bennett 1998), divorced from a broader structural analysis and prescription (FT54 1997; Kleinman 1998; Levitas 1998; Lister 1998a).

Although Blair's speech to launch the unit spoke of 'our national purpose to tackle social division and inequality,' the discourse he used was one of social cohesion (SID) rather than social justice (RED). Social division and inequality undermine social cohesion. But the emphasis is more on behaviour and values than structures. In Blair's view, 'the only way to rebuild social order and stability is through strong values, socially shared, inculcated through individuals, family, government and the institutions of civil society' (Blair 1996, 8). Launching the Social Exclusion Unit, he explained: 'My political philosophy is simple. Individuals prosper in a strong and active community of citizens. But Britain cannot be a strong community, cannot be one nation, when there are so many families experiencing a third generation of unemployment, when so many pensioners live on crime-ridden housing estates and are afraid to go out, when thousands of truant children spend their days hanging round on street corners. The public knows only too well the dangers of a society that is falling apart. They know that worsening inequality, hopelessness, crime and poverty undermine the decency on which any good society rests. They know how easily shared values and rules can unravel' (Blair 1997a). Likewise, in an article to mark the launch of the Social Exclusion Unit, Blair explained that it 'will embody a core new Labour value: "community" or "one nation" ... Our contract with the people was about opportunity and responsibility going together' (Blair 1997b).

From Rights to Responsibilities

The emphasis on responsibility underlines the social integrationist paradigm that frames Labour's analysis of and approach to tackling social exclusion. It contrasts with the definition of social exclusion provided by the European Commission's European Observatory on National Policies for Combating Social Exclusion, which was 'first and foremost in relation to the social rights of citizens' (Room 1992, 14).

The statement of values, which replaced the totemic Clause IV of the Labour Party's constitution, sets as its ideal a community 'where the rights we enjoy reflect the duties we owe.' In a series of speeches and essays, Blair has set out to reorient the party's conceptualization of citizenship, emphasizing the centrality of obligation and responsibility to the New Labour project. Back in 1995, in a Spectator Lecture, for example, he took as his subject people's 'duties to one another as citizens': 'duty,' he declared, 'is an essential Labour concept. It is at the heart of creating a strong community or society.' He distanced himself from 'early Left thinking' in which the 'language of responsibility [was] spoken far less fluently' than that of rights. He spoke of a 'covenant between society and each of its citizens within which duty must be set; and it involves duties from society to citizen as well as the other way about.' This 'allows us to be much tougher and hard-headed in the rules we apply; and how we apply them' (Blair 1995).

This 'hard-headedness' can be found in a range of social policy areas, most notably social security (see below), including a preoccupation with 'cracking down' on fraud, but also anti-social behaviour and crime and disorder where the emphasis is on the responsibilities of families and parents (Lister 1998b). The New Labour philosophy was summed up well by Frank Field, when minister for welfare reform: 'our reform agenda is dominated by a new emphasis on responsibilities as well as rights: the responsibility of parents, absent and present, to care, emotionally and materially for their children; the responsibility of adults of working age to work; the responsibility of welfare recipients to take opportunities to escape from dependency' (Field 1997).

This emphasis on the responsibilities rather than the rights of citizenship is an expression of what David Marquand (1996) has described as a 'new kind of moral collectivism' on the centre-left. It reflects the influence on New Labour of the popular communitarianism of Amitai Etzioni and David Selbourne and on Blair himself of the philosophy of John Macmurray, which emphasizes moral responsibilities rooted in community (Freeden 1999; Heron and Dwyer 1999). In an analysis, which distinguishes between a number of levels and dimensions of communitarianism, Stephen Driver and Luke Martell argue that 'Labour increasingly favours conditional, morally prescriptive, conservative and individual communitarianisms. This is at the expense of less conditional and redistributional socioeconomic, progressive and corporate communitarianisms' (Driver and Martell 1997, 27; see also Hughes 1996; Hughes and Little 1999).

Blair's Christian Socialism, a central tenet of which is personal responsibility, is commonly identified as the other main influence on his political philosophy (Deacon 1997a). There have also been suggestions that Blair's belief in responsibility and community is redolent of late-nineteenth-century 'new' or social liberalism, which also influenced Macmurray (Beer 1998; Marr 1998). Brian Lund (1997), in an analysis of a number of new liberal writers, maintains that '"new" Labour has absorbed elements of "new" Liberal thinking on character, rights and obligations but has neglected "new" Liberal ideas on the redistribution of income' rooted in a distinction between 'social' and 'unsocial' wealth.

Critics point to the dangers of an imbalance in the allocation of responsibilities and rights in an unequal society. The influential commentator Will Hutton, while accepting a link between rights and obligations, has pointed out that 'most of the obligations that accompany rights in a New Labour order are shouldered by the bottom of society rather than those at the top, which is let off largely scot-free' (*The Observer*, 5 July 1998). More fundamentally, from a critical academic social policy stance, Tony Fitzpatrick asks: 'Does not the language of responsibilities, when divorced from a radical political economy, risk ossifying existing power imbalances, often in the name of *empowering* the poorest?' (Fitzpatrick 1998, 27). What is involved, he suggests, is a collectivization of duties, centred on the duty to pursue independence through work, combined with a retreat from collectively underpinned rights. For all the emphasis on community, the answer is seen to lie in individual responsibility.

'Reforming Welfare around the Work Ethic'

Work, or to be more precise paid work, lies at the heart of the New Labour trinity of Responsibility, Inclusion, and Opportunity. 'Reforming welfare around the work ethic' has become another New Labour mantra. The pivotal role that work plays in the government's policies to promote social inclusion and opportunity is brought out in a speech on 'the Government's priorities for tackling social exclusion' by the then Social Security Secretary, Harriet Harman:

> work is central to the Government's attack on social exclusion. Work is the only route to sustained financial independence. But it is also much more. Work is not just about earning a living. It is a way of life ... Work is an important element of the human condition ... Work helps fulfil our aspirations – it is a key to independence, self-respect and opportunities for advancement ... Parents don't just work to support their families financially, they also work to set an example to their children. Work brings a sense of order that is missing from the lives of many young unemployed men. Work provides access to social networks ... Work rather than worklessness is the difference between a decent standard of living and benefit dependency. And between a cohesive society and a divided one. (Harman 1997)

The evils of 'benefit dependency' are a common refrain in the RIO discourses of New Labour, as they were under the Tories, despite the lack of empirical evidence to support the notion of a 'dependency culture' (Lister 1996). In both cases, the fingerprints of U.S. New Right thinkers can be discerned. With echoes of Charles Murray, for instance, Frank Field, the former New Labour minister and now prominent backbencher, has laid great emphasis on the ways in which the social security system shapes attitudes, character, and behaviour: 'At the moment the structure of welfare all too often conditions, even expects, dependency. Instead we should reward those values which underpin civil society – honesty, integrity and independence,' underpinned wherever possible 'by work rather than the passive handout of welfare' (Field 1997).[5]

As an antidote to 'welfare dependency,' the responsibility on benefit claimants to take up opportunities for paid work and training is stressed continually by ministers. The Green Paper on welfare reform (discussed further below) holds out a vision of 'a new welfare contract' in which the first two duties of the individual are to 'seek training or work where able to do so' and to 'take up the opportunity to be independent if able to do so.' The first duties on government are to 'provide people with the assistance they need to find work' and to 'make work pay' (not to ensure work is available) (DSS 1998a, 80).

The vehicle for exercising these responsibilities is the government's flagship policy, dubbed the New Deal and described in its First Annual Report as 'a huge piece of radical welfare reform' (Prime Minister 1998, 12). The New Deal exemplifies what is commonly and somewhat misleadingly known as 'welfare to work.' Alan Deacon summarizes the objectives of welfare to work strategies:

> First, to increase the job opportunities available to welfare claimants by means of employment subsidies, job creation measures, or training and work experience schemes. Second, to improve the motivation and skills of particularly the long-term unemployed through an expansion of personal counseling and advice services along with educational and training provision. Third, to reform the structure of social security benefits so as to give claimants a greater financial incentive to take advantage of the opportunities thereby created. This third objective can be achieved by enhancing the benefits paid to those in work, by imposing stiffer sanctions upon those who refuse to participate in the schemes, or by a combination of both of these approaches. (Deacon 1997a, 35)

The New Deal comprises a series of 'welfare-to-work' programs targeted on young people aged eighteen to twenty-four, unemployed for six months or more, together with their partners where there are no children; those aged twenty-five plus, unemployed for two years or more (to be extended to those unemployed for eighteen months); and, on a voluntary basis, lone-parent families with school-age children (or younger if the parent wishes to participate), partners of unemployed people aged twenty-five or over, and disabled people. The great bulk of the resources are earmarked for the young unemployed.

The first of the objectives set out by Deacon, namely to increase job opportunities, is to be met for young unemployed people through a series of guaranteed New Deal options comprising either a job, subsidized for up to six months; a six-months placement with an environmental task force or voluntary organization for which either a wage or benefit plus £15 is paid; or full-time education for up to a year. [6] Support is also available for those who wish to pursue self-employment. For the older long-term unemployed, subsidies are available for six months to employers who recruit from this group and long-term unemployed claimants are allowed to undertake up to a year's full-time job-related education or training while on benefit. From 2001, they will be offered a set of options similar to those available to the young unemployed. Additional help is available for unemployed people aged over fifty.

The second objective of improving motivation and skills is pivotal to the New Deal approach, reflecting New Labour's emphasis on personal counselling aimed at behavioural change. Young people enter a 'gateway' lasting up to four months, during which those who are not 'job-ready' will receive 'careers advice and guidance, assessment of training needs, work trials with employers and tasters of other options' (DSS 1998a, 25). An 'after-care' service is also provided during the placement and afterwards, if the participant returns to unemployment. A similar intensive, individualized approach is being piloted for older unemployed people and pilot 'employment zones' have been created in which 'local partnerships will draw up plans to give unemployed people opportunities to improve their employability and move back into and remain in employment' (DSS 1998a, 27). Participants are able to draw on 'personal job accounts,' made up of money available for benefits and training, in order to access 'innovative advice, job creation, learning and business support programs, which local partnerships have been encouraged to develop' (Finn 1998, 116). Advice and assistance are the key elements of the voluntary New Deals for lone parents, partners, and disabled people. (Following the 2000 Budget, provision for lone parents is, however, to be extended to embrace training and a ladder of supported paid work options from a few hours while on benefit to full-time work.)

As suggested by Deacon, the third objective of social security reform is being pursued through a combination of 'stick' and 'carrot.' Under the Conservatives, the 'stick' applied to unemployed benefit claimants had become progressively tougher, with increasingly tight availability and seeking work rules, culminating in the replacement of the unemployment benefit (paid on a contributory basis for twelve months) by the jobseeker's allowance (JSA) (paid for only six months on a contributory basis and means-tested thereafter). The JSA obliges claimants to enter into a contract and gives officials wide discretionary powers to issue a 'jobseeker's direction,' requiring changes in behaviour, or even appearance.

Labour has accepted the JSA and the tougher sanctions regime associated with it. It has made clear that for young people there will be 'no fifth option of an inactive life on benefit.' It has progressively tightened up the sanctions applied to young people who fail to comply and has extended them to the over-twenty-fives, in what a government insider told *The Times* is 'the strongest ever attack on the workshy' (17 September 1999). Hardship payments are more limited than previously. In future, it will be a requirement of benefit receipt that all claimants of working age (with some very limited exceptions) should attend an interview at specified intervals with a personal adviser to discuss the prospects of finding work. The interviews will be administered by a new ONE service, which brings together the Employment Service and Benefits Agency for those of working age. According to the Prime Minister, 'the new agency will have a new culture and will be firmly focused on helping people to become independent' (DSS/DfEE Press Release, 16 March 2000).

On the 'carrot' side, there is a series of measures designed 'to make work pay.' Most notable among these are the introduction for the first time of a statutory minimum wage (albeit at a level lower than campaigned for by trade unions and the 'poverty lobby'); a number of improvements in benefits for children; a new children's tax credit in place of the existing married couple's tax allowance; and the replacement of family credit (a means-tested in-work benefit for families with children paid to mothers) by a significantly more generous working families tax credit (incorporating also a childcare credit) paid, in most cases, through the wage-packet.

This last measure has been controversial because of the transfer of resources it will involve, in many cases, from mothers to fathers (Goode, Callender, and Lister 1998). However, there is now a more ambitious proposal to combine all the income-related sources of support for children into an integrated child credit, paid in and out of work, to the caring parent, probably from 2003.[7] This would be complemented by a new employment tax credit for low-paid working adults.

Other measures include a disabled person's tax credit (again replacing a means-tested in-work benefit) and reform of national insurance contributions aimed 'to encourage job creation at the lower end of the labour market' (HM Treasury 1998, 5). The government's work-centred strategy is also being promoted through an ambitious childcare strategy (see below); and strengthened employment rights. In the latter case, its espousal of 'flexible' labour markets limits the extent to which New Labour is willing to apply a regulatory moderating hand (Kelly and Oppenheim 1998).

The New Deal reflects a broad consensus, both in the United Kingdom and the wider European Union, that paid employment represents the best route out of poverty for those able to take it. 'Welfare to work' was promoted by a number of independent commissions; likewise the need for work (as a right rather than an obligation) was also stressed by the Citizens' Commission on the Future of the Welfare State.[8] Nevertheless, there are critics. One area of concern is the degree of compulsion involved (see Deacon 1997a, 1997b, 1997c). Another is the priority which the strategy gives to employability, and 'the responsibility that every individual has to do all they can to improve their employability' (Bradley 1998), over employment.

Demand-side policies to reduce unemployment have effectively been abandoned in the face of the constraints believed to be imposed by globalizing economic forces (Deacon 1997a). Macro-economic policy, dubbed by Arestis and Sawyer (1998) as the 'new monetarism,' currently prioritizes low inflation over low unemployment. Although the overall unemployment level has fallen, some critics point to the inadequacy of reliance on 'supply-side' strategies alone in certain parts of the country, where there are simply not the jobs there for the various groups covered by the New Deal, who tend to be concentrated in the same low-employment areas (Webster 1997; Peck 1998; Turok and Webster 1998; Turok and Edge 1999). A further cause for concern is the sustainability of employment opportunities opened up by the New Deal (raised in the European Commission's Joint Employment Report 1998).

Even more fundamentally, a few, largely unheard, voices have queried the underlying philosophical premise of 'welfare to work' – that paid work can be equated with social inclusion and that it represents the primary obligation for all those of working age. Ruth Levitas (1998), for example, has questioned the value of 'integration' or 'inclusion' into a profoundly unequal labour market, tempered only by a pretty minimal minimum wage. As A.B. Atkinson has observed, 'employment does not ensure social inclusion; whether or not it does so depends on the quality of the work offered. "Marginal" jobs may be no solution' and 'if the expansion of employment is obtained at the expense of a widening gap between those at the bottom of the earnings scale and the overall average, then it may not end social exclusion' (Atkinson 1998, i & 9). Prior to the introduction of the minimum wage in 1999, the pay gap has widened in recent years in the United Kingdom and research suggests that the quality of work offered to workless people is generally poor, with few ladders into better jobs (White and Forth 1998).

New Labour's messianic espousal of the work ethic, as giving meaning to life, has also provoked a reaction in some quarters (see, e.g.,

Daniel 1998). A key criticism has been that the definition of work used, which confines it to paid work, discounts the value of community and voluntary activities and the unpaid work of reproduction and care carried out in the home, mainly by women (Levitas 1998; Lister 1998c). From the perspective of gender equity, the model pursued is primarily that described by Nancy Fraser as 'the universal breadwinner model,' in which the breadwinner role is universalized so that women can be citizen-workers alongside men, as opposed to the 'caregiver parity' or 'universal caregiver' models, which respectively support informal care work and encourage men to combine caring and paid work in the same way that women currently do (Fraser 1994, 1997; Fitzpatrick 1998). The launch of a childcare strategy as an integral part of economic policy, comprising both childcare provision and family friendly employment policies, can be seen as supporting the universal breadwinner model. Nevertheless, for all the strategy's limitations, including those of resources, the symbolic importance of government recognition, in the United Kingdom, that childcare is at least partially a public responsibility is not to be underestimated. The launch of the strategy has been widely welcomed.

Lone parents taking up paid work are targeted as among the main beneficiaries of the childcare strategy, in the face of evidence suggesting that lack of affordable and suitable childcare acts as a major barrier to lone parents' employment (Bradshaw et al. 1996).[9] It is in relation to lone parents (the great majority of whom are women) that the government's work-biased approach has come under greatest criticism, despite broad support for policies that make it easier for lone mothers to move into paid work if they want to. An unpopular decision to implement a Tory plan to abolish additional benefits for lone parents (originally proposed as a means of supporting the institution of marriage) was justified in part with reference to the paid work opportunities opened up by the New Deal and the childcare strategy. This was interpreted by many lone parents and their supporters as a denial of the importance of the unpaid work they do caring for their children. Research suggests that complex 'gendered moral rationalities' influence lone parents' own views of the role of paid work in good parenting (Duncan and Edwards 1999; Ford 1996).

The government recognizes its role in supporting caring responsibilities, in particular through its childcare and family-friendly employment policies and a strategy for carers. However, these are normally provided when the recipient is doing paid work. It has so far failed to address adequately what Levitas identifies as 'a profound contradiction between treating paid work as the defining factor in social inclusion, and recognising the value of unpaid work' (Levitas 1998, 145). Underlying that contradiction is a narrow, gendered interpretation of the obligations of citizenship.

The emphasis on paid work at the expense of unpaid work is a central issue for the Government's welfare reform strategy and raises the wider question of what kind of support should be provided for those unable to undertake paid work for whatever reason. This group will include not only those outside the labour market because of age, incapacity or severe disability, or caring responsibilities. It will also include those covered by the voluntary New Deal schemes who choose not to participate and those required to seek work but who cannot find it. In fact, those able to move from 'welfare to work' represent only a minority of benefit claimants (TUC 1998).

'Work for Those Who Can; Security for Those Who Cannot': The 'Welfare' Reform Agenda[10]

In theory, support for those unable to undertake paid work is covered by the central principle guiding the Green Paper on welfare reform, *New Ambitions for Our Country: A New Contract for Welfare* : 'work for those who can; security for those who cannot.'[11] In practice, a number of question marks remain over the government's strategy to ensure 'security for those who cannot' undertake paid work.

From the outset, the stakes on welfare reform were high. Blair's Foreword to the Election Manifesto declared that New Labour 'will be the party of welfare reform.' His appointment of the maverick Frank Field as minister for welfare reform, with almost cabinet minister status, was widely interpreted as a green light to 'think the unthinkable.' All the signs were that the unthinkable would mean cuts in social security spending, as the Manifesto pledged to divert spending from 'the bills of economic and social failure' (read social security) into education.

The government's first move on the social security front was to introduce a piece of legislation originally proposed by the Conservatives, ignoring many of the criticisms that had been made in response to the Green Paper that had preceded it (Sainsbury 1998). This legislation included the abolition of the lone parent benefit addition paid with child benefit, which together with the abolition of the other additional benefits for lone parents, proved to be the government's baptism of fire. The government refused to bow down in the face of fierce opposition both outside and inside Parliament and made matters worse by shifting the grounds of justification for the cuts. The result was a much bigger than expected backbench revolt at the end of 1997, which left the government shaken. Leaks of cuts in benefits for disabled people provoked a further outcry, with disabled people chaining themselves to the Downing Street railings and covering themselves in red paint. As *The Observer* (28 December 1997) commented, 'the pictures were shocking. Symbols matter; and it is important that the most vigorous protests about New Labour's early policy initiatives have come not from the strong and the rich but from the poor and the weak.'

As an air of crisis enveloped Labour's welfare reform plans, Blair announced that he was to take personal charge as chair of a new ministerial committee. The New Year saw Blair and other ministers taking to the road to sell the case for welfare reform and the publication of a series of Welfare Reform Focus Files with the not so subliminal message that social security spending was out of control (which is not, in fact, the case). By the time the welfare reform Green Paper finally appeared in March, the only concrete proposals it contained had already been announced in Gordon Brown's Budget. The 1998 Budget represented an attempt to repair the damage created by the cuts in lone-parent benefits. Improvements in benefits for families generally meant that the great majority of lone parents affected would eventually end up no worse off (at the same time fuelling the suspicion that the underlying agenda was one of support for the traditional two-parent family rather than affordability). Particularly welcome was an announcement of an increase in the universal child benefit to be funded by a reduction in the married couple's tax allowance, a policy that had been pressed by feminists and the 'poverty lobby' for many years. (The 1999 and 2000 Budgets built on these measures, with further improvements in the level of support for families with children.)

What had become clear by the spring of 1998 was that the government had managed the initial reform process very badly, with the Green Paper coming at the end of the initial phase of the process rather than the beginning. By starting with benefit cuts, it had raised fears of a cuts agenda, which created a climate of suspicion. By the time the Green Paper attempted to reassure that the strategy is 'reform-driven' and not 'cuts-driven,' the damage had been done.

The Green Paper itself was structured around eight principles concerning work; partnership between public and private sectors; high quality services; support for disabled people; family support and child poverty; social exclusion and poverty; openness and honesty; and flexible and efficient delivery. It offered a rather partial analysis of the problems with the current system and outlined the changing context for reform (which significantly failed to mention the development of a multiracial, multicultural society). It ended with what it described as 'Welfare 2020,' built on 'three core values of work, security and opportunity' (DSS 1998a, 79). 'At the heart of the modern welfare state,' it declared, 'will be a new contract between the citizen and the Government based on responsibilities and rights' (DSS 1998a, 80), although, in line with the philosophy outlined earlier, the emphasis was more on the former than the latter.[12] Responsibility and enlightened self-interest were its leitmotifs (Deacon 1998a).

In his foreword and introduction, Blair made clear that the aim is not to offer a blueprint but to 'return to first principles,' marking the beginning of a national debate. He described the essence of the Green Paper as a 'Third Way,' which was spelt out in the Green Paper in terms of the welfare state facing 'a choice of futures.' On the one side is 'a privatised future' with a residual safety net for the poorest, which is rejected as divisive. On the other is a status quo supported by those who 'believe that cash is the answer to most of the problems, that poverty is alleviated by more money rather than more opportunity. They defend the *status quo*, but want benefits for all to be more generous. They believe that poverty is relieved exclusively by cash hand outs.' This too is rejected in favour of the Third Way: 'a modern form of welfare that believes in empowerment not dependency' (DSS 1998a, 19). This is to be achieved through paid work for those able to work; security for those unable to work because of disability, old age, or caring responsibilities, and a partnership between public and private provision.

Through its biased presentation of the choice of futures, which the Third Way is supposed to transcend, the Green Paper in fact failed to offer a strategy for the reform of the structure of social security as opposed to a strategy for reducing the numbers reliant on benefit. The overarching model of social security which the government intends to build remains unclear. With regard to the crucial question of whether this model is closer to that of a comprehensive social security system based on notions of solidarity, typical of continental Europe, or that of a more residual safety net, the document seemed to point both ways.

On the one hand, the residual safety net future was rejected and a commitment to the universality of certain benefits for children and disabled people and to a welfare state 'from which we all benefit' was reaffirmed (although it was not always clear when the term 'welfare state' was being used in its broad sense and when in the narrower sense of social security). But on the other hand, there was no commitment to reduce the heavy reliance on means-testing, one of the common criticisms made of the current system, and central to its '20–20 vision' was a larger role for private forms of provision. While the aim may be to avoid a 'low grade safety net for the destitute' as Blair put it, a two-tier model of provision does appear to be indicated.

Two big holes in the Green Paper, in particular, have been identified. First, the future of the national insurance scheme, which stood at the heart of the Beveridge model and which represents the spirit of a welfare contract par excellence, is unclear. No mention was made in the Green Paper of the earlier proposals from the Commission on Social Justice (see note 8) for a modernized, more inclusive social insurance system, better attuned to women's needs and employment patterns, despite the identification of the changes in women's position as one of the key contextual trends. A subsequent 'policy appraisal' of women's position in the social security system by the Department of Social Security was again stronger on analysis of women's position than on prescription for improving it (DSS 1998b). The appraisal was an example of a wider policy of 'mainstreaming' women's perspectives in policy development and evaluation, promoted by a new Women's Unit in order to ensure that 'the different needs of women are reflected in government policy' (DSS 1998b, 24). Subsequent legislative changes involving restrictions on entitlement to benefits for long-term sick and disabled people will, nevertheless, hit women particularly hard.

While some limited improvements have also been announced, on balance, the reforms enacted following the Green Paper indicate a clear retreat from Labour's traditional commitment to social insurance and increased reliance on means-testing. This was summed up by *The Economist* as a crossing of 'the Rubicon from ... the left bank of welfare-for-all to the right bank of means-testing' (6 March 1999).

Second, the Green Paper had nothing to say about the adequacy of benefits other than the caricature, cited above, of those pressing the case for higher benefits. This case was made, for example, by the FT54 (see above) who criticized the false dichotomy created by ministers between an opportunity-based approach on the one hand and directly improving the living standards of those experiencing poverty on the other (Lister 1998a). What is remarkable is that, despite the mounting evidence of the failure of benefits to meet the needs of recipients and a succession of social security reviews over the past two decades, there has been no public official review of the adequacy of benefit levels since they were set by Beveridge. Improving benefit levels has been dismissed as an Old Labour approach that encourages 'welfare dependency,' although it has been conceded that there is a case for improving the position of those who cannot be expected to seek work, with targeted benefit increases for severely disabled people, the poorest pensioners, and children.

Initial speculation that the flagship reform program had become badly stalled when the two key ministers in the Department of Social Security were moved during the summer of 1998 was quickly dispelled as the new Secretary of State, Alistair Darling, moved swiftly to maintain the momentum, with a series of more specific legislative proposals. Some of these, particularly those affecting disability benefits, proved to be highly controversial, provoking considerable opposition both inside and outside Parliament.

Darling was moved from the Treasury, which is playing an increasingly pro-active role in the development of social policy (Deakin and Parry 1998). On coming to power, the Chancellor had decreed that Labour would work within Conservative spending limits (widely seen as unrealistically tight) for its first two years in power, during which a 'comprehensive spending review' would be undertaken. While maintaining tight overall controls on public spending, in the name of a budgetary balance or even surpluses and 'prudent' levels of national debt, the spending review did lead to the promise of significant increases in spending on education and health (although not financed by cuts in social security spending, as originally signalled). Even more significant increases, especially in health spending, were announced in the 2000 Budget.

The spending review also included funds for a previously announced New Deal for Communities, aimed at tackling poverty and unemployment on deprived estates; some limited measures to address pensioner poverty; and an innovative 'Sure-Start program,' targeted on helping families with young children in deprived areas, influenced by U.S. models. This last measure is the product of a Treasury review of early years provision and is another example of the government's desire to break down departmental boundaries in policy making and execution and also to strengthen families.

Despite the partial rehabilitation of public expenditure as a positive social and economic tool of government, the government continues to operate within the low tax, and to a lesser extent, limited public spending ideological paradigm espoused by the Thatcher government. In this way, it has deliberately distanced itself from 'Old Labour' 'tax and spend' policies (although, it was, in fact, the 1974–9 Labour government which started the retreat from public spending in the face of demands from the IMF [Hills 1998b]).

In Search of the 'Big Idea'

The use of the term New Labour acts as a deliberate, constant reminder that this is not the Labour Party of old. A metamorphosis, involving something of a philosophical paradigm shift, described above, has taken place (Shaw 1998). As Blair made clear on claiming victory, his party had fought the election as New Labour and would govern as New Labour. The promotion of New Labour is buttressed by a discourse of modernization and change, which runs through all its policy documents and political statements. Thus, for instance, in its First Annual Report, 'modernisation' is bracketed with 'fairness' as constituting 'the guiding aims of our strategy in the key policy areas' (Prime Minister 1998, 10). The discourse is particularly marked in the speeches of Social Security Secretary, Alistair Darling, who has called for 'principled modernisation of the welfare state' (Darling 1998). It is a discourse which brooks no opposition, for who wants to appear as old-fashioned and backward-looking? (Clarke 1998; see also Finlayson 1998; Andrews 1999; Rose 1999).

John Clarke and Janet Newman, who have analysed the deployment of this modernizing narrative in three major social policy documents,[13] suggest that it represents 'the site of significant continuities between the New Right and New Labour' (1998, 10). Global and societal change have been invoked by both in order to advocate the need for changes in thinking and policy. Nevertheless, in its search for a 'big idea' to make sense of its new ideological and policy stance, New Labour has attempted to distinguish itself from the New Right as well as the Old Left. In bewilderingly rapid succession, a number of potential 'big ideas' were taken up and discarded in the period between Blair becoming leader and then prime minister, surviving only at the rhetorical level. Citizenship was soon followed by 'community,' which in turn gave way to the 'stakeholder society' and then to the 'decent society' and 'one nation' (the last borrowed from Tory paternalism) (Lister 1997).

Finally, Blair appears to have found his 'big idea' in the notion of 'a third way,' borrowed from Bill Clinton. This provided the impetus for fevered, though not sustained, debate among intellectuals keen to put theoretical and policy flesh on a concept that has been defined in terms of what it is not – that is, it is 'different from the old left and the new right' (Giddens 1998a, 18) – rather than what it is. Blair encouraged this debate, including through an on-line discussion organized by the New Labour network, NEXUS,[14] and a seminar at No. 10 Downing Street. When asked in an interview with *The Guardian*'s U.S. correspondent whether this meant that he was still trying to formulate the idea, Blair responded:

> No. My view of this idea is very very clear. It is that it offers a way between not merely the politics of the new right – *laissez-faire*, leave everything to markets, social indifference – and the politics of the old left – state control, run everything through the centre – but that it also offers a way forward between the two types of left politics traditionally, one of which was principled, but was based on old left positions, and the other of which was 'pragmatic' but which basically involved saying we just want to get the same things more gradually. It's an attempt to say there's a principled position which is also entirely sensible, and it is about taking the values of the left – social justice, solidarity, community, democracy, liberty – and recasting them and reshaping them for the new world. (*The Guardian*, 15 May 1998)

The new world is a globalized world above all else and, as Will Hutton has argued, proponents of the Third Way 'offer no effective critique of the market economy and economic operation of contemporary capitalism – they accept it, hook, line and sinker' (*The Observer*, 5 July 1998). Thus a key example given by Blair of Third Way policies is 'the embracing of globalisation as inevitable and also as desirable' so that competitiveness in this global market is combined with 'active' labour market and education and training policies 'to equip people for that' (*The Guardian*, 15 May 1998; see also Arestis and Sawyer 1998). In his launch of the NEXUS on-line debate, David Halpern (co-director of NEXUS) posed as questions 'the real scope of choice in political economy, not least in the face of global economic forces. How far can a Third Way combine dynamism and equity in the political economy of the 21st century?' (Halpern 1998, 4).

Halpern opened with the claim that 'The Third Way implies a political philosophy and economy that is distinctive but is defined by its relationship to the alternative models,' while noting that 'we can already see the outline of rival interpretations of what the Third Way should be (ibid.). At the end of the on-line discussion, no agreed definition or approach had emerged. Some emphasized a more practical, pragmatic interpretation of the Third Way derived from the policies associated with it, such as the employment-centred social policy discussed above; 'the re-positioning of the state as a guarantor but not necessarily a provider of public services; a receptivity to new forms of mutualism; and a general deepening of democracy and accountability,' pursued through an ambitious agenda of constitutional reform (ibid., 43). Julian Le Grand characterized Third Way policies as exemplifying CORA: community, opportunity, responsibility, and accountability (Le Grand 1998), to which Halpern added 'a pragmatic, bottom-up orientation' (Halpern 1998, 43).

Others attempted to formulate a set of values and principles that would inform Third Way thinking. David Marquand, for instance, proposed 'well-being, solidarity, justice and freedom.' In his summing up of the discussion, though, Halpern observed that 'in general, the discussion focused on four slightly more applied principles or objectives: quality of life, rather than narrowly economic, objectives; the deeper valuing of democracy and accountability; the "partitioning of responsibility" between state, community and individuals ...; and the desire for greater social inclusion,' all four of which, he suggested, contain 'a strong social justice dimension' (ibid., 43–4). In an address to the No. 10 seminar, which also emphasized the need to develop a Third Way economics, Charles Leadbeater summed up the ethics of the Third Way as 'co-operative self-help,' 'self-improvement,' and 'creative individualism' (*The Observer*, 10 May 1998).

Anthony Giddens, the academic closest to Blair, has, in contrast, argued against the search for a 'big idea that would define the new politics,' in favour of the development of a 'framework that could be contrasted point by point with the two rival doctrines' of old left and new right. Giddens has developed this framework around notions of a 'radical centre' in place of the traditional left-right politics; a 'new mixed economy,' which balances regulation and deregulation; 'a new democratic state' based on the devolution of power; the 'democratic family' and an active civil society; 'equality as inclusion'; a 'new role for the nation in a cosmopolitan world'; and a 'social investment state,' which, while continuing to provide insurance against risks, is imbued with the principle of positive welfare: 'investment in human capital wherever possible, rather than the direct provision of economic maintenance' (Giddens 1998a, 1998b).

The exact location of the Third Way, in terms of its political geography, remains unclear. The attempt by its leading proponents to position it as distinct from the old left and new right has been criticized by those who see it as standing closer to the latter than to the former, rather than at some equidistant, dialectical point. More recently, however, both Blair (1998b) and Giddens (1998b) have appeared to be using the compass of a modernized social democracy in order to fix the Third Way's bearings. In this modernized social democracy, the old labels of 'left' and 'right' have less, if any, purchase, a position that has been denounced by Chantal Mouffe as implying that 'we live in a society which is no longer structured by social division' (1998, 13).

The move 'beyond left and right' also serves to distort existing political thinking on the left. All pre-New Labour thinking is lumped together as 'Old' and therefore by implication irrelevant to these new times. This writes out of political and intellectual history a body of political thinking that goes under various rubrics but would include the notions of 'radical democracy' and 'critical social policy.' Not only are they ignored in the distorted image of existing left thinking, but, even more importantly, their ideas do not appear to be informing in any systematic or fundamental way the construction of the Third Way alternative to it. The initial Third Way debate did not engage with attempts to forge a 'politics of difference' or 'recognition' in an acknowledgment, which is far from new, that class politics do not address a range of social divisions that might interact with class but cannot be read off from it. For all the talk of responding to social change, one element of which is recognized to be a more demanding citizenry, evoked in the image of 'the demanding sceptical citizen-consumer' (DSS 1998a, 16), there is no real acknowledgment of the increasingly vocal demands of various 'grassroots' groups and social movements not simply for equality but also to have their differences acknowledged and respected.

More recent tracts on the Third Way have, at least, made some mention of issues of difference. In particular, a pamphlet by Blair (1998b) himself acknowledged 'the value of a multicultural and multiethnic society' and the new awareness of 'the capacity of, for example, disabled and elderly people, as they assert their own rights and dignity' (3). It also declared that 'we seek a *diverse* but inclusive society' (12, my emphasis) but did not explore how this diversity could be nurtured (see also Giddens 1998b). The most discernible influence of 'recognition' claims has been in the establishment of the Women's Unit and Ministers for Women (in fact, an 'Old Labour' policy somewhat watered down in its execution) and in the acknowledgment of the demands of the disabled people's movement for civil rights and more effective disability discrimination legislation. Progress in promoting racial and gay and lesbian equality has been mixed.[15]

The politics of difference or recognition has never been adequately represented through the formal political system. Highly pertinent, therefore, is another New Labour ideal of an 'inclusive politics.' However, in an *Observer* interview with Roy Hattersley, Blair seemed to be interpreting an inclusive left politics as one that appealed to the aspirational, the successful, and the powerful (3 May 1998). This may make narrow electoral sense, but a wider conception of politics suggests that it is the relatively powerless rather than the powerful that an 'inclusive politics' should be trying to reach. The formal political system tends to exclude minority ethnic groups, disabled people, people in poverty and, despite the breakthrough in the last election, women. While New Labour has made a concerted attempt to feminize its image, and the existence of a number of 'out' gay and lesbian members of Parliament, including two ministers, suggests a greater openness around sexuality, it is still a very white government and there have been a number of criticisms of the failure to reflect the country's multi-ethnic composition in political and quasi-political appointments.

The political exclusion of those in poverty has intensified alongside their social and economic exclusion. Electoral politics has increasingly been conducted on the battleground of 'Middle England,' so that it was left to the churches to speak out on behalf of those in poverty during the 1997 election campaign. There is, however, a growing demand among some activists and academics that debates about social exclusion, anti-poverty strategies, and the reform of welfare should find ways of engaging those in poverty whose voices are rarely heard in such debates (Russell 1996; Beresford et al. 1999; Lister and Beresford 2000).

This brings us back to issues of income inequality. Most commentators point to the shift in Labour's thinking on inequality, discussed earlier, as definitive of Third Way thinking, although there are proponents of the Third Way who accept and argue the case for a continued role for more traditional forms of redistribution (White 1998). When pressed, some will acknowledge that the extent of inequality requires some (unspecified) form of redistribution but not the traditional kind.[16] Halpern, accurately, highlighted this unresolved area of disagreement within 'the broad envelope of the Third Way' as likely to be the subject of future political battles (Halpern 1998, 45).

Conclusion

The saliency of the issue of income inequality will be heightened by the continued impact of both global economic forces and underlying labour market trends, which will aggravate existing inequalities of income and wealth. Yet it is still within the power of individual national governments to counteract these trends. It would be premature to attempt a serious assessment of how successful the New Labour government's pursuit of RIO will be in tackling 'division and inequality,' as promised in its Manifesto, and in creating the inclusive society to which it is committed.

Good omens are the commitments to eradicate child poverty in two decades (with an interim target to halve it in one decade), to tackle social exclusion and to raise the living standards of the poorest, together with 'an annual report on poverty in Britain and the success we are having in alleviating it' (Prime Minster 1998, 57). Policies such as the New Deal, improvements in benefits for children, and the establishment of the Social Exclusion Unit are indicators of its determination to act. David Piachaud has calculated that, on the basis of measures announced by the end of 1999, there should be a reduction of 1.85 million in the numbers in poverty between 1997 and 2002. As he says, this 'would be a significant achievement. But to put it in perspective, poverty would remain more than twice what it was in 1979 ... If the current rate of progress were maintained – a very big "if" – only about two-thirds of child poverty would be abolished in 20 years, and its extent would be no lower than it was in 1979' (Piachaud 1999, 157–8). Official estimates after the 2000 Budget suggest that, by 2001, 1.2 million children will have been lifted out of poverty, which still leaves 3.2 million in poverty.

The impact of the determined strategy to tackle child poverty and social exclusion could, however, be blunted, if social security policies lead further down the road to a divisive two-tier system. Unless electoral reform is embraced, the political exclusion of those in poverty and other marginalized groups could intensify.[17] More generally, the government's espousal of an economic and fiscal policy that prioritizes low inflation and low taxation over jobs and public spending, in the context of its embrace of economic globalization, imposes a handicap of its own making. Its rejection of greater equality as a goal and of seriously redistributive tax-benefit policies as a means raises serious questions about the government's ability to eradicate poverty and social exclusion in the face of entrenched inequalities of income, wealth, and power.

NOTES

1 I am grateful to Fran Bennett for her helpful comments on the first draft of this paper.

2 Steve Webb (1998) has demonstrated the flaws in this reasoning.

3 There has been a suggestion that the pledge could hold for a second Labour government (*The Independent*, 26 September 1998) and the basic income tax rate has been cut by 1 per cent to 22 per cent from April 2000, the lowest level for seventy years.

4 See their website: http://www.open.gov.uk/co/seu/seuhome.htm

5 Alan Deacon (1998b), however, points out that Field has also been influenced by his perceptions of what was happening in his constituency.

6 Those in a job or placement should also receive on the job or day release education or training and measures have been announced to increase the educational participation of sixteen to nineteen year olds.

7 The inspiration comes, in part, from the Canadian integrated child benefit.

8 These were the Commission on Social Justice, established by the former leader of the Labour Party, the late John Smith, to advise Labour (CSJ 1994); the Dahrendorf Commission, established to advise the Liberal Democrats (Dahrendorf 1995); and the Rowntree Inquiry into Income and Wealth, a non-partisan independent inquiry established by the highly regarded Joseph Rowntree Foundation (JRF Inquiry 1995); the Citizens' Commission was an independent commission made up of welfare state users (Beresford and Turner 1997).

9 Research suggests, however, that lone mothers' decision making around paid employment reflects a complex set of factors, of which the availability of affordable childcare is only one (Ford 1996; Duncan and Edwards 1999).

10 The use of the term welfare to mean social security is relatively recent in

the United Kingdom. It carries with it some of the pejorative overtones it carries in the United States, thereby contributing to the somewhat negative discourses in which social security is discussed. I nevertheless use it here interchangeably with social security as it is a rather less cumbersome term.

11 A Green Paper constitutes an official discussion document.

12 Nancy A. Naples has analysed the discursive power of the notion of the 'social contract' in the U.S. context. She argues that it has 'privileged individualist and coercive behavioural strategies such as workfare and inhibited the incorporation of structural analyses into the resultant welfare policy' (1997, 908).

13 A White Paper on the National Health Service (*The New NHS: Modern, Dependable*) and a Green Paper on public health (*Our Healthier Nation*), as well as the welfare reform Green Paper.

14 See their website: http://www.netnexus.org.

15 It has, however, been the subject of some public debate in the wake of a report on an official inquiry into the inadequate police response to the murder of a black teenager, Stephen Lawrence, and a series of nail bombs directed against the black, Asian, and gay communities.

16 In a debate at the LSE (20 May 1997), Giddens agreed that the Third Way has to involve a 'politics of redistribution': 'I do think redistributive politics is absolutely necessary to the third way. I just don't think it's going to take the same forms, or can do any longer, than it did in the classical social democratic period.' In his book, he rejects the model of equality of opportunity as 'not tenable' and talks instead of 'the redistribution of possibilities' and of 'equality as inclusion' (1998b, 101, 102).

17 Under the present 'first past the post' voting system used in national general elections, elections are increasingly fought over marginal seats which, by and large, are not those where Labour's traditional constituency lives.

REFERENCES

Andrews, G. 1999. 'New Left and New Labour: Modernisation or a New Modernity?' *Soundings* 13: 14–24.

Arestis, P., and M. Sawyer. 1998. 'New Labour, New Monetarism.' *Soundings* 9: 24–41.

Atkinson, A.B. 1998. 'Social Exclusion, Poverty and Unemployment.' In A.B. Atkinson and J. Hills, eds., *Exclusion, Employment and Opportunity*. London: Centre for Analysis of Social Exclusion.

Beer, S. 1998. 'The Roots of New Labour: Liberalism Rediscovered.' *The Economist* 7 February: 23–5.

Bennett, F. 1998. 'Comment: Unravelling Poverty.' In C. Oppenheim, ed., *An Inclusive Society: Strategies for Tackling Poverty*. London: Institute for Public Policy Research.

Beresford, P., D. Green, R. Lister, and K. Woodard. 1999. *Poverty First Hand: Poor People Speak for Themselves*. London: Child Poverty Action Group.

Beresford, P., and M. Turner. 1997. *It's Our Welfare, Report of the Citizens' Commission on the Future of the Welfare State*. London: National Institute for Social Work.

Blair, T. 1995. 'The Rights We Enjoy Reflect the Duties We Owe.' Spectator Lecture, London, 22 March.

– 1996. 'My Vision for Britain.' In G. Radice, ed., *What Needs to Change: New Visions for Britain*. London: HarperCollins.

– 1997a. Speech given regarding the launch of the Government's new Social Exclusion Unit, Stockwell Park School, 8 December.

– 1997b. 'Why We Must Help Those Excluded from Society.' *The Independent*, 8 December.

– 1998a. 'Why Britain Needs a New Welfare State.' *The Times*, 15 January.

– 1998b. *The Third Way: New Politics for the New Century*. London: Fabian Society.

Bradley, K. 1998. 'From New Hope to the New Deal.' Speech at University of Wisconsin-Madison (when Social Security Minister).

Bradshaw, J., et al. 1996. *The Employment of Lone Parents: A Comparison of Policy in 20 Countries*. London: Family Policy Studies Centre.

Brown, G. 1996. 'New Labour and Equality.' The Second John Smith Lecture, Edinburgh: 19 April.

Clarke, J. 1998. The Trouble with Normal: Looking for the Social in Social Policy. Inaugural Lecture, Open University, March.

Clarke, J., and J. Newman. 1998. A Modern British People? New Labour and the Reconstruction of Welfare. Paper presented to the Discourse Analysis and Social Research Conference, Copenhagen, September.

CSJ. 1994. *Social Justice: Strategies for National Renewal*. London: Vintage Press.

Dahrendorf, R. 1995. *Report on Wealth Creation & Social Cohesion in a Free Society*. London: Commission on Wealth Creation & Social Cohesion.

Daniel, C. 1998. 'Working to Live or Living to Work?' *New Statesman* 10 April.

Darling, A. 1998. Speech to Fabian Society Conference, London, October.

Deacon, A. 1997a. '"Welfare to Work": Options and Issues.' In M. May, E. Brunsdon, and G. Craig, eds., *Social Policy Review 9*. London: Social Policy Association.

– 1997c. 'The Case for Compulsion.' *Poverty* No. 98.

– 1998a. 'The Green Paper on Welfare Reform: A Case for Enlightened Self Interest?' *Political Quarterly* 69(3).

– 1998b. 'Welfare Reform in the 51st State?: The Influence of US Thinking and Experience upon Welfare Debate in Britain.' Paper to 20th Annual Research Conference of the Association for Public Policy Analysis and Management, New York, October.

– ed. 1997b. *From Welfare to Work: Lessons from America*. London: Institute of Economic Affairs.

Deakin, N., and R. Parry. 1998. 'The Treasury and New Labour's Social Policy.' In E. Brunsdon, H. Dean, and R. Woods, eds., *Social Policy Review 10*. London: Social Policy Association.

Driver, S., and L. Martell. 1997. 'New Labour's Communitarianisms.' *Critical Social Policy* 17(3): 27–46.

– 1998. *New Labour: Politics after Thatcherism*. Cambridge: Polity Press.

DSS. 1998a. *New Ambitions for Our Country: A New Contract for Welfare*. London: The Stationery Office.

– 1998b. *Women & Social Security: A Policy Appraisal*. London: Department of Social Security.

– 1999. *Opportunities for All: Tackling Poverty and Social Exclusion*. London: Stationery Office.

Duffy, K. 1998. 'Combating Social Exclusion and Promoting Social Integration in the European Union.' In C. Oppenheim, ed., *An Inclusive Society: Strategies for Tackling Poverty*. London: Institute for Public Policy Research.

Duncan, S., and R. Edwards. 1999. *Lone Mothers, Paid Work and Gendered Moral Rationalities*. Basingstoke: Macmillan.

EOC. 1996. 'Pay.' *Briefings on Women and Men in Britain*. Manchester: Equal Opportunities Commission.

– 1997. 'Income and Personal Finance.' *Briefings on Women and Men in Britain*. Manchester: Equal Opportunities Commission.

– 1999. *Women and Men in Britain: Pay and Income*. Manchester: Equal Opportunities Commission.

Field, F. 1997. Speech for the Warwick Debate, London, 21 October.

Finlayson, A. 1998. 'Tony Blair and the Jargon of Modernisation.' *Soundings* 10: 11–27.

Finn, D. 1998. 'Labour's "New Deal" for the Unemployed and the Stricter Benefit Regime.' In E. Brunsdon, H. Dean, and R. Woods, eds., *Social Policy Review 10*. London: Social Policy Association.

Fitzpatrick, T. 1998. 'The Rise of Market Collectivism.' In E. Brunsdon, H. Dean, and R. Woods, eds., *Social Policy Review 10*. London: Social Policy Association.

Ford, R. 1996. *Childcare in the Balance*. London: Policy Studies Institute.

Fraser, N. 1994. 'After the Family Wage: Gender Equity and the Welfare State.' *Political Theory* 22(4): 591–618.
– 1997. *Justice Interruptus*. New York & London: Routledge.
Freeden, M. 1999. 'The Ideology of New Labour.' *Political Quarterly* 70(1): 42–51.
FT54. 1997. Letter to the *Financial Times*, 1 October.
Giddens, A. 1998a. 'After the Left's Paralysis.' *New Statesman*, 1 May: 18–21.
– 1998b. *The Third Way: The Renewal of Social Democracy*. Cambridge: Polity Press.
Goode, J., C. Callender, and R. Lister. 1998. *Purse or Wallet? Gender Inequalities and Income Distribution within Families on Benefits*. London: Policy Studies Institute.
Halpern, D., with D. Mikosz. 1998. *The Third Way: Summary of the Nexus On-Line Discussion*. London: Nexus.
Hansard. 1997. *House of Commons Hansard*. 30 October 1997, col. 859.
Harman, H. 1997. Speech to mark the launch of the Centre for Analysis of Social Exclusion, London School of Economics: 13 November.
Heron, E., and P. Dwyer. 1999. 'Doing the Right Thing: Labour's Attempt to Forge a New Welfare Deal Between the Individual and the State.' *Social Policy & Administration* 33(1): 91–104
Hills, J. 1998a. *Income & Wealth: The Latest Evidence*. York: Joseph Rowntree Foundation.
– 1998b. *Thatcherism, New Labour and the Welfare State*. London: Centre for the Analysis of Social Exclusion.
HM Treasury. 1998. *The Working Families Tax Credit and Work Incentives*. London: HM Treasury.
Hughes, G. 1996. 'Communitarianism and Law and Order.' *Critical Social Policy* 16(4): 17–41.
Hughes, G., and A. Little. 1999. 'The Contradictions of New Labour's Communitarianism.' *Imprints* 4(1): 37–62.
JRF Inquiry. 1995. *Income and Wealth*. York: Joseph Rowntree Foundation.
Kelly, G., and C. Oppenheim. 1998. 'Working with New Labour.' *Renewal* 6(3): 36–49.
Kleinman, M. 1998. *Include Me Out? The New Politics of Place and Poverty*. London: Centre for the Analysis of Social Exclusion.
Le Grand, J. 1998. 'The Third Way Begins with Cora.' *New Statesman* 6 March: 26–7.
Levitas, R. 1998. *The Inclusive Society? Social Exclusion and New Labour*. Basingstoke: Macmillan.
Lister, R. 1996. 'In Search of the "Underclass".' In R. Lister, ed., *Charles Murray*

and the Underclass: The Developing Debate. London: Institute of Economic Affairs in association with *The Sunday Times*.
– 1997. 'From Fractured Britain to One Nation? The Policy Options for Welfare Reform.' *Renewal* 5(3 & 4): 11–23.
– 1998a. 'Fighting Social Exclusion ... with One Hand Tied behind Our Back.' *New Economy* 5(1): 14–18.
– 1998b. 'Vocabularies of Citizenship and Gender: The UK.' *Critical Social Policy* 18(3): 309–31.
– 1998c. 'Introduction' to D. Thurley, ed., *Response to the Government's Green Paper*. London: Local Government Association Publications on behalf of the Social Security Consortium.
Lister, R., and P. Beresford. 2000. 'Where Are "the Poor" in the Future of Poverty Research?' In J. Bradshaw and R. Sainsbury, eds., *Researching Poverty*. Aldershot: Ashgate.
Lloyd, J. 1996. 'Now You See It, Now You Don't.' *New Statesman*, 12 July.
Lund, B. 1997. '"New" Liberalism, "New" Labour: Green, Hobhouse, Hobson or George?' Paper presented to Social Policy Association Annual Conference, Lincoln, July.
Mandelson, P. 1997. *Labour's Next Steps: Tackling Social Exclusion*. London: Fabian Society, first given as Fabian Society lecture, 14 August.
Marquand, D. 1996. 'Moralists and Hedonists.' In D. Marquand and A. Seldon, eds., *The Ideas That Shaped Post-War Britain*. London: Fontana.
– 1998. 'The Blair Paradox.' *Prospect*, May.
Marr, A. 1998. *The Observer*, 26 July.
Mouffe, C. 1998. 'The Radical Centre: A Politics without Adversary.' *Soundings* 9: 11–23.
Mulgan, G. 1998. 'Social Exclusion: Joined Up Solutions to Joined Up Problems.' In C. Oppenheim, ed., *An Inclusive Society: Strategies for Tackling Poverty*. London: Institute for Public Policy Research.
Naples, N. 1997. 'The "New Consensus" on the Gendered "Social Contract".' *Signs* 22(4): 907–45.
Peck, J. 1998. New Labourers? Making a New Deal for the Workless Class. Unpublished paper, Manchester University.
Piachaud, D. 1998. 'The Prospects for Poverty.' *New Economy* 5(1): 8–13.
– 1999. 'Progress on Poverty.' *New Economy* 6(3): 154–60.
Plowden, W. 1998. 'Unit costs.' *The Guardian*, Society Tomorrow: 7 January.
Prime Minister. 1998. *The Government's Annual Report 97/98*. London: Stationery Office.
Room, G. 1992. *Second Annual Report of the Observatory on National Policies to Combat Social Exclusion*. Lille: European Economic Interest Group.

– 1995. 'Poverty and Social Exclusion: The New European Agenda for Policy and Research.' In G. Room, ed., *Beyond the Threshold*. Bristol: Policy Press.

Rose, N. 1999. 'Inventiveness in Politics.' *Economy and Society* 28(3): 467–93.

Russell, H. 1996. *Speaking from Experience*. Manchester: Church Action against Poverty.

Sainsbury, R. 1998. 'Lost Opportunities: Benefit Decision-Making and the 1998 Social Security Act.' In E. Brunsdon, H. Dean, and R. Woods, eds., *Social Policy Review 10*. London: Social Policy Association.

Shaw, E. 1998. 'Safe in Our Hands': The Blair Government and the Future of the Welfare State. Paper presented to the European Consortium of Political Research, Warwick, March.

Stewart, M. 1997. 'Tackling Social Exclusion: A History of Failure?' *Poverty* 98: 3–4.

Thompson, A., and B. Holman. 1998. 'New Labour, BIG deal?' *Community Care* 13–19 August: 16–18.

TUC. 1998. *Comments on the Green Paper on Welfare Reform*. London: Trades Union Congress.

Turok, I., and N. Edge. 1999. *The Jobs Gap in Britain's Cities: Employment Loss and Labour Market Consequences*. Bristol: Policy Press.

Turok, I., and D. Webster. 1998. 'The New Deal: Jeopardised by the Geography of Unemployment?' *Local Economy* 13: 309–28.

Wallace, M. 1998. Speech to the Social Policy Association Annual Conference, Lincoln, July.

Webb, S. 1998. 'Crisis: What Crisis? Are We Really Spending Too Much Money on Social Security?' *New Economy* 5(3): 131–5.

Webster, D. 1997. 'Welfare to Work: Why the Theories behind the Policies Don't Work.' *Working Brief* June 10–11.

White, S. 1998. 'Interpreting the Third Way: Not One Road, But Many.' *Renewal* 6(2): 17–30.

White, M., and J. Forth. 1998. *Pathways through Employment*. York: Joseph Rowntree Foundation.

PART FOUR

THE MEDIA, PUBLIC OPINION, AND FINANCIAL INEQUALITY

11

The News Media and Civic Equality: Watch Dogs, Mad Dogs, or Lap Dogs?

ROBERT A. HACKETT

Why the Media Matter

The long-term prospects for sustainable democracy arguably depend on reducing the social and economic inequalities, within and between nations, which are generated by a market economy and intensified by globalization. In turn, the prospects for a political project of equality are related to public perceptions and attitudes regarding the meanings, extent, desirability, and attainability of equality. Those perceptions derive, in no small measure, from the news and information media, which provide audiences with a mental map of the social and political world beyond their own immediate experience. In a world of second-hand experience, mass media help to 'create the political reality that governs much of our political behavior.'[1]

What kind of political reality are the news media helping to construct? Do they promote or inhibit equality between the citizens of Canada as a democratic state?

Not so long ago, the answer seemed straightforward. Embedded in popular folklore and journalism's self-understanding, the standard view presents journalism as the Great Leveller – a builder of a sense of local and national community, but also a righter of wrongs, a humbler of the mighty, a watchdog against the abuse of power, an agent to 'comfort the afflicted and afflict the comfortable.' The commercial press of the 1800s, the modern world's first mass medium, was born with a profound democratic promise: to present information without fear or favour, to make it accessible to everyone, and to foster public rationality based on equal access to relevant facts.[2]

Historically, there is much to support this view. The emergence of journalism along with a middle-class public helped break down aristocratic privilege in early modern western Europe and authoritarian colonial rule in North America. Much more recently, independent journalism has sometimes played a similar role vis-à-vis dictatorships in eastern Asia, the former Soviet bloc, and elsewhere.

However, this interpretation of journalism as a watchdog for democracy and a promoter of civic equality is very much in question today. One avenue of critique sees journalism as having shifted from watchdog to mad dog, mindlessly attacking authority (especially governments), avoiding 'serious' news about public affairs in favour of scandals, celebrities, and 'infotainment.' In doing so, the media are reputedly blocking governments' efforts to communicate with citizens and even threatening the legitimacy of democratic public authority.[3] In this view, media are undermining rather than facilitating public discourse on matters of common concern, thus degrading and reducing the public sphere – those forums and interactions (such as politics, the media, and the workplace) where important public issues are debated and discussed, and where informed public opinion can in principle be created.

Another critique sees the media not as mad dogs, but as lap dogs, excessively subservient to the economic and political elite. Best known through Herman and Chomsky's propaganda model, the media are seen to legitimize the unjust policies and privileges of the state and corporations while muzzling the voices of fundamental dissent and marginalizing ordinary citizens from political debate, positioning them as passive spectators. For Herman and Chomsky, five filters ensure that media 'manufacture' the subordinate population's consent to elite domination: concentrated corporate media ownership, advertising, dependence on elite news sources, flak from right-wing institutes, and the 'national religion' of anti-Communism (in the United States) and free market fundamentalism.[4]

While the mad dog and lap dog theories suggest quite different media-authority relations, they are not as contradictory as they might appear. The mad dog theory suggests that the commercial media's infotainment orientation serves to distract broader publics from serious political issues and undermines the public sphere. In so doing, the media are reinforcing the political status quo by constraining oppositional mobilization, an impact consistent with the lap dog view. Similarly, if the media's alleged mad dog hostility to authority is selectively directed not against the private sector but against government bureaucrats and politicians (especially left-of-centre governments), then the media's impact is consistent with the lap dog theory: unaccountable corporate power is legitimized at the expense of a positive economic role for democratically elected governments.

There are, however, problems with this perspective. The North American left, especially in the United States, has tended to conceptualize the relationship between power, media, and public consciousness in terms of notions like propaganda, bias, and indoctrination. Such notions usefully direct us to the power imbalances in the media and political systems, but they have some significant drawbacks. They lead people on the left too easily to scapegoat the media for political failures and problems whose roots lie elsewhere and to ignore the real spaces for representing progressive views even in the corporate, commercial media.

Moreover, notions like propaganda and indoctrination are too simplistic. They imply intentional efforts to manipulate and persuade. Such efforts do of course exist; they are at the core of the massive advertising and public relations industries. But such general notions ignore the complexity of the processes through which news is produced in organizations and consumed (or interpreted) by audiences. The limits and pressures on the news system are broader than the commonsensical notion of media owner and advertiser influence. Concepts like agenda-setting, spiral of silence, cultivation, and ideology offer more useful ways to think about the media's impact on public orientations towards civic equality and other political values.

The media's agenda-setting role is a by-product of our collective dependence on mass media for information beyond our direct experience. It was Bernard Cohen who originally suggested that the press 'may not be successful much of the time in telling people what to think, but it is stunningly successful in telling its readers what to think about.'[5] Through their ability to focus public attention on some events and issues, and away from others, the media influence public perceptions of what exists, what is important, what is good and valuable, what is bad and threatening, and what is related to what.[6] While the media's definitions of reality have in the first instance a cognitive or perceptual impact, attitudinal consequences may well follow. For instance, if public perceptions of the extent of welfare fraud are heightened by sustained media coverage, negative public attitudes towards welfare recipients or social welfare programs could also be reinforced.

The flip side of agenda-setting is the spiral of silence.[7] Many people who hold views which they feel are in a minority and seldom expressed in public become reluctant to express them for fear of social isolation; without social reinforcement, their own adherence to these views declines. This social psychological mechanism suggests that if the media are (wittingly or not) avoiding significant topics or muzzling some viewpoints, these omissions can have substantial political consequences. In the long run, media help shape what counts as an acceptable or legitimate opinion.

The process of cultivation is similarly cumulative and long term. It is associated with the work of American communication scholar George Gerbner and his cultural indicators research. It suggests that prolonged use of media, particularly television, tends to cultivate a certain set of perceptions and sensibilities. The basic idea is that TV viewing 'gradually leads to the adoption of beliefs about the nature of the social world which conform to the stereotyped, distorted and very selective view of reality as portrayed in a systematic way in television fiction and news.'[8] For example, according to some studies, those who watch a lot of television are more likely than others to see the world as threatening, to overestimate crime rates, and to be less trustful of other people. The theory also holds that within its current industrial, commercial framework, television (at least in the United States), 'serves primarily to maintain, stabilize and reinforce rather than to alter, threaten or weaken conventional belief and behaviours.'[9]

Taken together, these concepts point to the ideological role of news media. Social theorists have generated dozens of different definitions of ideology, which will not be explored here. Instead, I simply suggest that ideology points to a connection between power and signification, the social process of producing meanings. Ideology can be understood as the production of meaning in the service of power;[10] but unlike propaganda, ideology is not produced with the intention to dominate, manipulate, or persuade. Rather, it typically involves unconscious or taken-for-granted value commitments and assumptions about reality, assumptions that seem to be natural, the way things are. News is ideological to the extent that, wittingly or otherwise, it constructs symbolic maps of the world which favour dominant values, institutions, elites, or (especially) social relations – at the expense of alternative mappings of social reality.

Does it make sense to say that news accounts in commercial media in modern democracies are ideological? Is the keystone of Western journalistic professionalism not its commitment to objectivity, to reporting 'the facts' impartially, and getting 'both sides' of any controversial story? The reality is more complex. Even at its most objective and with the best of professional intentions, journalism cannot escape judgments about what counts as a newsworthy 'story,' what are the pertinent issues in a dispute, who constitutes a relevant and credible source, what is the appropriate (even if implicit) context in which to place the story, and so on. Of particular importance are media 'frames' – 'persistent patterns of cognition, interpretation, and presentation, of selection, emphasis and exclusion, by which symbol-handlers routinely organize discourse, whether verbal or visual.'[11] A story can be balanced in the sense of quoting spokespeople from both sides of an issue, and yet ideological in the way it defines or frames the issue itself. (The reduction of complex issues to two sides is itself an ideological operation.)

One example of media framing: major Canadian dailies now routinely report the right-wing Fraser Institute's 'Tax Freedom Day' each year, which is based on dividing the year into two parts equivalent to the portion of Canadians' income paid to government and that part which they keep 'for themselves.' The typical press story might quote a critic of this media-oriented gimmick, but it also incorporates the Institute's highly debatable assumptions into the very text – for example, headlines like 'Finally you can stop working for Tax Collectors,' and 'Heavy burden: until Monday, all you earn this year goes to pay tax.' Largely absent are counter-balancing themes, such as the vastly different impact of taxation and spending on higher and lower income earners, the benefits average Canadians derive from well-targeted public spending, and the long-term increase of personal taxation and decline of corporate taxation. In contrast, the Canadian Labour Congress's Corporate-Tax Freedom Day, which occurs much earlier in the year than the Fraser Institute's Day, is virtually blacked out in the media.[12]

Representing Equality

In relation to civic equality, the media's ideological role has two broad dimensions: first, their construction or representation of equality as a political issue in news narrative, and second, the ways in which the very institutional structure of media reinforce social relations of equality or inequality. The ideological roles of the media are complex; here, I simply sketch in some of their aspects.

It would be inaccurate to suggest that the Canadian news media routinely present Canadian society as naturally, inevitably, and justifiably inegalitarian. If Canada's news media do in certain respects reinforce civic inequality, it is not because they typically endorse Marie Antoinette's 'let them eat cake' world-view. There is, after all, a very strong populist and anti-elitist streak in contemporary Canadian journalism, especially in the mass-market tabloid press and commercial television news. Rather, the problem resides in the ways the media tend to define equality and to present it as a largely achieved state of affairs.

The news draws from, and contributes to, the values and assumptions of its surrounding culture. Two decades ago, sociologist Herbert Gans described what he saw as the 'enduring values' of American journalism: ethnocentrism, meritocratic and altruistic democracy, responsible capitalism, small-town pastoralism, moderatism, and rugged individualism.[13] About the same time, Todd Gitlin argued that news is skewed towards representing people and frames compatible with the 'dominant hegemonic principles,' namely, private control of commodity production and the prerogatives of capital, the national security state, the right and ability of authorized agencies to manage conflict and reform, selected violations of the moral code, and individualism – within corporate and bureaucratic structures – as the measure of social existence.[14] Similarly, John Hartley argued that British journalism's underlying 'cultural maps' of the social world assume society to be fragmented into distinct spheres (politics, economy, sports, family life, etc.); composed of individual persons who are the authors of social and political action; hierarchical in the sense that some people, events, and spheres are more important than others; and diverse and pluralistic yet consensual by nature: that is, a fundamental agreement on certain basic values and institutions is assumed as a precondition for identifying what constitutes news.[15]

It seems reasonable to assume that similar values also inform journalism in Canada, another liberal democracy with a capitalist economy. These values resonate with a market-liberal conception of equality as formal, legal equality for individual citizens – equal rights for individuals under the law, equal opportunity to compete for jobs or other economic resources, and the equal right to vote in elections. Such an individual-centred definition of equality precludes an alternative conception of equality between collectivities, one which historically has been essential to the Québécois conception of Canada as a compact between two founding peoples. (The Parti Québécois's slogan for the 1980 sovereignty-association referendum was 'Egal à Egal.') Moreover, the dominant, liberal conception of equality does not address structural inequalities of material wealth and social condition – in short, of social class. Instead, the liberal conception means the equal legal right to compete economically in order to become unequal. The corrosive impact of significant economic inequality on a key democratic premise – meaningful political and legal equality – is not a subject high in the media agenda.

During the 1990s, most Canadian media enthusiastically embraced the liberal conception of equality, and much else of the market liberal agenda of privatization, deregulation, free trade, lower taxation, and cutbacks to public services and programs.[16] In so doing, the media helped to push the question of growing substantive economic inequality onto the political back burner. To the extent that the media did display a crusading zeal on equality issues, they focused on social equality for women, gays, and Aboriginal people. Income and class disparities were largely ignored.

Research conducted by News Watch Canada, a media monitoring project at Simon Fraser University, provides evidence of the media's emphasis on market liberalism and related corporate interests. One obvious clue has been the dominance as a source of news of corporate-funded, market liberal think-tanks in comparison with their left-wing rivals. A study analysing seven Canadian dailies found an overall ratio of more than two to one.[17] Similarly, in the op/ed pages of six major papers in 1998, market liberal viewpoints were twice as frequent as advocacy for social programs or other positive economic roles for government. In contrast, progressive viewpoints outweighed traditional conservative perspectives on moral issues, like abortion, which arguably impinge less on corporate priorities.[18]

The shift towards more market- and business-friendly journalism is evident in other ways as well. In Canada's third largest city, Vancouver, for instance, the *Vancouver Sun's* business news traditionally greatly outweighs labour news in both amount and favourability of treatment. That discrepancy increased in the 1990s. Labour news tended to be about 'negative' events, especially strikes; business news covered a much wider range of topics. Labour spokespeople were much more likely than those from business to be counterbalanced by opposing sources.[19]

Similarly, the Toronto dailies framed the 1996 Days of Action rallies against cutbacks in social programs by the Harris government as deviance and disruption rather than legitimate political protest. The dailies also exaggerated organized labour's role in the protests, largely ignoring the broad range of social advocacy groups who were involved.[20]

Another study focused on a comparison of news coverage of poverty in 1987 and 1997. In both years news representation of poverty, social inequality, and the poor was slight. To be sure, the poor were covered in each year in a relatively sympathetic light, although by 1997, a growing proportion of news stories portrayed the poor as threatening or undeserving. Overall attention to the issue of poverty declined, even though the official poverty rate in Canada had grown. Differences in the kinds of sources accessed in stories about the poor also emerged. Over the ten-year period spokespersons representing the poor declined somewhat, while business and (especially) government spokespeople increased.[21]

There was also a greater tendency to identify 'taxpayers' as a stakeholder group in stories about poverty. The positioning of the assumed average audience members as taxpayers is now a general phenomenon in news discourse and it has serious ideological implications. It displaces the concept of universal citizenship with an implication that only those sufficiently affluent to pay taxes have a right to a voice in public affairs. It easily coheres with market liberalism's obsession with alleged government inefficiency and waste, and with fiscal restraint as the key measure of all public policy.

Some caveats are in order. First, these patterns are not monolithic. In Vancouver, for example, the commercial dailies did report on a prolonged strike by projectionists, even though major theatre chains were big advertisers. Moreover, there is some diversity within and between different news outlets. To take one example, while free market policy institutes greatly outnumbered their progressive counterparts as news sources in most papers, there were differences related to the ownership and culture of media organizations. Right-wing institutes were only slightly favoured in Canada's largest daily, the *Toronto Star*, while in Thomson papers they were preferred 2 to 1, in Hollinger papers 3 to 1, and in the unabashedly conservative *Toronto Sun*, 29 to 1.[22]

Still, the News Watch research indicates that poverty and class inequality is a publicly significant but under-covered topic in Canada's press as a whole. The research suggests other, and often related, blind spots as well: the extent of Canada's involvement in militarism, and its negative consequences; environmental degradation as a systemic problem; the perspective of non-Québécois francophone minorities in Canada's constitutional debates; religion and traditional social values; human rights abuses by Canada's major trading partners; white-collar and corporate crime, which costs Canadians an estimated $30 billion annually; the power of the public relations industry; most news about labour, apart from disruptive strikes; alternatives to the market liberal policies of privatization and free trade; and the vested interests of media companies themselves.[23]

Structural Inequality in the Media

Are such blind spots haphazard? Do they reflect lack of public interest in these topics? Or is there a tendency to privilege some social and political voices, issues, and perspectives over others embedded in the institutional logic of the news media? Is inequality structurally entrenched in the news system?

According to conventional libertarians and market liberals, a private-sector, advertising-financed, market-oriented media system is the epitome of press freedom and democracy. It delivers media content inexpensively to consumers, it is responsive to consumer demand, and it offers a bulwark against government censorship, propaganda, and other abuses of power. So goes the standard argument, and as noted above, the press has indeed played a role in creating public space vis-à-vis authoritarian governments.

Nevertheless, in an era when a handful of transnational conglomerates dominate global media markets,[24] the context is vastly different. In liberal democracies, where legal freedom of the press from the state is quite secure, corporate and commercial pressures upon and within the media system may well constitute the greatest threat to the democratic functions of the press.

Since the federal government's enquiry on the Canadian media in 1970, critics within the media and without have been warning that the structure of the press may be at odds with democratic values like equality, represenitive diversity, and civic participation.[25] Consider daily newspaper journalism which, even in the Internet era, remains the agenda-setting base of the information pyramid. Critics have pointed to some troubling trends: the links between media owners and the rest of the business elite; the disproportionate political power of corporate-financed advocacy groups as sources of news; the decline of competition within local newspaper markets; the growing regional and national concentration of the industry, with the Hollinger chain owning about 55 of Canada's 105 dailies as of August 1999, when it sold many of them to I.H. Asper's CanWest Global Communication Corp.; the displacement of the family-owned firms of yesteryear by shareholder-driven, bottom-line-oriented conglomerates on the one hand, and influence-seeking right-wing press barons on the other.

Critics also note the continued dependence of dailies on advertising for up to 80 per cent of revenues, and their orientation towards upscale readers whom advertisers want to reach. Moreover, critics argue, as competition for ad revenue grows fiercer, editors' autonomy from commercial pressure declines, and journalism shifts from a civic culture of public service towards a market-survey culture of infotainment.

Potential consequences include a conservative or pro-business bias in the press, potential power over the public agenda residing in fewer hands, the loss of editorial diversity as chains rationalize their resources, and a disconnection between chain newspapers and local communities. Moreover, independent public affairs journalism may be eclipsed by attention-grabbing scandals, eroded by drastic downsizing in smaller market papers, and stifled by the avoidance of negative news about major advertisers or media-owning corporate empires. (For instance, fear of reprisals from condominium developers – whether through an advertiser boycott or libel suits is a contested point – apparently prevented timely whistle-blowing on Vancouver's leaky condo fiasco. Some *Vancouver Sun* reporters had begun (un)covering this story as early as 1993, but the *Sun* and most other Vancouver media largely neglected it until it exploded in 1997 as a billion dollar disaster.)

One cannot deny that at its best, commercially oriented media in liberal democracies have positive economic, social, and indeed political functions, such as promoting more open government. Moreover, corporate imperatives are certainly not journalism's whole reality. Other influences include journalists' news values, organizational routines, cultural meta-narratives, and much else.[26]

Nevertheless, the corporate-dominated, profit-driven global media system at the start of the twenty-first century subtly but profoundly institutionalizes undemocratic values. Today, the primary justification for the commercial media system is that of 'consumer sovereignty' – the idea that the media respond effectively to consumer choice and thus 'give people what they want.' 'If there's not enough international news and too much Jerry Springer,' media apologists might say, 'don't blame us. That's what people choose to watch.'

There are two problems with this argument. First, it assumes that media audiences are primarily consumers rather than citizens. From a democratic standpoint, the two concepts (and the media programming they imply) are radically different. 'Citizen' implies active participation in civic affairs; 'consumer' implies the more private and passive role of material consumption. Citizens in a democratic state are in principle equal; consumers in a market economy are unequal, since their ability to consume commodities depends upon their purchasing power. Second, the 'consumer sovereignty' argument does not work even on its own terms. It conveys an image of unified and determined consumers barking orders to compliant media corporations, who then produce the programming that consumers want.

In reality, many structural factors refract or undermine the expression of consumer preferences in commercial media content. As various scholars have noted,[27] these structural factors include high entry costs and oligopoly (the small number of competitors) in media markets; the political biases and interests of media owners, interests which are not simply reducible to commercial considerations; the dispersion and diversity of media audiences, whose power is thus far more diffused than that of media corporations; and audiences' routinized use of media, much media being a matter of habitual choices rather than strong preferences for the programming offered.

The brand-name recognition, access to distribution networks, and the cross-promotional strategies of large media corporations also reduce consumer choice by driving alternative media products to the margins. Moreover, the need to recoup over large markets the huge production costs of blockbuster films and television programs limits consumer sovereignty. It has been plausibly argued that the main reason that so many Hollywood films overflow with violence is that such films are the easiest genre to export to foreign markets; they require little cultural or linguistic translation.[28]

Similar economy-of-scale reasons account for the prevalence of American rather than home-grown programming on prime-time Canadian commercial television. Evidence suggests that given a choice of two programs with similar production values, Canadian audiences would prefer the domestic program. However, Canadian broadcasters can import U.S. programs which have already recovered their production costs in the huge American market far more cheaply than they can finance the production of similar programs within the much smaller Canadian market. A parallel economic logic also puts Canadian magazines at a disadvantage with the 'split run' editions of their American competitors.

Finally, the consumer sovereignty argument ignores the crucial role of advertising. Economically, the commercial media's bread is buttered not by audiences as such, but by advertisers who pay for access to audiences of the right kind. The commercial imperative to attract the right kinds of audiences whose attention can be sold to advertisers has had decidedly inegalitarian consequences. Advertisers are interested in reaching not just anyone, but those people most likely to buy their products – in particular, affluent people such as professionals, investors, and executives. The commercial media have an incentive to tailor their content to appeal to the cultural and political sensibilities of the affluent, sensibilities which on economic issues tend to be conservative.

Affluent consumers thus have a disproportionate influence in determining what kinds of media content and media outlets will economically flourish, and which ones will be driven to the wall. In the history of the British and North American press, there have been radical and progressive papers that reached a substantial working-class readership, but they could not survive once the popular press became a mainly advertising-dependent medium in the late 1800s; their readers were not of particular interest to advertisers. Not surprisingly, as a Canadian Royal Commission on Newspapers pointed out, 'It was left-wing viewpoints that tended to be under-represented as commercialism increased its hold.'[29]

For other reasons as well, advertising has made the political content of commercial media more conservative. Press history suggests that large advertisers 'disliked liberal and radical-left views that might raise questions about the role of big business.'[30] By toning down such views in their editorials, news selection, and investigative initiatives, newspapers are more likely to attract conservative-minded advertisers. Advertising-based media also face economic incentives to avoid divisive issues and to offer political blandness, for fear of alienating portions of their intended audience, and to promote consumerist values and lifestyle issues over other social values (like ecological sustainability), which might contradict the advertising messages.

Small wonder that some scholars describe advertisers as '*a de facto* licensing authority,' the ultimate force behind a system of market censorship. The logic of democracy is one person, one vote; the logic of market-driven media, however, is one dollar, one vote.[31] The commercial media do not simply 'give people what they want.' They give some of the people part of what they think they want: programming that media corporations find economical and convenient to offer, that is generally compatible with a consumerist stance, and that affluent and/or mass consumers (who lack ready access to the full range of potential alternatives) are prepared to accept as a reward for joining the audience. The commercial media satisfy primarily those communication needs compatible with the marketing of commodities, largely ignoring those needs that no one can make money from or that threaten a consumerist culture. These include the need, in a democracy, for a reasonably egalitarian forum for civil public discourse.[32]

The inegalitarian structural biases of the commercial media are not likely to be corrected through market forces. Such forces, I have argued, are the problem, not the solution. Nor can we count on the much-touted Internet or the Information Superhighway to provide a more egalitarian communication network. For all its democratic and interactive potential, the Internet is becoming colonized by the same commercial logic and corporate giants (joined by telecommunications and computer conglomerates as well) that dominate the traditional information media, in the absence of a countervailing public policy.[33]

What is required is a new public policy to reform the media system so that it promotes rather than inhibits egalitarian, democratic public debate. Governments, however, are unlikely to act in the absence of a widespread popular movement demanding such reform. Fortunately, there are signs that coalitions for media democratization are beginning to emerge – for example, the Friends of Canadian Broadcasting, the Cultural Environment in the United States, and the Campaign for Press and Broadcasting Freedom in the United Kingdom. For several decades, the political right has taken very seriously the need to monitor, massage, and even intimidate the media, as part of its project of establishing the hegemony of market liberalism.[34] Those who wish to build a commitment to civic equality in public policy debate need to help democratize the power and structure of the commercial information media. The left needs to convey the message of equality through the media; democracy needs to reinvigorate structures of equality in the media.

NOTES

1 George Comstock, S. Chaffee, N. Katzman, M. McCombs, and D. Roberts, *Television and Human Behavior* (New York: Columbia University Press, 1978), 315.

2 Robert A. Hackett and Yuezhi Zhao, *Sustaining Democracy: Journalism and the Politics of Objectivity* (Toronto: Garamond, 1998), 32; Dan Schiller, *Objectivity and the News* (Philadelphia: University of Pennsylvania Press, 1981), 87, 181.

3 For a much-discussed (though limited) critique of this kind, see James

Fallows, *Breaking the News: How the Media Undermine American Democracy* (New York: Pantheon, 1996).

4 Edward S. Herman and Noam Chomsky, *Manufacturing Consent: The Political Economy of the Mass Media* (New York: Pantheon, 1988).

5 Bernard C. Cohen, *The Press and Foreign Policy* (Princeton: Princeton University Press, 1963), 13.

6 This formula is adapted from George Gerbner, 'Toward "Cultural Indicators": The analysis of mass mediated public messages systems,' in G. Gerbner, O.R. Holsti, K. Krippendorff, W.J. Paisley, and P.J. Stone, eds., *The Analysis of Communication Content* (New York: John Wiley, 1969), 121–32.

7 This concept was introduced by Elizabeth Noelle-Neumann in the 1970s. For a summary, see Denis McQuail, *Mass Communication Theory: An Introduction*, 3rd ed., (London: Sage, 1994), 361–3.

8 McQuail, *Mass Communication*, 364–5.

9 L.P. Gross, 'Television as a Trojan Horse,' *School Media Quarterly* (Spring 1977): 175–80; cited in McQuail, *Mass Communication*, 364.

10 John B. Thompson, *Studies in the Theory of Ideology* (Berkeley: University of California Press, 1984), 73–147.

11 Todd Gitlin, *The Whole World Is Watching: Mass Media in the Making and Unmaking of the New Left* (Berkeley: University of California Press, 1980), 7.

12 This example derives from Hackett and Zhao, *Sustaining Democracy*, chap. 6.

13 Herbert J. Gans, *Deciding What's News* (New York: Vintage Books, 1980), 42–52.

14 Gitlin, *The Whole World Is Watching*, 258, 271.

15 John Hartley, *Understanding News* (London: Methuen, 1982), 81–3.

16 Hackett and Zhao, *Sustaining Democracy*, chap. 6.

17 Unpublished News Watch research, conducted for News Watch Canada by Nathan Elliott and Jodi Patsch, 1999.

18 Unpublished News Watch research, conducted by John Boyd, Susan Postma, Chris Skerik, and Amanda Wood, 1999.

19 Donald Gutstein with Robert Hackett and News Watch Canada, *Question the Sun! A Content Analysis of Diversity in the Vancouver Sun before and after the Hollinger Take-over* (Burnaby, B.C.: News Watch Canada, July 1998). The report can be found on the Internet at http://newswatch.cprost.sfu.ca. The original study of labour news was conducted by Dianne Birch and Trevor Hughes. Also in Robert A. Hackett and Richard Gruneau, with Donald Gutstein, Timothy A. Gibson, and Newswatch Canada, *The Missing News: Filters and Blind Spots in Canada's Press* (Toronto: Garamond and Ottawa: Canadian Centre for Policy Alternatives, 2000), 194–5.

20 James Compton, 'Toronto Papers Misrepresented Last Year's Days of

Action,' *News Watch Monitor*, 1, (2) (Fall 1997), iv. Also in Hackett et al., *The Missing News*, 196–7.

21 Gutstein et al., *Question the Sun!*, 31–8. The research was undertaken by Scott Uzelman, Louise Barkholt, and Christine Krause. Also in Hackett et al., *The Missing News*, 197–201.

22 Unpublished News Watch research, conducted by Nathan Elliott and Jodi Patsch, 1999.

23 Robert A. Hackett, 'Missing News,' in Peter Phillips and Project Censored, *Censored 1999: The News that Didn't Make the News* (New York: Seven Stories Press, 1999), 143–4; see also Hackett et al., *The Missing News*, chaps. 6 and 7.

24 Edward S. Herman and Robert W. McChesney, *The Global Media: The New Missionaries of Global Capitalism* (London and Washington: Cassell, 1997).

25 The critiques of the newspaper industry derive from a variety of sources: Canada, Special Senate Committee on the Mass Media, *Report*, vol. 1, *The Uncertain Mirror* (Ottawa: Information Canada, 1970); Wallace Clement, *The Canadian Corporate Elite* (Toronto: McClelland & Stewart, 1975); Canada, Royal Commission on Newspapers, *Report* (Hull, Que: Supply and Services Canada, 1981); Paul Audley, *Canada's Cultural Industries* (Toronto: Lorimer, 1983), chap. 1; Doug Underwood, *When MBAs Rule the Newsroom* (New York: Columbia University Press, 1993); James Winter, *Democracy's Oxygen: How Corporations Control the News* (Montreal: Black Rose Books, 1996); Ben Bagdikian, *The Media Monopoly*, 5th ed. (Boston: Beacon Press, 1997); John Miller, *Yesterday's News* (Halifax: Fernwood, 1998); Hackett and Zhao, *Sustaining Democracy*, chap. 3; Robert W. McChesney, *Corporate Media and the Threat to Democracy* (New York: Seven Stories Press, 1997); Herman and McChesney, *The Global Media*.

26 For a very useful synthesis of research on factors which influence news selection and presentation, see Pamela Shoemaker and Stephen Reese, *Mediating the Message: Theories of Influences on Mass Media Content*, 2nd ed. (White Plains, N.Y.: Longman, 1996).

27 James Curran, 'Mass Media and Democracy Revisited,' in James Curran and Michael Gurevitch, eds., *Mass Media and Society*, 2nd ed. (London: Arnold, 1996), 801–19; Herman and McChesney, *Global Media*, 190–1.

28 George Gerbner, 'Introduction,' in Kate Duncan, ed., *Liberating Alternatives: The Founding Convention of the Cultural Environment Movement* (Cresskill, N.J.: Hampton Press, 1999), 8–9.

29 Canada, Royal Commission on Newspapers, 15.

30 Bagdikian, *Media Monopoly*, 129–30; Hackett and Zhao, *Sustaining Democracy*, 69.

31 James Curran and Jean Seaton, *Power without Responsibility* (London and New York: Methuen, 1985), 41; McChesney, *Corporate Media*, 45; Hackett and Zhao, *Sustaining Democracy*, 185–8.

32 Hackett and Zhao, *Sustaining Democracy*, 188.

33 Ibid., 190–200; McChesney, *Corporate Media*, 30ff.; Herman and McChesney, *Global Media*, chap. 4.

34 The most obvious example of such market-liberal media mobilization in Canada is the Fraser Institute's National Media Archive, which churns out report after report implying that the news media – most especially, the public-funded CBC – is too left wing.

12

Growing Inequality: What the World Thinks

DANIEL SAVAS[1]

Disparity in wealth is increasing everywhere, both within and between countries. Americans (and a few others) see this as the natural order. But most do not and most approve of state intervention to reduce the gap between richest and poorest. Many observers interpret this widening chasm as a wake-up call, a signal that the beast of disparity is prepared to move in unpredictable and menacing ways. But in some quarters there is still a sense of dreamy contentment.

Social policy and development experts warn that such contentment is, indeed, a dream. They point to the legions of disenfranchised and disaffected, even in the midst of plenty, and say worse is yet to come. The growing inequality among people within and between countries could, if unchecked, lead to instability, conflict, and fear. Increasingly, members of the world development community are rallying around strategies they feel have a good chance of relieving the disparity without compromising national sovereignty or stunting economic growth.

The *Angus Reid World Monitor* has explored public sentiment in thirty-two countries around the globe on two related disparity issues: whether some individuals have a right to amass great wealth while others have little, and whether the state has an obligation to reduce the imbalance between the haves and have-notes. Overall, there is a slim consensus against massive wealth accumulation in the face of poverty and, where the natural order needs a nudge, an acknowledgment that government intervention is proper.

But this consensus is fashioned from hugely disparate viewpoints.

Alone in one corner stands the United States, where extremes are the norm. In an Angus Reid World Poll conducted in May and June 1998, nearly two in three U.S. respondents (65 per cent) agreed with the

TABLE 12.1
Should the rich get richer? Public sentiment in most of the 32 countries polled found unfettered wealth accumulation unacceptable

Not acceptable (%)	Country	Acceptable (%)
21	Taiwan	74
32	U.S.	65
36	Israel	60
41	Poland	52
45	Malaysia	51
47	China*	50
44	Australia	49
48	Canada	49
45	Czech Republic	48
51	Turkey	45
48	South Korea	43
50	South Africa*	43
52	U.K.	43
54	Norway	43
58	Thailand*	41
50	Russia*	39
57	Denmark	39
59	Greece	38
63	Belgium	35
64	Brazil*	35
55	Japan	34
65	Germany	33
68	Sweden	30
68	Mexico**	30
68	Italy	27
74	Indonesia**	24
71	Argentina	23
75	Colombia*	23
74	France	22
73	Spain	21
78	Netherlands	20
80	India**	17

*Urban samples
**Urban middle/upper SECs

statement: 'People should be allowed to accumulate as much wealth as they can, even if some make millions while others live in poverty.' The average across all thirty-two countries polled was 42 per cent in favour of the unimpeded pursuit of plenty and 52 per cent opposed.

TABLE 12.2
Dealing with disparity. Should government reduce the income gap?

Yes, intervene (%)	Country	No, leave alone (%)
28	U.S.	69
51	Canada	47
55	Denmark	39
57	South Africa	39
60	Netherlands	38
58	Czech Republic	37
58	Japan	36
60	U.K.	35
60	Australia	35
63	France	34
63	Israel	33
64	Belgium	33
67	Sweden	31
68	Mexico	29
72	Thailand	28
65	Poland	28
69	South Korea	26
73	Italy	23
74	Colombia	22
76	India	22
75	Germany	21
76	Malaysia	21
70	Russia	20
71	Spain	19
77	Taiwan	18
78	China	17
79	Greece	17
80	Norway	17
81	Indonesia	17
83	Brazil	17
84	Turkey	12
84	Argentina	11

While America's libertarian view was shared by most of those polled in Taiwan (74 per cent) and Israel (60 per cent), a second, related question set the United States apart. When confronted with the proposition, 'It is the responsibility of the government to reduce the differences in income between people with high incomes and those with low incomes,' there were thundering objections from citizens of the world's only superpower. Almost seven in ten U.S. respondents (69 per cent) disagreed with the statement. This is double the survey average and makes the United States the only one of thirty-two countries surveyed in which this is the majority view. The American aversion to state intrusion was powerful and pervasive, cutting across lines of gender, age, and even personal income.

Perhaps not surprisingly, given the U.S. influence on Canada, America's northern neighbour exhibited the next strongest discomfort with government intervention (47 per cent resistant, 51 per cent in favour). But consider the difference in scope between the two otherwise reasonably similar countries: the 47 per cent of Canadians opposed to state measures to reduce economic disparity is a significant twenty-two percentage points lower than the 69 per cent in the United States.

Indeed, outside of the United States, a government role in narrowing the income gap was supported by a majority in every country surveyed – from 51 per cent in Canada to 84 per cent in Argentina and Turkey. Even in Taiwan and Israel, where unfettered wealth accumulation was deemed acceptable, 77 per cent and 63 per cent respectively approved of state-sponsored levelling.

Examining the numbers more closely, other powerful threads emerge. For example, the richer people are, the less willing they are to part with their assets. Within and across countries, top-income earners are most likely to favour the piling up of wealth and to oppose redistribution measures.

In fact, when respondents are grouped into thirds according to household income, spreads of more than twenty percentage points on both questions emerge between the richest and poorest groups within countries as diverse as Canada, the Czech Republic, and South Africa. In the United States, fully 70 per cent of the wealthiest respondents called for unrestricted wealth accumulation compared to 57 per cent of the poorest third. Only one in five of the top U.S. earners saw a useful role for government in spreading wealth around – half the proportion in the lowest-income group.

A similar, if somewhat more complex, correlation holds true for countries. Taken as a bloc, the highly industrialized OECD nations were more likely to favour the accumulation of personal wealth (44 per cent) than the less developed non-OECD portion of the survey (39 per cent). At the same time, the OECD grouping was much less enamoured with official redistribution policies (55 per cent), compared to the poorer countries (74 per cent). However, the libertarian impetus within the

OECD is driven principally by countries outside of western Europe, which by itself demonstrated strongly egalitarian sentiments.

The data also reinforce the image of women as 'the gentler sex.' With notable consistency, women in virtually every country favoured societies in which wealth is shared more equitably. The percentage-point gender gap was in the double digits in several countries polled, led by Belgium, Norway, urban Brazil, the Czech Republic, the Netherlands, Sweden, and the United States.

Age is also linked to attitudes on private wealth accumulation. In most countries surveyed, there was a distinct trend towards egalitarianism with rising age, although the trend was reversed in the recently dynamic economies of Thailand and Malaysia and a few other countries as well. The correlation between age and egalitarianism was most pronounced and consistent in eastern Europe, where the over-fifty-five cohort had grown up with communism. Indeed, the generation gap between this oldest group and respondents aged eighteen to thirty-four ranged from fifteen percentage points in Poland to thirty-five points in Russia, where the two generations hold completely opposite views.

On the other hand, the relationship between the age of respondents and their perceptions about the obligations of the state in rectifying disparity varied considerably and inconsistently across countries. Again, only eastern Europe revealed a strong and clear trend line, with faith in the state rising dramatically with age. There was 80–per-cent support for a government role in income redistribution among eastern Europeans aged over fifty-five, versus a more modest 58 per cent among their younger compatriots.

The two World Poll questions on wealth disparity were intentionally broad in scope. For instance, the questions were not limited to domestic economic disparity; they could just as easily have referred to imbalances between countries – the developed and the developing world, as an obvious example. Nor did the poor offer clues as to the form of any government action to redress disparities.

There are clearly both moral and economic dimensions to the disparity issue. Apart from the wasted economic potential, the statistics provoke serious ethical questions. For instance:

- Among the world's 192 countries, per capita gross national product (GNP) ranges from $80 to $45,360. At a time when the global economy is worth a total of $25 trillion, 1.3 billion people are living on less than $1 a day. (All figures in this article are in U.S. dollars.)

TABLE 12.3
What's mine is mine

		Gender		Age			Relative income		
	Overall (%)	Men (%)	Women (%)	18–34 (%)	35–54 (%)	55+ (%)	Lower (%)	Middle (%)	Higher (%)
Unfettered Wealth Accumulation Is Not Acceptable									
Overall	52	50	55	52	51	55	56	53	48
English-speaking	18	34	41	41	33	40	43	37	32
Western Europe	69	66	71	68	69	68	71	70	66
Eastern Europe	47	43	50	36	47	59	52	46	42
Asia	53	53	54	53	54	52	57	52	48
Latin America	70	67	72	66	72	74	73	69	64
Government Should Reduce Income Gap									
Overall	60	58	62	63	58	59	64	64	54
English-speaking	37	34	39	45	33	34	44	40	26
Western Europe	70	67	72	71	69	70	73	72	66
Eastern Europe	68	65	70	58	67	80	76	72	59
Asia	67	65	69	68	67	64	75	78	76
Latin America	78	76	80	76	78	81	78	78	77

Notes: Japan is excluded from relative income analysis; data not available. 'English-speaking' includes U.S., U.K., Australia, and Canada (including the one in four Canadians who are French-speaking). The above country groupings, while they include the appropriate countries from the survey sample, are necessarily incomplete since not all countries belonging in these groupings were included in the survey.

- The share in global income of the poorest 20 per cent of the world's people now stands at 1.1 per cent, halved from 2.3 per cent in 1960. The ratio of the incomes of the richest 20 per cent to the poorest 20 per cent rose from 30:1 in 1960 to 78:1 in 1994.
- The death rate of children under five ranges from 4 per 1,000 live births to 320 per 1,000. Every year, nearly 12 million children under five die in developing countries, more than half of them through malnutrition. In war-ravaged Sudan, at the time of the survey, more than 200,000 children were on the brink of starving to death.
- Primary school enrolment varies from 24 per cent of young people in some developing countries to 100 per cent in most developed countries. About 110 million children are out of school, and nearly a billion people are illiterate.

If the inequities between the industrialized and the developing world are stark, they are no less unjust within nations. Within the wealthy nations, they should be regarded as scandalous. Consider the following:

- In the United States, the world's strongest economy, some 14 million children in 1996 were living in households with incomes below the official poverty line.
- It is estimated that about three million people in the fifteen countries of the European Union do not have a permanent home. Homelessness is also pervasive in other wealthy nations; some 750,000 people are homeless in the United States.
- Eastern Europe and countries of the former Soviet Union have seen the greatest deterioration in the past decade. Where once only a small part of the population had poverty-level incomes, now about a third do – 120 million people in all.
- In industrialized countries, a total of 37 million people are looking for work.
- In India and Turkey, the gap between the proportions of boys and girls enrolled in primary school exceeds twenty percentage points.

The Gini coefficient, an economic measure of domestic income disparity,can be used to gauge inequity. The higher the coefficient, the more concentrated the wealth in a few hands. In South Africa, for instance, wealth is distributed more equitably among whites (a Gini coefficent of 48) than among the whole population (a coefficient of 62).

TABLE 12.4
For richer, for poorer. The degree of inequality in national wealth distribution

Country	Gini coefficient*	Country	Gini coefficient*
Argentina	48	Japan	35
Australia	36	South Korea	31
Belgium	29	Malaysia	48
Brazil	63	Mexico	57
Canada	33	Netherlands	29
China	38	Norway	27
Colombia	51	Poland	33
Czech Republic	28	South Africa	62
Denmark	29	Russia	30
France	34	Spain	26
Germany	26	Sweden	26
Greece	38	Taiwan	32
India	32	Thailand	54
Indonesia	32	Turkey	44
Israel	36	U.K.	32
Italy	27	U.S.	39

*The Gini coefficient describes the distribution of a nation's wealth across five population strata. The lower the number, the greater the equity of national wealth distribution; the higher the number, the more unequal that distribution. These Gini coefficients were gathered from a number of sources, notably the Luxembourg Income Study database and World Bank researchers Milanovic and Ying.

South Africa was one of eight countries in the survey where income disparity was more pronounced than in the United States (a coefficient of 38.5); the others were Thailand, Malaysia, Turkey, and the four Latin American countries, Mexico, Colombia, Brazil, and Argentina.

Such disparities are growing, even as the economic picture is improving throughout most of the world.

Per capita GNP in the dozen fastest-growing industrialized countries more than doubled between 1980 and 1995. In developing countries, too, output grew in the past year by 5.6 per cent, the highest rate in two decades.

The economic boom has generally also improved the standard of living. Life expectancy everywhere has risen more in the past forty years than in the previous four thousand. In the developing countries, child death rates have been more than halved since the 1960s. There have been dramatic improvements in nutrition and primary school education, and the proportion of rural families without access to safe water has fallen from nine-tenths to about one-quarter. Indeed, the United Nations Development Program predicted in its 1997 *Human Development Report* that by the end of the twentieth century, some three to four billion of the world's people will have experienced substantial improvements in their standards of living.

However, economists are divided on the nature of the link between economic growth and disparity. Economic growth can be an effective tool to reduce poverty, but its benefits are not automatic. For example, Argentina's annual per capita economic growth was 2 per cent throughout the 1950s, yet poverty as measured by household incomes rose. Similarly, the United Kingdom and the United States experienced good average growth during the period 1975 to 1995, yet the proportion of people living in poverty increased. Whether disparity impedes growth or is a by-product of it is a subject of endless academic debate.

Klause Deininger and Lyn Squire, both of the World Bank's Policy Research Department, recently wrote in the Bank's quarterly magazine, *Finance & Development*, that economic growth may not be tied to income inequality at all. The real culprit is an unequal distribution of fixed assets – principally land in developing countries. With possession of such fixed assets, even the income-poorest individuals gain better access to capital and are thus able to invest, improve their standard of living, and contribute to economic prosperity.

While the causes of inequality are contested, globalization and ruthless economic policies are seen as the leading contenders by many experts in the development community. Their argument is that economic advances founded on job cuts and wage reductions fuel growing income disparity, as the winners climb on the backs of the losers. Writing in *The Progress of Nations*, 1998, a UNICEF publication, Philip Alston draws attention to the disappearance of secure, full-time jobs – often in manufacturing – which has served to undermine family and community stability. Alston, who as chair of the UN Committee on Economic, Social and Cultural Rights, also criticizes the 'demonization of caring government,' which he says leads to declining public investment in social services and the non-profit sector, all in the name of global competitiveness. 'This has been accompanied by a parallel demonization of the poor themselves – with women who receive welfare cheques dismissed as "welfare queens" – which makes it easier for communities to cut funds and programs designed to assist the most fragile of its members.'

Such concepts as the existence of a social contract, of community, of concern for the long-term good, or even of public morality are discarded as people ignore the growing, simultaneous presence of high levels of prosperity on the one hand and homelessness on the other. The principles of economic and social rights are trampled without regard or regret.

While globalization has clearly helped reduce poverty in some of the largest and strongest economies – China and India among them – the greatest benefits have tended to be garnered by a more fortunate minority. And the continuation of discriminatory trade policies and protectionism by industrialized nations has hampered developing nations in taking full advantage of the shrinking global village. Clearly, fairer trade policies, in combination with investment in human development, must be part of any global solution.

Rich countries can also assist through debt relief, technical cooperation, and other forms of assistance. However, their record on direct development aid has been spotty at best. OECD figures show that aid contributions from industrialized countries amounted to $55.5 billion in 1996, down 16 per cent from 1992. As a proportion of GNP, official development aid from OECD countries fell to an average of 0.25 per cent in 1996 compared to 0.34 per cent in 1990. If this rate of decline continues, official development assistance will cease to exist by 2015.

One solution is to find better ways to concentrate aid and investment on basic services such as health and education and on opening up economic opportunities for employment. Just as important are strategies to help national economies mature. These include measures to enforce laws and fight corruption, rehabilitate infrastructure, develop financial and civic institutions, and encourage good governance and political involvement by the broadest spectrum of citizens.

Is life, liberty, and the unhampered pursuit of personal wealth what life is all about? James D. Wolfensohn, president of the World Bank, warned in a speech delivered in 1997 that wealthy nations can insulate themselves from the global poverty crisis for a time, but the bomb is ticking. Within thirty years, as many as five billion people could be living on the equivalent of less than two dollars a day. He warned that the tensions wrought by misery will spill over into terrorism and conflict which will not be restricted to distant corners of the Third World: no walls or gates will protect the haves from the have-nots, even in the most civil Western society. As the 'tragedy of exclusion' grows, so will crime, violence, and danger. No society will be spared the angry resentment of the marginalized and disenfranchised. He went on to say,

'Without equity, we will not have global stability. Without a better sense of social justice, our cities will not be safe and our societies will not be stable. Without inclusion, too many of us will be condemned to live separate, armed and frightened lives. Whether you broach it from the social or the economic or the moral perspective, this is a challenge we cannot afford to ignore.'

In addition to his moral argument, Wolfensohn issued an economic warning to the developed nations. The next twenty-five years will see a doubling of the share of global output by developing and transition economies such as China, India, Indonesia, Brazil, and Russia. Today these countries represent 50 per cent of the world's population, but only 8 per cent of its gross domestic product (GDP). Their share of world trade is only a quarter that of the European Union today. Yet by 2020, that share could be 50 per cent more than Europe's. In short, the tables could be turned. Current complacency by industrialized nations over yawning disparity is not only naïve, but myopic. Without appropriate global action, some of them could wind up on the wrong side of the wealth chasm.

NOTE

1 *World Poll, 1998,* presented by Daniel Savas on behalf of Angus Reid Group Inc., Vancouver, Canada. Article written by staff of writers of *Angus Reid World Monitor.*

13

The Economic Consequences of Financial Inequality

JIM STANFORD

Introduction

One of the greatest sources of inequality in Canadian society has become the lopsided ownership of financial wealth. Financial markets are portrayed in advertising and popular culture as the economic equivalent of the neighbourhood playground – something that is there for any child to play in regardless of his or her socio-economic status. But this portrayal is actually quite inaccurate. The large bulk of financial wealth is not owned through the pension funds of ordinary people or other quasi-'collective' forms of ownership. Most is owned the old-fashioned way: directly by individuals. And among those individual investors, the vast majority of shares are in the hands of a small elite of very well-off families.

The myth of 'people's capitalism' is a convenient one for those with vested interests in the continuing expansion and profitability of the financial industry. Financial industry advertising and briefs to government miss no opportunity to tell the public that what is good for the stock market must also be good for Canada. But in reality, the community of financiers is not at all inclusive. Indeed, the highly unequal distribution of financial wealth has distorted the operation of Canada's entire financial system, leading to an emphasis on macroeconomic and regulatory policies that enhance the value of narrowly held financial wealth at the expense of economic growth and job creation. In short, both the growing importance of financial wealth and its maldistribution have become barriers to the development and expansion of Canada's real economy – that is, the industries that produce the real goods and services that we consume every day and that determine our actual standard of living.

Conservatives argue that inequality is good for economic growth, as it creates incentives for harder work and innovation. In practice, however, the striking financial inequality which has arisen in Canada over the past two decades has distorted the incentive structure of Canada's economy and hampered growth. It has become consistently more profitable for investors to purchase paper assets instead of investing in real businesses. And the concentrated vested interest represented by the surprisingly small club of big-money financial investors represents a powerful constituency standing in the way of measures that would put more emphasis on real growth and job creation.

The Distribution of Wealth

Who owns the financial wealth of a country is a matter of considerable social and economic importance. Thus it is disturbing that Canada does not collect official statistics on the comparative ownership of wealth (including financial wealth) across different categories of households. Statistics Canada did compile such data in the past, but the last edition of this important research was published in 1984. Subsequent surveys were cancelled in the wake of the Mulroney government's budget cuts to the agency. Fifteen years later, Statistics Canada is finally implementing a new survey of household wealth, the first results of which are scheduled to be reported early in the new century. In the meantime, however, we can only guess at the true distribution of wealth on the basis of less official data.

Even before the Statistics Canada wealth survey was cancelled, it was already apparent that a dangerously unbalanced pattern of wealth ownership in Canada was emerging. The results of the final 1984 survey are summarized in Table 13.1. The richest quintile of all Canadian households owned over two-thirds of all household wealth. Excluding the value of residences, land, and other real assets, the top quintile's share of financial wealth (stocks, bonds, and other financial assets) was even larger: they owned fully three-quarters of all net financial wealth. The bottom 60 per cent of households, on the other hand, together accounted for just 6 per cent of net financial wealth – one-tenth of its share of the population. Not surprisingly, the poorest segments of society actually reported negative net financial wealth. It is important to note that the distribution of financial wealth is consistently more uneven than the distribution of total wealth. While the ownership of some real assets (especially primary residences) is reasonably widespread in Canadian society, the ownership of financial wealth is not.

TABLE 13.1
Distribution of wealth in Canada, 1984

Household category	Share of all household wealth (%)	Share of net financial assets (%)
1st Quintile (bottom 20%)	−0.3	−3.5
2nd Quintile	2.4	2.2
3rd Quintile (middle 20%)	9.3	7.3
4th Quintile	19.8	19.3
5th Quintile (top 20%)	68.8	74.7

Source: Statistics Canada Catalogue 13-588, *Changes in the Distribution of Wealth in Canada, 1970–1984*, June 1987.

The growing relative importance of financial wealth in the overall wealth of Canada, therefore, coincides with the growing maldistribution of overall wealth.

Has the evenness of the distribution of wealth improved since the last official survey on this subject in 1984? Not likely. Canada's real economy since the early 1980s has demonstrated an ongoing pattern of underperformance, as policy makers shifted their emphasis from reducing unemployment and spurring real growth in favour of controlling inflation and reducing the size of government. Chronic unemployment has increased, and so has the poverty rate. Incomes at the top end of society, meanwhile, have grown. In fact, the top quintile of households is the only segment which enjoyed higher income, after inflation, for most of the 1990s. Very high returns on financial assets during the low-inflation 1980s and 1990s explain a good part of the economic success that those in the higher-income brackets have enjoyed.

Despite the absence of official statistics, there are several clues available which hint at the extent to which financial wealth has become concentrated in the hands of the wealthiest households in the land. In each case, this evidence contrasts sharply with the popular image advanced by the financial industry that Canada is now a nation of personal investors – a community filled with frugal financiers, happily accumulating for the good of both themselves and the economy. The self-serving nature of the mythology of people's capitalism is clear: don't question any policies or decisions that may seem to be enhancing the economic prospects of a lucky few at the expense of the many, because in fact we all have a stake in the paper boom. Concerned about excessive bank profits? Don't worry, the executives say: one in two

Canadians owns at least one share of those banks through their mutual funds or pension funds, so in essence we all share in those profits. (Of course, it might take slightly more than one share before the benefits of being a bank 'owner' offset the costs of being a bank consumer, but that is another matter.) Concerned about more lay-offs at a company like CN Rail, which cut its workforce by 30 per cent between 1994 and 1998, yet more than doubled its profits? Don't be. It's been great for shareholders (the price of CN shares tripled between its initial privatization in 1995 and the announced round of lay-offs late in 1998), and that means it's good for you and me.[1] Concerned about economic and fiscal policies which have placed far more importance on maximizing the profitability of financial investments (through low inflation, high real interest rates, and financial deregulation) than on stimulating real growth and job creation? According to the theory of people's capitalism, everyone is both a worker and an investor. You might lose out in the workplace due to lay-offs and downsizing. But you'll be a winner on the stock market.

Individuals and Institutions

In reality, fewer than half of Canadians hold any direct stake in the stock market, and the total holdings of most of those who do own shares are economically trivial. What follows are a few of the clues which help to illustrate the extent to which financial wealth has become concentrated in the hands of a small group of families clustered at the top of the income ladder in Canada.

The largest single players in Canada's financial markets are now institutional investors: organizations such as mutual funds or pension funds, which represent the pooled assets of numerous much smaller investors. These institutional investors control huge sums of capital. The largest private pension fund in Canada, the Ontario Teachers' Pension Plan Board, held $65 billion in assets at the end of 1998. The largest mutual fund in Canada, the Templeton Growth Fund, controlled some $10 billion in assets at the same time. These large pools of accumulated capital naturally suggest a degree of concentrated decision-making power much larger than for other market players. Company executives regularly make the rounds of the important institutional investors, detailing their earnings forecasts and business plans and working hard to maintain the goodwill of these most powerful of financiers.

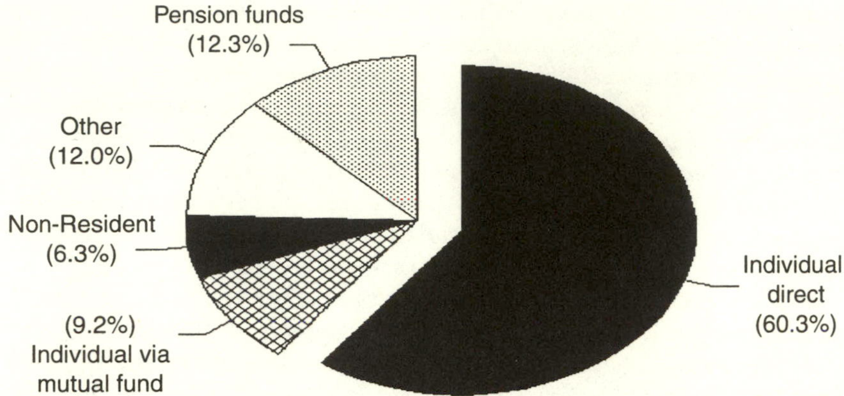

Source: Statistics Canada Catalogue 13-214, *National Balance Sheet Accounts.*

Figure 13.1. Ownership of corporate equities by sector, Canada, 1997.

In the wake of the growth of these institutional investors, it is often suggested that modern capitalism is moving towards a strange new form of collective ownership, in which average citizens come to own the companies they work for through their pension and mutual funds. Futurist Peter Drucker even titled his 1975 book on this subject, *The Unseen Revolution: Pension Fund Socialism in America.* This view implies a degree of popular participation in financial markets that is not justified by the evidence. Despite the importance of particular large funds, pension and mutual funds in general account for only a minority of total financial wealth in Canada. And, in fact, that share is likely to decline in coming years.

The size and visibility of particular large institutions does not necessarily mean that wealth ownership in this new era has somehow become a more 'collective' and participatory undertaking. Institutional investors, despite their large individual size, still account for a minority of total equity ownership. Figure 13.1 indicates the total ownership of corporate equities in Canada, as described by the national wealth accounting system of Statistics Canada. Despite their visibility and concentrated decision-making power, pension funds owned just 12 per cent of all equities as of the end of 1997. Mutual funds, which represent the pooled purchase of assets by individual investors, accounted for another 9 per cent. The large majority of all equities – 60 per cent as of the end of 1997 – is still owned by Canadians who purchase company shares directly. Other assorted investors – including non-residents, banks, insurance companies, and governments – hold the remaining 18 per cent of equities.

So the direct ownership of shares by individuals is still the dominant form of corporate ownership in Canada. And there is some evidence that this dominance may become even more marked in the future. For example, the proportion of Canadian workers covered by workplace pension plans has declined in recent years, from 45 per cent in 1993 to 42 per cent in 1997. This reflects the growth of various forms of employment (such as part-time work, contract and temporary positions, small business jobs, and burgeoning self-employment) which are unlikely to provide pension coverage and other standard occupational benefits. It is unlikely that the collective importance of pension funds in equity markets will grow in coming years; it may even shrink. More than twice as much money is now invested in personalized RRSPs each year as flows into registered pension funds.

Most company shares are owned directly by individuals, yet ironically the direct ownership of corporate shares is one of the least common forms of financial investment in Canada. A 1996 survey sponsored by the Toronto Stock Exchange indicated that just 21 per cent of adult Canadians own any corporate shares directly (and only 37 per cent of Canadians own any shares whatsoever, whether directly or through a mutual fund). The more burdensome information requirements, transactions costs, and risk associated with purchasing the shares of individual companies has made mutual funds the equity investment vehicle of choice for most personal investors. This already hints at the extent to which financial wealth in Canada is concentrated among a small share of the population: only about one-fifth of households own any corporate shares directly, but those direct holdings alone collectively account for 60 per cent of all equity ownership (not even counting the shares owned by these same households through indirect means, such as mutual funds).

Income Tax Data

As I have noted, Canada does not collect official statistics on the distribution of wealth. However, we do have ample official data on the distribution of income, including the distribution of different types of income (from work, from government sources, and from the ownership of financial wealth). An ongoing stockpile of wealth generates annual

TABLE 13.2
Investment income by level of total income (1995 tax returns)

Income level	Under $20,000	Under $50,000	Over $50,000	Over $100,000
Number of taxfilers	10.8 million	18.1 million	2.4 million	300,000
Share of all taxfilers	52.7%	88.3%	11.7%	1.5%
Sources of investment income:				
Share of dividend income	4.5%	29.1%	70.9%	45.3%
Share of capital gains	4.0%	14.7%	85.3%	70.2%
Share of other investment income	24.1%	63.6%	36.4%	16.8%
Share of total investment income[1]	15.7%	46.2%	53.8%	33.6%
Investment-related tax subsidies:				
Dividend tax credit	4.5%	29.1%	70.9%	45.3%
Capital gains tax exemption	0.8%	7.0%	93.0%	80.6%
Carrying charges	7.4%	31.0%	69.0%	41.6%

Source: Author's calculations from Revenue Canada, *Tax Statistics on Individuals*, 1995 Tax Year.
1 Excludes retirement income such as RRSPs and annuities.

flows of income which individuals are obligated to declare on their tax returns. Of course, unlike taxes collected from workers (which are usually deducted at source long before the worker ever sees his or her pay cheque), taxes on most investment income must be declared and paid voluntarily by the taxpayer. This raises a problem of the possible underreporting of investment income, which would distort any data on this subject derived from income tax statistics.

Nevertheless, the income tax system provides one of the better sources of data regarding the distribution of investment income (which in turn is an indirect indicator of the distribution of those investments). Investment income can include interest on savings accounts or government bonds, dividends paid to shareholders of a company, net income from investment properties (such as rental apartments), and capital gains resulting from the sale of some asset (such as a stock, a bond, or a home) for a price greater than was paid for it.

Income tax data describing a range of investment income indicators are summarized in Table 13.2. We consider three broad sources of investment income: dividends, capital gains, and 'other investment income' (which includes income received from savings deposits, bonds, rental properties, and other investments). The top 11.7 per cent of

Canadian individuals in 1995 (those earning more than $50,000) accounted for 54 per cent of all investment income – roughly five times greater than their share of the population. Just the top 1.5 per cent of taxpayers (those earning over $100,000 in 1995) accounted for an incredible 34 per cent of all investment income, twenty-two times their share of the population. In contrast, the bottom 88 per cent of individuals accounted for 46 per cent of all investment income – about one-half its share of the population. And the bottom 53 per cent of Canadians (those earning less than $20,000 in 1995) received only about 15 per cent of all investment income.

When investment income is disaggregated into its components, it becomes clear that income derived from stock market investments, mutual funds, and other securities is much more concentrated than common savings deposits, savings bonds, and other run-of-the-mill interest-bearing assets. For example, the top 11.7 per cent of households claimed 71 per cent of all dividend income and 85 per cent of all reported capital gains. The economic elite earning over $100,000 (accounting for just 1.5 per cent of taxpayers) claimed 45 per cent of all dividends, and 70 per cent of all capital gains. In contrast, the bottom nine-tenths of taxpayers accounted for less than 30 per cent of all dividend income, and only 15 per cent of all capital gains.

The conclusion that financial wealth is particularly concentrated in the upper end of the income ladder is reaffirmed by an analysis of claims for tax deductions related to stock market and other investments. These are summarized in the lower part of Table 13.2. The most common investment-related tax claims are the dividend tax credit (which refunds a portion of the taxes paid on dividend income), the capital gains deduction (through which taxpayers pay tax on only a portion of the capital gains income earned from the purchase and subsequent resale of various assets), and the deduction of carrying charges (interest payments, brokerage fees, and other expenses) which investors incur in the course of generating their investment income. As indicated in the table, these various tax subsidies are even more concentrated at the upper end of the income ladder than is investment income itself. The distribution of the dividend tax credits mirrors the distribution of dividend income (since the credit is allocated proportionately to total dividend income); 45 per cent of the credits were claimed by just the top 1.5 per cent of individuals. Similarly, 93 per cent of capital gains deductions were claimed by the top 11.7 per cent of taxpayers – and an incredible 81 per cent by just the top 1.5 per cent alone. Finally, 69 per cent of all carrying charges were deducted by those earning above $50,000, close to two-thirds of that by those earning over $100,000.

Why are investment-related tax deductions even more concentrated in high-income households than investment income itself? Lower-income households may not know about the tax deductions available, and given their much smaller holdings of financial wealth, they may not incur a proportionate share of carrying charges, or they may simply not go through the trouble to claim the deductions. One conclusion is clear, however: the rich range of tax subsidies that supports various forms of private investment activity deliver the largest benefits to upper-income households. Perversely, from the point of view of equity, in the case of carrying charges and other deductions, the value of each dollar deducted is actually higher for the high-income taxpayers who claim most of the deductions anyway: since they pay income tax at a higher rate than their less well-heeled counterparts, the final value of their tax deductions is enhanced accordingly. So an even greater share of the total public cost of the tax deductions is concentrated at the top end of the income ladder than is implied by the data provided in Table 13.2.

RRSP Contributions

Canada's RRSP (Registered Retirement Savings Program) may qualify as the most 'democratic' form of private financial investment in our economy. But this does not imply that RRSPs are equalizing in their effects: the majority of RRSP funds are owned by high-income Canadians, while most lower and middle-income households own economically trivial amounts or no RRSPs at all.

Like the tax deduction for carrying charges, RRSP tax subsidies are distributed to households in a manner that exacerbates inequality: the RRSP holdings of high-income investors are subsidized at a higher rate than those of other Canadians. Unlike many other tax subsidy programs (such as the child tax credit for poor families), the RRSP subsidy is calculated as a tax deduction (in which the legal amount of RRSP contributions is deducted from income before the investor's tax bill is calculated), rather than as a tax credit (in which the subsidy is added back in at the end of the income tax form, after the individual's taxes have already been calculated). The value of a tax deduction depends on the rate of tax the investor would otherwise be paying on the income that is deducted. Higher-income taxpayers pay a higher rate of tax;

hence, the RRSP deduction is worth proportionately more to them, and hence, they receive a sweeter subsidy for their RRSP investments. For years progressive tax reformers have called for the conversion of the RRSP deduction into a fairer RRSP tax credit (in which all taxpayers, regardless of their income level, would receive the same rate of subsidy). But the RRSP deductions are so beloved by the upper-middle-class and high-income communities which rely on them most intensively that no government has dared to implement this change in practice.

Despite these inequalities, however, the fact that RRSP investments are subsidized, and that the total tax-subsidized contribution is limited (at present to a maximum of 18 per cent of the previous year's earned income, to a ceiling of $75,000), means that RRSP investments are distributed far more equally across households than other financial investments. Most working and middle-income Canadians do not come close to using up the total value of RRSP subsidies available to them. In 1997, a total of 5.6 million Canadians (less than a quarter of all tax-filers) contributed an aggregate $22.8 billion to their RRSPs. But this staggering total represented just 13 per cent of what Canadians could have contributed if all taxpayers had used up the full RRSP 'room' available to them. Only one in ten of Canadian taxpayers contributed the maximum allowed to their RRSPs. Most of this unused RRSP room is concentrated at the bottom of the income spectrum, where a shortage of disposable income constrains household saving potential. For those who can afford it, contributing the maximum allowable into an RRSP is the first commandment of personal investing: virtually every financial adviser demands that 'maxing out' their RRSP accounts is among the very first things that personal investors should do with discretionary funds. So almost all personal financial wealth held by lower and middle-income Canadians (such as it is) is held within RRSPs. But for high-income households which have exhausted their RRSP contribution room, RRSPs will represent simply a portion (and sometimes a small portion) of total wealth holdings. For all of these reasons, the distribution of RRSP holdings across households is far more equal than the distribution of financial wealth generally.

However, upon further analysis, the distribution of RRSPs turns out not to be very equal at all. A couple of data sources support this conclusion. The income tax data cited earlier breaks down total RRSP contributions by income category. High-income individuals are far more likely to invest in an RRSP than those with less income. Less than one-

TABLE 13.3
RRSP investments by level of total income (1995 tax returns)

Income level	Under $20,000	Under $50,000	Over $50,000	Over $100,000
Number of taxfilers	10.8 million	18.1 million	2.4 million	300,000
Share of all taxfilers	52.7%	88.3%	11.7%	1.5%
Proportion who invested in RRSPs	8.4%	22.4%	69.4%	76.6%
Average RRSP contribution	$1,610	$2,598	$6,369	$12,326
Share of total RRSP contributions	6.9%	49.9%	50.1%	13.6%
Approx. share total RRSP subsidies[1]	3.0%	35.0%	65.0%	18.0%

Source: Author's calculations from Revenue Canada, *Tax Statistics on Individuals*, 1995 Tax Year, and unpublished Revenue Canada data.
1 Current-year subsidy to new investments only; excludes value of tax-sheltering for accumulated funds.

quarter of Canadians who earned less than $50,000 contributed to an RRSP in 1995, compared to 70 per cent of those who earned over $50,000. The average level of contributions also rises dramatically with income. RRSP contributors earning less than $50,000 put away $2,500 each in their plans, compared to over $6,000 each for those earning over $50,000, and $12,000 each for those pulling in more than $100,000. The end result: in 1995, a full 50 per cent of RRSP contributions was claimed by just the top 11.7 per cent of taxfilers (those earning over $50,000). The top one-tenth of taxpayers, in other words, accounted for about five times more than their per capita share of RRSP contributions. The top 1.5 per cent of taxfilers (those earning over $100,000 in 1995) accounted for 14 per cent of all RRSP contributions, about ten times greater than their share of the population.

Because of the inequitable fact that these same high-income taxpayers are actually subsidized by the government at a higher rate for their personal investing, they account for an even larger proportion of the subsidies handed out to support new RRSP contributions.[2] It would be safe to conclude that those earning over $50,000 received 65 per cent of total RRSP subsidies, while those earning over $100,000 received about 18 per cent. Even for this most 'democratic' form of (subsidized) financial investment, the clear majority of the gains is concentrated in the highest-income segment of society. If anyone needs help with their personal saving, it is average-income Canadians whose savings have been pinched between stagnant incomes and the rising cost of living; in fact, the average saving rate for all Canadian households fell to a record low of just 1.4 per cent of disposable income in 1999. However, an unreformed RRSP system continues to focus its incentive on the upper-income Canadians who would save a lot even without its generous tax subsidies.

This picture of the unbalanced pattern of RRSP investment in Canada is further confirmed by a second source of data: Statistics Canada's biennial reports on pension fund investments, including RRSPs. According to this data, those Canadians reporting 1995 total income in excess of $80,000 – the top 2.7 per cent of taxpayers that year – accounted for almost 20 per cent of all RRSP contributions (and, once again, an even higher share of all RRSP subsidies). In contrast, those taxfilers earning under $40,000 in 1995 (accounting for 80 per cent of all taxfilers) contributed just one-third of all RRSP money deposited that year and received an even smaller share of total RRSP subsidies. Even within Canada's RRSP system, which in theory is supposed to support the retirement savings of average citizens, the ownership of financial wealth is highly concentrated. Yet the total stock of RRSPs – some $200 billion by the end of 1995 – still accounts for a small share (perhaps one-eighth) of all household financial investments in Canada. Outside of the RRSP system, wealth is distributed far more unequally; few lower and middle-income Canadians have any financial assets at all apart from their RRSP holdings.

Other Data Sources

There are a few other sources of indirect data regarding the wealth holdings of different classes of Canadians, and these once again serve to contradict the myth that personal investing is now a virtually universal Canadian activity. Many financial institutions conduct their own private surveys of investment and wealth-ownership patterns, to support their wealth management and financial advising services. These surveys, when they are made public, tend to confirm the notion that despite the pseudo-populist culture of personal investing, most Canadians sit on the sidelines of this game. A 1996 poll conducted by the Toronto Stock Exchange confirmed that only about one-third of Canadians own any equities whatsoever (whether directly or through mutual funds). Stock ownership was especially rare among lower-income households: only 8 per cent of families with income under $25,000 per year owned either shares or mutual funds, compared to over 70 per cent of those with incomes above $75,000. And the total holdings of those lower-income households which do invest in equities are trivial in economic terms.

Another 1998 survey by Royal Trust showed that 55 per cent of those Canadians who do possess RRSPs own less than $25,000 in total assets. One-third of respondents held total RRSP assets of less than $10,000. No matter how hard these personal investors had to scrimp and save in order to accumulate their nest-eggs, the cold truth of the matter is that these savings are next to meaningless within the big-money world of pension funding. Given recent interest rates and investment returns, it typically costs over $25,000 to purchase a pension annuity paying $150 per month, assuming retirement age of sixty-five, guaranteed until the purchaser reaches ninety years of age, but not protected against inflation. By this criteria, then, even a $25,000 RRSP would generate a monthly pension of less than $150 (or $1,800 per year). But only 45 per cent of those Canadians who do own RRSPs have financial wealth exceeding that $25,000 threshold, and that does not include the roughly 50 per cent of Canadians who own no RRSPs whatsoever. By this reckoning, then, perhaps one-fifth of Canadians possess sufficient private financial wealth to purchase themselves a private monthly pension equal to a measly $150.[3] Despite the hype of the RRSP industry, the ability of most Canadians to finance their own personal pensions is negligible and will almost certainly remain so.

Rules of Thumb

All of these data sources provide only indirect information regarding the distribution of financial wealth in Canadian society. It would be preferable to have a complete and accurate survey of the subject, and it is hoped that Statistics Canada's upcoming wealth survey will provide precisely that. This survey should shed needed light on the distribution of the benefits of the paper boom of the 1990s. Have they been shared broadly within Canadian society – or have they been primarily the preserve of the elite?

The preceding data sources all paint a fairly consistent picture, one that is unlikely to be refuted by official data in the future. The notion that financial investment is a universal, equalizing and thus democratic phenomenon in Canadian society is clearly invalid. The clear majority of Canadians own no significant stockpiles of personal financial wealth.

Such wealth remains highly concentrated in a relatively small group at the top of the income ladder. Approximate, conservative rules of thumb can be constructed, based on the preceding data sources. The top 10 per cent of Canadian society probably owns about 50 per cent of all wealth (including real assets such as homes), and something closer to 70 per cent of all financial wealth. The top 1 per cent of society probably owns about one-quarter of all wealth, and something approaching 40 per cent of all financial wealth.

These exclusive constituencies are the ones that have enjoyed most of the benefits of the spectacular boom in private finance that dominated Canada's economy during the 1990s. And their vested interest in maintaining the types of policies and institutions that favour the protection and enhancement of financial wealth – high real interest rates, ultra-low inflation, financial industry deregulation, global financial liberalization – constitutes an important barrier to measures that would promote the development of Canada's real economy. In short, the surprising degree of financial inequality in Canadian society is holding back our economy from reaching its full productive potential. Inequality and efficiency have become contradictory, not complimentary.

Wealth and Income

The preceding data indicate that the distribution of financial wealth in Canada is very unequal. Indeed, the distribution of wealth is far more unequal than the distribution of annual income (a fact with which most Canadians are quite familiar). How is it that an initial imbalance in income distribution can become so amplified in the far more unequal distribution of accumulated wealth? If all Canadians started from a position of zero savings, saved an equal proportion of their income, no matter how much they made, and then invested those savings in equally profitable personal investments, the distribution of wealth would perfectly match the distribution of income: no more equal, no less equal. None of those conditions, however, prevail in reality. In the first place, most wealthy households inherited a significant proportion of their total wealth from their parents or other relatives. Secondly, higher-income investors probably obtain slightly higher average returns on their investments, simply because they tend to have more financial knowledge and more resources with which to pursue sophisticated investment opportunities. Most importantly, high-income households are able to allocate a much larger share of their initial income to savings

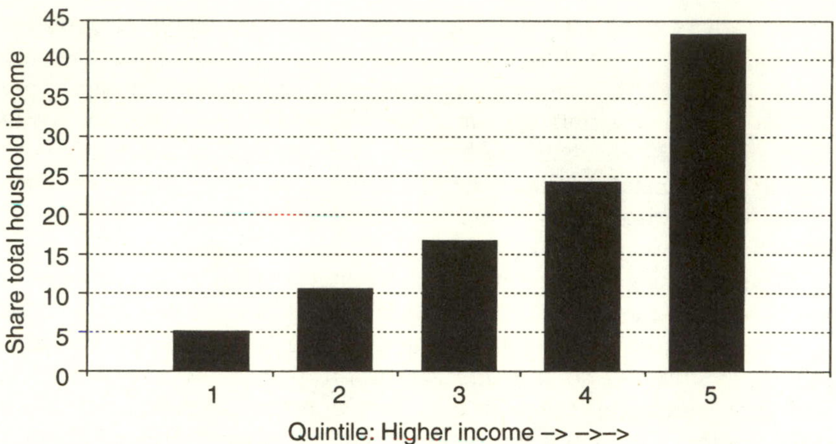

Figure 13.2. The distribution of income in Canada (by household quintile, before tax, 1996).
Source: Author's calculations from Statistics Canada Catalogue 62-555, *Family Expenditure in Canada*, 1996.

and wealth accumulation than most other households. Higher income households also spend larger sums of money on various types of consumption – housing and furnishings, cars, clothing, entertainment, travel – than their less well-heeled counterparts. But this personal consumption spending tends to grow with income at a less-than-proportional rate. Hence, the proportion of income allocated to savings tends to increase with the level of a household's income.

The reason for this is straightforward. There are certain simple necessities of life that must be paid for as a condition of basic subsistence, regardless of an individual's income level. Everyone must eat, be clothed, and housed. If their current income is inadequate to cover even these basic necessities, individuals must dip into their savings or go into debt. Rich people spend more on food than poor people, obviously, but there are limits to how much they can eat, and even to how much they can spend on luxury food products. Thus someone who earns $200,000 per year will spend more on food than someone earning $20,000, but not ten times as much. After paying for the necessities of life (and even the non-necessities), higher-income households have more income left over after the bills are paid, and hence a higher savings rate, than those with lower income.

This relationship is dramatized in Figures 13.2 and 13.3. Figure 13.2

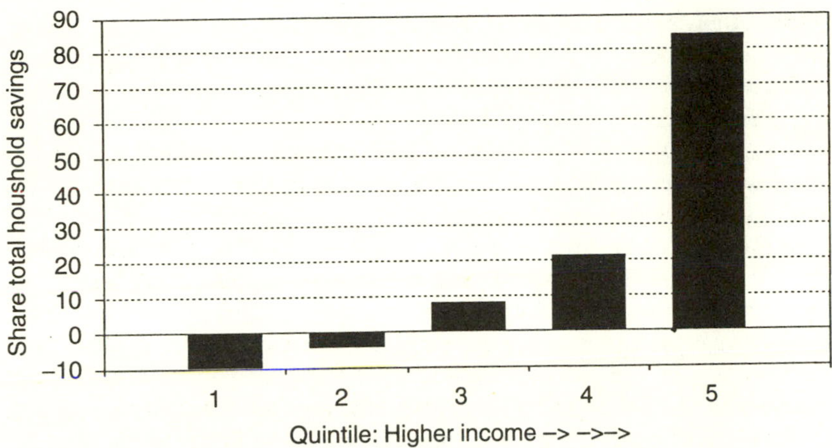

Figure 13.3. The distribution of savings in Canada (by household quintile, 1996).
Source: Author's calculations from Statistics Canada Catalogue 62-555, *Family Expenditure in Canada*, 1996.

indicates the distribution of income across different income groups in Canadian society. This distribution is significantly uneven. The top fifth of households take in more than 43 per cent of total income (including government transfer payments such as pensions and welfare benefits), or about 8.5 times as much as the lowest fifth. This inequality is moderated somewhat as a result of Canada's tax system (since high-income earners pay a higher-than-proportional share of total taxes), and hence the distribution of after-tax income is somewhat more equal than the distribution of before-tax income. The share of the top fifth of households drops from 43 to 40 per cent after taxes are taken into account. Figure 13.2 only illustrates the lopsided distribution of income across all households in Canada; this maldistribution is all the more striking when we consider gender, race, and rural-urban differences in income.[4]

That same top tier of households, meanwhile, accounts for only about one-third of total current personal expenditure by Canadian families – significantly less than their share of total income. The top tier enjoys average incomes 8.5 times as large as the lowest tier, but only spends about 4 times as much on personal consumption (you can only buy so much). As a result, the top fifth of households accounts for 81 per cent of total Canadian savings (Figure 13.3). At the same time, lower and even many middle-income Canadians have no savings whatsoever: their modest incomes are just sufficient to pay for current costs, with nothing left over for RRSPs or mutual funds. These households therefore experience negative savings rates, either drawing down existing assets or (more likely) going deeper into debt.

It is not until we reach the middle quintile of society – families earning an average of about $45,000 per year in 1995 – that any positive savings are generated. Moreover, most of those middle-class savings take the form of gradual decreases in the outstanding balances of residential mortgages. (In accounting terms, paying off a long-term debt like a mortgage is equivalent to positive saving.) Virtually all of the net financial saving of Canadian households, therefore, takes place within the top 40 per cent of households, and the great bulk of that is accounted for by the top tier. Since they account for the vast majority of savings, year in and year out, before long these households also account for the vast majority of accumulated wealth.

The fact that most personal saving is undertaken by the richest minority of households also sheds light on other current economic issues. It explains, for example, why consumption or sales taxes (like Canada's GST) are regressive – that is, they collect a higher rate of tax from lower-income households, the ones who can least afford to pay. High-income households can avoid paying the GST on that significant portion of their incomes which they save, rather than spend. For a related reason, a policy that redistributed income from rich to poor could have stimulative effects on the economy. Lower-income households spend every available dollar on current consumption, while their better-heeled counterparts have relatively high savings rates. Taking $100 from a rich household and giving it to a poor one, therefore, would tend to increase the total amount of consumption spending (since the rich family might have spent only $50 of the $100, while the poor family would spend all of it). This extra consumption spending in turn could generate new demand and new jobs throughout the economy.[5] Income tax reductions for high-income earners, by the same logic, can actually have a dampening effect on economic growth. Higher-income households pay most of Canada's income taxes, and hence they receive the greatest share of the benefits from any general income tax cut.[6] But they subsequently spend only a portion of their tax savings on goods and services, and allocate the rest to their growing stockpiles of financial wealth. And when tax cuts are offset by equivalent reductions in government spending on various public services and social programs, the overall effect is to dampen demand, growth, and employment.

The Implications of Financial Concentration

The concentration of private savings in Canada in the hands of the highest-income elite has led inevitably to a concentration of financial wealth in those same hands. The political power represented by these well-off sectors of society has in turn promoted the adoption of policies that have generally rewarded savings and financial investment, often at the expense of real investment, growth, and job creation. These policies have included the introduction of a major new sales tax (GST), the shift in the relative tax burden from progressive personal income taxes to regressive sales taxes, the payment of juicy tax subsidies for personal savings and investment, and the broader macroeconomic policies (such as high real interest rates and cutbacks in government spending) that generally helped to fuel the paper boom of the 1990s in private financial markets.

This lopsided concentration of financial wealth among a small elite of Canadian society is a cause for concern on numerous grounds. In terms of equity, it is clearly unfair. It also provides a jarring refutation of the recent ideology of people's capitalism, an ideology that pretends that personal investing has become almost as universal as the suffrage itself. The concentration of wealth has also created a dangerous and destructive political dynamic. A small but powerful constituency of financial investors has been able to lobby successfully for the implementation of policies that have clearly enhanced the value and profitability of finance, but at the expense of real growth and job creation. They have also shaped the framework of political debate on economic policy. Think of many of the debates that have occurred in recent years in Canada. How hard should we crack down on inflation? How should we reduce government deficits, and how fast? Should we try more aggressively to prop up the Canadian dollar, or even move towards a joint currency with the United States? In case after case the fundamental issue seems to boil down to a clash between those who own or manage significant quantities of financial wealth (and hence demand low inflation, less debt, a strong currency, and a free-wheeling financial market) and those who do not (and who hence would benefit from policies that emphasized job creation over the protection of financial returns).

For those who own and control finance, the stakes are huge in cementing the general direction that Canadian economic policies have followed over the past fifteen years. Financiers will never forget the

1970s, when the value of their stockpiles of wealth was badly eroded by inflation, falling stock market prices, unprecedented labour militance, and negative real interest rates. Some have described the period of deliberately restrictive, pro-finance economic policy that has been experienced in most Western economies in the wake of this turbulent time as the 'revenge of the rentiers.'[7] The rentier class – those who live off the proceeds of accumulated wealth rather than the sweat of current labour activity – organized itself effectively to shift economic policy in a fundamentally different direction, to ensure that the 'horror' of the 1970s did not repeat itself.

For the rest of us, in retrospect, the 1970s were actually not so bad, despite accelerating inflation and moderate financial instability. Real wages in Canada grew by an average of about 1.5 per cent per year during the decade, and the unemployment rate averaged just 5.9 per cent, barely half its level during the 'financially responsible' 1990s. But the fact that most Canadians have clearly been harmed economically by the pro-finance policies of the 1980s and 1990s has hardly affected the speed and determination with which this policy agenda continues to be implemented. In short, there is little doubt that the concentration of financial wealth in Canada also led to a disproportionate political influence and a disturbing tendency for our democracy to be governed more by the sentiments of the 'market' than by the sentiments of ordinary voters – even though the market is nothing other than a symbolic representation of the vested economic interests of one small but powerful constituency of society. The motto of 'one dollar, one vote' seems to be replacing the democratic principle of 'one person, one vote.'

It will require a significant rearrangement of our economic priorities in order to put the top emphasis of economic policy making back on real indicators (such as real capital formation, productivity growth, and job creation) rather than paper ones (such as inflation, interest rates, and financial markets). Most Canadians have no significant stake in the lucrative financial hyperactivity that has propelled stock markets and other financial arenas to unprecedented highs. For the vast majority of Canadians it is their ability to find and keep a well-paying job that will determine their economic well-being and retirement security, not their choice of a mutual fund. At best the paper boom in financial markets has been largely irrelevant to the development of our real economy; at worst, during times of upheaval and financial fragility, it clearly stands in the way. Through economic education and political activism, democratic citizens can be mobilized to challenge the daunting economic, political, and cultural power of high finance. A good place to start is by exposing the falsity of the claim that everyone has an equal stake in the markets.

NOTES

1 In fact, the majority of CN shares is now owned in the United States. More experience with the economics of the private railway industry led United States investors to spot the huge potential at CN (once it was privatized) to boost profits through relentless cost-cutting, and they snapped up the majority of shares quickly after privatization. While the benefits of higher share prices have largely been exported, therefore, the negative economic impacts of 10,000 lay-offs in five years have been felt closer to home.

2 The federal government will lose tax revenues of about $8 billion due to the RRSP deduction in 2000, and the provincial governments lose another $4 billion. Both levels of government provide an additional subsidy to the RRSP system by allowing interest and dividends to accumulate tax-free within RRSP shelters; this costs the two levels of government an additional $8 billion per year. The second type of subsidy for accumulated RRSP funds is distributed even less fairly than the subsidy for current-year contributions. Many lower- and middle-income Canadians use RRSPs not for retirement savings but as an income-averaging device: they contribute to their RRSPs during good years, and withdraw funds (at lower tax rates) in years of unemployment or underemployment. For this reason, their RRSP balances tend to rise and fall over time (rather than rising steadily as is usually the case for higher-income regular contributors). Hence their share of accumulated RRSP money (and the government subsidies to those moneys) is even smaller than their share of current RRSP contributions in any single year. It should be noted that about one-fifth of the cost of the overall RRSP program – less than $4 billion per year at present – is offset by income taxes collected on withdrawals from RRSP accounts and post-retirement RRSP payouts. See *Government of Canada Tax Expenditures* (Ottawa: Department of Finance, 1998), Table 1, for more details.

3 If 50 per cent of Canadians own RRSPs, and only 45 per cent of those with RRSPs own a total portfolio exceeding $25,000, then only about 22 per cent of Canadians own RRSP portfolios worth more than $25,000.

4 A range of recent data sources attest to the continuing inequality of income distribution experienced by women and visible minorities in Canada. See, for example, Monica Townson, *A Report Card on Women and Poverty* (Ottawa:

Canadian Centre for Policy Alternatives, 2000), for details of the continuing income gap between men and women. Recent research has also highlighted the growing concentration of poverty in inner-city neighbourhoods in Canada, experienced particularly by people of colour; see Kevin Lee, *Urban Poverty in Canada: A Statistical Profile* (Ottawa: Canadian Council on Social Development, 2000). Since women and visible minorities experience lower lifetime incomes, they will tend to accumulate even smaller personal nest-eggs of financial wealth.

5 Conservatives argue that the lower aggregate savings rate resulting from this redistribution of income would harm the economy. The economic evidence suggests, however, that it is a lack of investment demand, not a lack of savings, that explains Canada's poor investment performance during the 1990s; for more details on this argument see Jim Stanford, *Paper Boom: Why Real Prosperity Requires a New Approach to Canada's Economy* (Ottawa: Canadian Centre for Policy Alternatives, 1999), chap. 10.

6 Income tax cuts can be targeted so that more of their benefits are received by lower-income households, through such measures as increasing targeted tax credits (such as the GST credit or the child tax benefit), or reducing the lowest tax rate. Any general income tax cut, however (such as that implemented by the Harris government in Ontario between 1995 and 1998), will inevitably deliver most of its benefits to high-income households simply because these households pay far more income tax than anyone else.

7 See John Smithin, 'Cause and Effect in the Relationship between Budget Deficits and the Rate of Interest,' *Économies et Sociétés*, Jan.–Feb. 1994, 151–69.

Index

Note: Page numbers followed by an 'f' indicate a figure. Page numbers followed by a 't' indicate a table.